P9-BID-074

Where do I go for answers to my travel questions?

What's the best and easiest way to plan and book my trip?

frommers.travelocity.com

Frommer's, the travel guide leader, has teamed up with **Travelocity.com,** the leader in online travel, to bring you an in-depth, easy-to-use resource designed to help you plan and book your trip online.

At **frommers.travelocity.com**, you'll find free online updates about your destination from the experts at Frommer's plus the outstanding travel planning and purchasing features of Travelocity.com. Travelocity.com provides reservations capabilities for 95 percent of all airline seats sold, more than 47,000 hotels, and over 50 car rental companies. In addition, Travelocity.com offers more than 2,000 exciting vacation and cruise packages. Travelocity.com puts you in complete control of your travel planning with these and other great features:

> **Expert travel guidance from Frommer's** - over 150 writers reporting from around the world!
>
> **Best Fare Finder** - an interactive calendar tells you when to travel to get the best airfare
>
> **Fare Watcher** - we'll track airfare changes to your favorite destinations
>
> **Dream Maps** - a mapping feature that suggests travel opportunities based on your budget
>
> **Shop Safe Guarantee** - 24 hours a day / 7 days a week live customer service, and more!

Whether traveling on a tight budget, looking for a quick weekend getaway, or planning the trip of a lifetime, Frommer's guides and Travelocity.com will make your travel dreams a reality. You've bought the book, now book the trip!

A New Star-Rating System & Other Exciting News from Frommer's!

In our continuing effort to publish the savviest, most up-to-date, and most appealing travel guides available, we've added some great new features.

Frommer's guides now include a new star-rating system. Every hotel, restaurant, and attraction is rated from 0 to 3 stars to help you set priorities and organize your time.

We've also added seven brand-new features that point you to the great deals, in-the-know advice, and unique experiences that separate travelers from tourists. Throughout the guide look for:

Finds	Special finds—those places only insiders know about
Fun Fact	Fun facts—details that make travelers more informed and their trips more fun
Kids	Best bets for kids—advice for the whole family
Moments	Special moments—those experiences that memories are made of
Overrated	Places or experiences not worth your time or money
Tips	Insider tips—some great ways to save time and money
Value	Great values—where to get the best deals

Frommer's®

PORTABLE
New Orleans

5th Edition

by Mary Herczog

Hungry Minds™

Best-Selling Books • Digital Downloads • e-Books
Answer Networks • e-Newsletters • Branded Web Sites • e-Learning
New York, NY • Cleveland, OH • Indianapolis, IN

ABOUT THE AUTHOR

Mary Herczog is a freelance writer who also works in the film industry. She is the author of *Frommer's Las Vegas* and *Las Vegas For Dummies* and has covered Bali for *Frommer's Southeast Asia*. She would never leave New Orleans if it weren't for July and August.

Published by:

HUNGRY MINDS, INC.

909 Third Ave.
New York, NY 10022

ISBN 0-7645-6521-4
ISSN 1090-316X

Editor: Alexis Lipsitz Flippin
Production Editor: Bethany André
Photo Editor: Richard Fox
Cartographer: Roberta Stockwell
Production by Hungry Minds Indianapolis Production Services

SPECIAL SALES

For general information on Hungry Minds' products and services, please contact our Customer Care department; within the U.S. at 800-762-2974, outside the U.S. at 317-572-3993 or fax 317-572-4002. For sales inquiries and reseller information, including discounts, bulk sales, customized editions, and premium sales, please contact our Customer Care department at 800-434-3422.

Manufactured in the United States of America

5   4   3   2   1

Contents

List of Maps

An Invitation to the Reader

In researching this book, we discovered many wonderful places—hotels, restaurants, shops, and more. We're sure you'll find others. Please tell us about them, so we can share the information with your fellow travelers in upcoming editions. If you were disappointed with a recommendation, we'd love to know that, too. Please write to:

Frommer's Portable New Orleans, 5th Edition
Hungry Minds, Inc. • 909 Third Avenue • New York, NY 10022

An Additional Note

Please be advised that travel information is subject to change at any time—and this is especially true of prices. We therefore suggest that you write or call ahead for confirmation when making your travel plans. The authors, editors, and publisher cannot be held responsible for the experiences of readers while traveling. Your safety is important to us, however, so we encourage you to stay alert and be aware of your surroundings. Keep a close eye on cameras, purses, and wallets, all favorite targets of thieves and pickpockets.

What the Symbols Mean

The following abbreviations are used for credit cards:

AE	American Express	DISC	Discover	V	Visa
DC	Diners Club	MC	MasterCard		

FROMMERS.COM

Now that you have the guidebook to a great trip, visit our website at www.frommers.com for travel information on nearly 2,000 destinations. With features updated regularly, we give you instant access to the most current trip-planning information available. At Frommers.com, you'll also find the best prices on airfares, accommodations, and car rentals—and you can even book travel online through our travel booking partners. At Frommers.com, you'll also find the following:

- Daily Newsletter highlighting the best travel deals
- Hot Spot of the Month/Vacation Sweepstakes & Travel Photo Contest
- More than 200 Travel Message Boards
- Outspoken Newsletters and Feature Articles on travel bargains, vacation ideas, tips & resources, and more!

Planning Your Trip to New Orleans

Whatever your idea of the ideal New Orleans trip, this chapter will give you the information to make informed plans and help point you toward some additional resources.

1 Visitor Information

Even a seasoned traveler should consider writing or calling ahead to the **New Orleans Metropolitan Convention and Visitors Bureau,** 1520 Sugar Bowl Dr., New Orleans, LA 70112 (© **800/672-6124** or 504/566-5055; www.neworleanscvb.com). The staff is extremely friendly and helpful, and you can easily get any information you can't find in this book from them.

Another source of information is the **New Orleans Multi-cultural Tourism Network,** Louisiana Superdome, 1520 Sugar Bowl Dr., New Orleans, LA 70112 (© **504/523-5652**); you may be particularly interested in their self-directed tours of African-American landmarks.

2 Money

Prices for everything from accommodations to zydeco clubs skyrocket during major events and festivals (see "Planning a Visit for Mardi Gras or Jazz Fest," later in this chapter). New Orleans is also quite popular in the fall during what has become the convention season. The heat and humidity of the summer months (July and Aug) keep tourism in the city to its yearly low, so if the weather doesn't bother you, you can find some incredible bargains, especially at hotels.

ATMs   Almost all New Orleans ATMs are linked to a national network that most likely includes your bank at home. **Cirrus** (© **800/ 424-7787;** www.mastercard.com/atm) and **PLUS** (© **800/843-7587;** www.visa.com/atms) are the two most popular networks; check the back of your ATM card to see which network your bank belongs to (these days, most banks belong to both).

Some centrally located ATMs in New Orleans are at the **First National Bank of Commerce,** 240 Royal St.; **Hibernia National Bank,** 701 Poydras St.; and **Whitney National Bank,** 228 St. Charles Ave. There are now ATMs all over the French Quarter, a big change from 10 years ago when there was just one.

Expect to pay a $1 to $2 service charge each time you withdraw money from an ATM in addition to what your home bank charges.

3 When to Go

With the possible exception of July and August (unless you happen to thrive on heat and humidity), just about any time is the right time to go to New Orleans. Mardi Gras is, of course, the time of year when it's hardest to get a hotel room, but it can also be difficult during the various music festivals throughout the year, especially during Jazz Fest (see below). It's important to know what's going on when; the city's landscape can change dramatically depending on what festival or convention is happening, and prices can also reflect that. The best time of year, in our opinion, is December, before and during Christmas. The town is gussied up with decorations, there are all kinds of seasonal special events, the weather is nice—but for some reason, tourists become scarce. Hotels, eager to lure any business, lower their rates dramatically, and most restaurants are so empty that you can walk in just about anywhere without a reservation. Take advantage of it.

THE WEATHER

The average mean temperature in New Orleans is an inviting 70°, but it can drop or rise considerably in a single day. (We've experienced 40° and rain one day, 80° and humidity the next.) Conditions depend primarily on two things: whether it rains and whether there is direct sunlight or cloud cover. Rain can provide slight and temporary relief on a hot day; for the most part, it hits in sudden (and sometimes dramatically heavy) showers, which disappear as quickly as they arrived. Anytime the sun shines unimpeded, it gets much warmer. The region's high humidity can make even mild warms and colds feel intense. Still, the city's semitropical climate is part of its appeal—a slight bit of moistness makes the air come sensually alive.

It will be pleasant at almost any time of year except July and August, which can be exceptionally hot and muggy. If you do come during those months, you'll quickly learn to follow the natives' example, staying out of the noonday sun and ducking from one air-conditioned building to another. Winter is very mild by American standards but is punctuated by an occasional cold snap, when the mercury can drop below the freezing point.

In the dead of summer, T-shirts and shorts are absolutely acceptable everywhere except the finest restaurants. In the spring and fall, something a little warmer is in order; in the winter, you should plan to carry a lightweight coat or jacket. Umbrellas and cheap rain jackets are available everywhere for those tourists who inevitably get caught in a sudden, unexpected downpour.

New Orleans Average Temperatures & Rainfall

	Jan	Feb	Mar	Apr	May	June	July	Aug	Sept	Oct	Nov	Dec
High (°F)	69	65	71	79	85	90	91	90	87	79	70	64
Low (°C)	21	18	22	26	29	32	33	32	30	26	21	18
Days of Rainfall	10	9	9	7	8	10	15	13	10	5	7	10

NEW ORLEANS CALENDAR OF EVENTS

For more information on **Mardi Gras, Jazz Fest,** and other major area events, see below. For general information, contact the **New Orleans Metropolitan Convention and Visitors Bureau,** 1520 Sugar Bowl Dr., New Orleans, LA 70112 (📞 **800/672-6124** or 504/566-5055; www.neworleanscvb.com).

January

Nokia Sugar Bowl Classic. First held in 1934, this is New Orleans's oldest yearly sporting occasion. The football game is the main event, but there are also tennis, swimming, basketball, sailing, running, and flag-football competitions. Fans tend to be really loud, really boisterous, and everywhere during the festivities. For information, contact Nokia Sugar Bowl, 1500 Sugar Bowl Dr., New Orleans, LA 70112 (📞 **504/525-8573;** www.nokiasugarbowl.com). January 1.

February

Lundi Gras. An old tradition that has been revived in the last decade or so. Celebrations take place at Spanish Plaza. It's free, it's outdoors, and it features music (including a jazz competition) and the arrival of Rex at 6pm, marking the beginning of Mardi Gras. For more information, contact New Orleans Riverwalk, 1 Poydras St., New Orleans, LA 70130 (📞 **504/522-1555**). Monday before Mardi Gras (in 2002, it'll be Feb 11).

Mardi Gras. The culmination of the 2-month-long carnival season, Mardi Gras is the big annual blowout, a citywide party that takes place on Fat Tuesday (the last day before Lent in the

Christian calendar). The entire city stops working (sometimes days in advance!) and starts partying in the early morning, and the streets are taken over by some overwhelming parades—which, these days, go through the Central Business District instead of the French Quarter. Day before Ash Wednesday (in 2002, it'll be Feb 12). See below for more details.

Black Heritage Festival. Honors the various African-American cultural contributions to New Orleans. Write or call the Black Heritage Foundation, 4535 S. Prieur St., New Orleans, LA 70125 (© **504/827-0112**) for more info. Specific events usually begin about 2 weeks after Carnival.

March

St. Patrick's Day Parades. There are two: One takes place in the French Quarter beginning at Molly's at the Market (1107 Decatur St.), and the other goes through the Irish Channel neighborhood following a route that begins at Jackson Avenue and Magazine Street, goes over to St. Charles Avenue, turns uptown to Louisiana Avenue, and returns to Jackson Avenue. The parades have the flavor of Mardi Gras, but instead of beads, watchers are pelted with cabbages, carrots, and other veggies. For information on the French Quarter parade, call **Molly's at the Market** (© **504/525-5169**). The Irish Channel parade takes place in early March.

St. Joseph's Day Parade. In addition to the parade, which takes place March 19, you may want to visit the altar devoted to St. Joseph at the American Italian Museum and Library, 537 S. Peters St. The altar is on display from March 17 to March 19. For more information, call © **504/522-7294.**

Super Sunday. This is the annual Mardi Gras Indians showdown, which takes place on the Sunday following St. Joseph's Day.

Tennessee Williams New Orleans Literary Festival. A 5-day series celebrating New Orleans's rich literary heritage, it includes theatrical performances, readings, discussion panels, master classes, musical events, and literary walking tours dedicated to the playwright. By the way, the focus is not confined to Tennessee Williams. Events take place at venues throughout the city. For info, call © **504/581-1144** or go to www.tennesseewilliams.net. Late March.

Spring Fiesta. The fiesta, which begins with the crowning of the Spring Fiesta queen, is more than half a century old and takes place throughout the city—from the Garden District to the French Quarter to Uptown and beyond. Historical and architectural tours of many of the city's private homes, court-yards, and plantation homes are offered in conjunction with the 5-day event. For the schedule, call the Spring Fiesta Association (© **504/581-1367**). Last two weekends in March.

April

The French Quarter Festival. For hard-core jazz fans, this is rapidly becoming an alternative to Jazz Fest, where actual jazz is becoming less and less prominent. It kicks off with a parade down Bourbon Street. Among other things, you can join people dancing in the streets, learn the history of jazz, visit historic homes, and take a ride on a riverboat. Many local restaurants set up booths in Jackson Square, so the eating is exceptionally good. Events are held all over the French Quarter. For information, call or write French Quarter Festivals, 100 Conti St., New Orleans, LA 70130 (© **504/522-5730**). Middle of the month.

The New Orleans Jazz & Heritage Festival. A 10-day event that draws musicians, music fans, cooks, and craftspeople to celebrate music and life, Jazz Fest rivals Mardi Gras in popularity. Lodgings in the city tend to sell out up to a year ahead, so book early. Events take place at the Fair Grounds Race Track and various venues throughout the city. For information, call or write the **New Orleans Jazz and Heritage Festival,** 1205 N. Rampart St., New Orleans, LA 70116 (© **504/522-4786;** www.nojazzfest. com). Usually held the last weekend in April and first weekend in May. Look for more information below.

The Crescent City Classic. This 10-kilometer road race, from Jackson Square to Audubon Park, brings an international field of top runners to the city. For more info, call or write the Classic, P.O. Box 13587, New Orleans, LA 70185 (© **504/861-8686;** www.ccc10k.com). Saturday before Easter (Mar 3, 2002).

May

Greek Festival. At the Holy Trinity Cathedral's Hellenic Cultural Center, it features Greek folk dancing, specialty foods, crafts, and music. For more information about the 3-day event, call or write Holy Trinity Cathedral, 1200 Robert E. Lee Blvd., New Orleans, LA 70122 (© **504/282-0259**). Last weekend of May.

June

The Great French Market Tomato Festival. A celebration of tomato diversity, this daylong event features cooking and tastings in the historic French Market. For more information, call or write the French Market, P.O. Box 51749, New Orleans, LA 70151 (© **504/522-2621**). First Sunday in June.

Reggae Riddums Festival. This 3-day gathering of calypso, reggae, and *soca* (a blend of soul and calypso) musicians is held in City Park and includes a heady helping of ethnic foods and arts and crafts. For more information, call or write Ernest Kelly, P.O. Box 6156, New Orleans, LA 70174 (© **888/767-1317** or 504/367-1313). Second week of June.

July

Go Fourth on the River. The annual Fourth of July celebration begins in the morning at the riverfront and continues into the night, culminating in a spectacular fireworks display. For more information, call or write Anna Pepper, 610 S. Peters St., Suite 301, New Orleans, LA 70130 (© **504/587-1791**).

New Orleans Wine and Food Experience. Antiques shops and art galleries throughout the French Quarter hold wine and food tastings, wine makers and local chefs conduct seminars, and a variety of vintner dinners and grand tastings are held for your gourmandistic pleasure. More than 150 wines and 40 restaurants are featured every day. For information and this year's schedule, call or write Mary Reynolds, P.O. Box 70514, New Orleans, LA 70172 (© **504/529-9463;** www.nowfe.com). Five days in July.

September

Southern Decadence. All over the French Quarter, thousands of folks—drag queens, mostly—follow a secret parade route, making sure to stop into many bars along the way. People travel from far and wide to be a part of the festivities. There is only an informal organization associated with the festival, and it's hard to get anyone on the phone. For information, try the website (www.southerndecadence.com) or contact *Ambush Magazine* (© **800/876-1484** or 504/522-8047; fax 504/522-0907). Labor Day weekend.

Words & Music: A Literary Feast in New Orleans. A highly ambitious literary and music conference (originated in large part by the folks behind Faulkner House Books) offering 5 days' worth of roundtable discussions with eminent authors (with varying connections to the city), original drama, poetry readings, master classes, plus great music and food. For authors seeking guidance and inspiration and for book lovers in general, call © **504/586-1609** for dates. Generally held beginning September 20.

Festivals Acadiens. This is a series of happenings that celebrate Cajun music, food, crafts, and culture in and near Lafayette, Louisiana. (Most of the events are in Lafayette.) For more info, contact the **Lafayette Parish Convention and Visitors Commission,** P.O. Box 52066, Lafayette, LA 70505 (**℗ 800/ 346-1958** in the U.S., 800/543-5340 in Canada, or 337/232-3737; www.lafayettetravel.com). Third week of the month.

Swamp Festival. Sponsored by the Audubon Institute, the Swamp Festival features long days of live swamp music performances (lots of good zydeco here) as well as hands-on contact with Louisiana swamp animals. Admission to the festival is free with zoo admission. For information, call or write the Audubon Institute, 6500 Magazine St., New Orleans, LA 70118 (**℗ 504/861-2537;** www.auduboninstitute.org). Last weekend in September and first weekend in October.

The Rayne Frog Festival. Cajuns can always find an excuse to hold a party, and in this case, they've turned to the lowly frog as an excuse for a *fais do-do* (dance) and a waltz contest. Frog races and frog-jumping contests fill the entertainment bill—and if you arrive without your amphibian, there's a Rent-a-Frog service. A lively frog-eating contest winds things up. For dates and full details, contact Lafayette Parish Convention and Visitors Commission, P.O. Box 52066, Lafayette, LA 70505 (**℗ 800/ 346-1958** in the U.S., 800/543-5340 in Canada, or 337/232-3808; www.lafayettetravel.com).

October

Art for Arts' Sake. The arts season begins with gallery openings throughout the city. Julia, Magazine, and Royal streets are where the action is. For more information, contact the Contemporary Arts Center, 900 Camp St., New Orleans, LA 70130 (**℗ 504/ 523-1216;** fax 504/528-3828; www.cacno.org). Throughout the month.

Louisiana Jazz Awareness Month. There are nightly concerts (some of which are free), television and radio specials, and lectures, all sponsored by the Louisiana Jazz Federation. For more information and a schedule, contact the Louisiana Music Commission (**℗ 504/835-5277;** www.louisianamusic.org).

Gumbo Festival. This festival showcases one of the region's signature dishes and celebrates Cajun culture to boot. It's 3 days of gumbo-related events (including the presentation of the royal court of King and Miss Creole Gumbo) plus many hours of Cajun music. The festival is held in Bridge City, on the outskirts of New Orleans. For more information, contact the Gumbo Festival, P.O. Box 9069, Bridge City, LA 70096 (**℗ 504/436-4712**). Second weekend in October.

New Orleans Film Festival. Canal Place Cinemas and other theaters throughout the city screen award-winning local and international films and host writers, actors, and directors over the course of a week. Admission prices range from $4 to $6. For dates, contact the New Orleans Film and Video Society, 843 Carondelet, no. 1, New Orleans, LA 70130 (② **504/524-5271;** www.neworleansfilmfest.com). Mid-month.

Halloween. Rivaling Mardi Gras in terms of costumes, Halloween is certainly celebrated more grandly here than in any other American city. After all, New Orleans has a way with ghosts. Events include Boo-at-the-Zoo (Oct 30 and 31) for children, costume parties (including a Monster Bash at the Ernest N. Morial Convention Center), haunted houses (one of the best is run by the sheriff's department in City Park), the Anne Rice Vampire Lestat Extravaganza, and the Moonlight Witches Run. You can catch the ghoulish action all over the city—many museums get in on the fun with specially designed tours—but the French Quarter, as always, is the center of the Halloween-night universe. October 31.

December

Christmas New Orleans Style. New Orleans loves to celebrate, so it should be no surprise that they do Christmas really well. The town is decorated to a fare-thee-well, there is an evening of candlelight caroling in Jackson Square, bonfires line the levees along the River Road on Christmas Eve (to guide Papa Noël, his sled drawn by alligators, on his gift-delivering way), restaurants offer specially created multicourse Réveillon dinners, and hotels throughout the city offer "Papa Noël" rates. Why? Because despite all the fun and the generally nice (read: not hot and humid) weather, tourism goes *waaay* down at this time of year, and hotels are eager to lure you all in with cheaper rates. For information, contact French Quarter Festivals, 100 Conti St., New Orleans, LA 70130 (② **504/522-5730**). All month.

Celebration in the Oaks. Lights and lighted figures, designed to illustrate holiday themes, bedeck sections of City Park. This display of winter wonderment is open for driving and walking tours. Driving tours are $8 per family car or van, and walking tours are $3 per person. For information, contact Celebration in the Oaks, 1 Palm Dr., New Orleans, LA 70124 (② **504/483-9415**). Late November to early January.

New Year's Eve. The countdown takes place in Jackson Square and is one of the country's biggest and most reliable street parties. In the Southern equivalent of New York's Times Square, revelers

watch a lighted ball drop from the top of Jackson Brewery.
December 31.

4 Planning a Visit for Mardi Gras or Jazz Fest

MARDI GRAS

The granddaddy of all New Orleans celebrations is Mardi Gras.
Thanks to sensational media accounts that zero in on the salacious
aspects, its rep has gone downhill in the last few years—while the
accounts have attracted more and more participants looking for wild
action rather than tradition. But despite what you may have heard,
Mardi Gras remains one of the most exciting times to visit. You can
spend several days admiring and reveling in the traditions and never
even venture into the frat-party atmosphere of Bourbon Street.

THE SEASON   The date of Fat Tuesday is different each year, but
Carnival season always starts on **Twelfth Night,** January 6, as much
as 2 months before Mardi Gras. On that night, the Phunny Phorty
Phellows kick off the season with a streetcar ride from Carrollton
Avenue to Canal Street and back.

Two or three weeks before Mardi Gras, parades begin chugging
through the streets with increasing frequency. There are plenty of
parodies, like the parade of the **Mystick Krewe of Barkus**. Barkus
is, as you might guess, a krewe for pets that parades through the
Quarter (some of the dogs get quite gussied up) and is a total hoot.

If you want to experience Mardi Gras but don't want to face the
full force of craziness, consider coming for the weekend 10 days
before Fat Tuesday (the season officially begins the Fri of this weekend). You can count on 10 to 15 parades during the weekend by
lesser-known krewes like Cleopatra, Pontchartrain, Sparta, and
Camelot. The crowds are more manageable during this time.

The following weekend there are another 15 parades—the big-
gies. Everything's bigger: The parades are bigger, the crowds are
bigger; the city has succumbed to Carnival fever. After a day of
screaming for beads, you'll probably find yourself heading
somewhere to get a drink or three. The French Quarter will be the
center of late-night revelry; all of the larger bars will be packed. The
last parade each day (on both weekends) usually ends around
9:30pm or later.

LUNDI GRAS   In the 19th century, Rex's **King of Carnival**
arrived downtown from the Mississippi River on this night, the
Monday before Fat Tuesday. Over the years, the day gradually lost
its special significance, becoming just another day of parades. In the

1980s, however, Rex revived Lundi Gras, the old tradition of arriving on the Mississippi.

These days, festivities at the riverfront begin in the afternoon with lots of drink and live music leading up to the King's arrival at around 6pm. Down the levee a few hundred feet, at Wolfen-berg Park, Zulu has its own Lundi Gras celebration with the king arriving at around 5pm. In 1999, for the first time, King Zulu met up with Rex in an impressive ceremony. That night, the **Krewe of Orpheus** holds their parade. It's one of the biggest and most popular parades, thanks to the generosity of the krewe's throws. It holds fast to old Mardi Gras traditions, including floats designed by master float creator Henri Schindler. For Mardi Gras 2000, venerable Proteus returned to parading, right before Orpheus.

Because Lent begins the following night at midnight, Monday is the final dusk-to-dawn night of Mardi Gras. A good portion of the city forgoes sleep so as not to waste the occasion—which only adds to the craziness.

MARDI GRAS The day begins early, starting with the two biggest parades, **Zulu** and **Rex,** which run back to back. Zulu starts near the CBD at 8:30am; Rex starts Uptown at 10am. Generally, the best place to watch parades on St. Charles Avenue is between Napoleon and Jackson avenues, where the crowds are somewhat smaller and consist mostly of local families and college students.

It will be early afternoon when Rex spills into the Central Business District. Nearby at about this time, you can find some of the most elusive New Orleans figures, the **Mardi Gras Indians.** The "tribes" of New Orleans are small communities of African Americans and black Creoles (some of whom have Native American ancestors), mostly from the inner city. Their elaborate (and that's an understatement) beaded and feathered costumes, rivaling Bob Mackie Vegas headdresses in outrageousness and size, are entirely made by hand.

After the parades, the action picks up in the Quarter. En route, you'll see that Mardi Gras is still very much a family tradition, with whole families dressing up in similar costumes. Marvel at how an entire city has shut down so that every citizen can join in the celebrations. Some people don't bother hitting the streets; instead, they hang out on their balconies watching the action below or have barbecues in their courtyards. If you are lucky and seem like the right sort, you might well get invited in.

In the Quarter, the frat-party action is largely confined to Bourbon Street. The more interesting activity is in the lower

Quarter and the Frenchmen section of the Faubourg Marigny (just east of the Quarter), where the artists and gay community really know how to celebrate. The costumes are elaborate works of art. Although the people may be (OK, probably *will* be) drunk, they are boisterous and enthusiastic, not (for the most part) obnoxious.

PLANNING A VISIT DURING MARDI GRAS

LODGING   You can't just drop in on Mardi Gras. If you do, you may find yourself sleeping in Jackson Square or on a sidewalk somewhere. Accommodations in the city and the nearby suburbs are booked solid, *so make your plans well ahead and book a room as early as possible.* Many people plan a year or more in advance. Prices are usually much higher during Mardi Gras, and most hotels and guesthouses impose minimum-stay requirements.

CLOTHING   As with anything in New Orleans, you must join in if you want to have the best time. Simply being a spectator is not enough. And that means a **costume** and **mask.** Once you are masked and dressed up, you are automatically part of it all. (Tellingly, the Bourbon Street participants usually do not wear costumes.) As far as costumes go, you need not do anything fancy. If you've come unprepared, several shops in town specialize in Mardi Gras costumes and masks. One of the most reasonable is the **Mardi Gras Center,** 831 Chartres St. ((✆ **504/524-4384**).

DINING   If you want to eat at a restaurant during Mardi Gras, make reservations as early as possible. And pay very close attention to **parade routes,** because if there is one between you and your restaurant, you may not be able to cross the street, and you can kiss your dinner goodbye. This might work to your advantage; often restaurants have a high no-show rate during Mardi Gras for this reason, and so a well-timed drop-in may work.

PARKING   Even though the huge crowds everywhere add to the general merriment, they also grind traffic to a halt all over town. So our admonition against renting a car is even stronger during Mardi Gras. *Don't drive.* Instead, relax and take a cab or walk. Remember, the fun is everywhere, so you don't really have to go anywhere. Parking along any parade route is not allowed 2 hours before and 2 hours after the parade. In addition, although you'll see people leaving their cars on "neutral ground" (the median strip), it's illegal to park there, and chances are good that you'll be towed. Traffic in New Orleans is never worse than *in the hour after a parade.*

Tips **For More Information . . .**

You'll enjoy Mardi Gras more if you've done a little home-work before your trip. You'll want to get your hands on the 2002 edition of *Arthur Hardy's Mardi Gras Guide* as early as possible. Your best bet is to call the magazine directly (© 504/838-6111; mardihardy@aol.com). It is an invaluable guide full of history, tips, and maps of the parade routes.

Also a terrific buy is the **MardiCard,** a combination map and Mardi Gras schedule full of insider tips to help you find the best stuff to see during the greatest free show and party in the country. It folds up into pocket size and is most handy for taking around during the day. Check out the website for additional informational resources: **www.mardicard.com**. You can buy the MardiCard at, among other places, Accent Annex (633 Toulouse St.), the House of Blues gift shop (225 Decatur St.), Lenny's News (5420 Magazine St. and 622 Carrollton Ave.), and Martin's Wine Cellar (3827 Baronne St.).

SAFETY   Many, many cops are out, making the walk from uptown to downtown safer than at other times of year, but, not surprisingly, the streets of New Orleans are a haven for pickpockets during Mardi Gras. Take precautions.

CAJUN MARDI GRAS

Mardi Gras in New Orleans sounds like too much for you, no matter how low-key you keep it? Consider driving out to Cajun country, where Mardi Gras traditions are just as strong but consid-erably more, errr, wholesome. **Lafayette,** the capital of French Acadiana, celebrates Carnival in a different manner, one that reflects the Cajun heritage and spirit. Three full days of activities lead up to Cajun Mardi Gras, making it second in size only to New Orleans's celebration. There's one *big* difference, though: The Cajuns open their final pageant and ball to the general public. Don your formal wear and join right in!

Things get off to a joyous start with the **Children's Krewe** and **Krewe of Bonaparte** parades and ball, held on the Saturday before Mardi Gras following a full day of celebration at Acadian Village. On Monday night, Queen Evangeline is honored at the **Queen's Parade.** The **King's Parade,** held the following morning, honors King Gabriel and opens a full day of merriment. Lafayette's African-American community stages the **Parade of King Toussaint**

L'Ouverture and Queen Suzanne Simonne at about noon, just after the King's Parade. Then the Krewe of Lafayette invites everyone to get into the act as its parade winds through the streets. Krewe participants trot along on foot or ride in the vehicle of their choice—some very imaginative modes of transportation turn up every year. The Mardi Gras climax, a formal ball presided over by the king and queen and their royal court, takes place that night. Everything stops promptly at midnight, when all depart to begin observance of Lent.

MASKED MEN AND A BIG GUMBO   In the Cajun countryside that surrounds Lafayette, there's yet another form of Mardi Gras celebration, one tied to the rural lifestyle. Cajuns firmly believe in sharing, so you're welcome to come along. The celebration goes like this: Bands of masked men dressed in raggedy patchwork costumes (unlike the New Orleans costumes, which are heavy on glitter and shine) and peaked hats known as *capichons* set off on Mardi Gras morning on horseback, led by their *capitaine*. They ride from farm to farm, asking at each, *"Voulez-vous reçevoir le Mardi Gras?"* ("Will you receive the Mardi Gras?") and dismounting as the invariable *"Oui"* comes in reply. Each farmyard then becomes a miniature festival as the revelers *faire le macaque* ("make monkeyshines") with song and dance, much drinking of beer, and other antics loosely labeled "entertainment." As payment for their show, they demand, and get, "a fat little chicken to make a big gumbo" (or sometimes a bag of rice or other ingredients).

When each band has visited its allotted farmyards, they all head back to town where there is dancing in the streets, rowdy card games, storytelling, and the like until the wee hours, and you can be sure that all those fat little chickens go into the *"gumbo gros"* pot to make a very big gumbo indeed.

You can write or call ahead for particulars on both the urban and rural Mardi Gras celebrations. For the latter, the towns of Eunice and Mamou stage some of the most enjoyable celebrations. Contact the Lafayette Parish Convention and Visitors Commission, P.O. Box 52066, Lafayette, LA 70505 (© 800/346-1958 in the U.S., 800/543-5340 in Canada, or 337/232-3737; www.lafayettetravel.com).

THE NEW ORLEANS JAZZ & HERITAGE FESTIVAL

People call it "Jazz Fest," but the full name is the New Orleans Jazz and Heritage Festival, and the heritage is about as broad as it can get. Stand in the right place and, depending on which way the wind's blowing, you can catch as many as 10 musical styles from several continents, smell the tantalizing aromas of different food offerings, and meet a U.N.–like spectrum of fellow fest goers all at once.

While such headliners as Dave Matthews, Bob Dylan, and Paul Simon have drawn record-setting crowds in recent years, serious Jazz Fest aficionados savor the lesser-known acts. They range from Mardi Gras Indians to old-time bluesmen who have never played outside the Delta, from Dixieland to African artists making rare U.S. appearances to the top names in Cajun, zydeco, and, of course, jazz.

Gone are the days when only a few hundred people came to celebrate. Now filling the infield of the Fair Grounds horse-racing track up near City Park, the festival (which covers the last weekend in Apr and the first in May) is set up about as well as such an event can be. When the crowds get big, though—the second Saturday traditionally is the busiest—it can be tough to move around, especially if the grounds are muddy from rain. However, the crowds are remarkably well behaved—to make a sweeping generalization, these are not the same types who come for Mardi Gras.

EVERY DAY A GOOD DAY   Hotel and restaurant reservations, not to mention choice plane flights, fill up months (if not a year) in advance, but the schedule is not announced until a couple of months before the event. That may mean scheduling your visit around your own availability, not an appearance by a particular band. Just about every day at Jazz Fest is a good day, however, so this is not a hardship—at least, until you learn about an extraordinary group that is playing on a day you won't be in town. Or you could do like we do: Go for the whole 10 days so you won't miss a thing.

The second Saturday does attract some of the top acts, and each year it sets a record for single-day attendance. But we feel the fun tends to diminish with that many people. Still, the tickets are cheap enough that going early in the day and leaving before the crowds get too big is a viable option. The Thursday before the second weekend is traditionally targeted to locals, with more local bands and generally smaller crowds because fewer tourists are around than on the weekends. It's a great time to hit the best food booths and to check out the shopping in the crafts areas.

Contact the **New Orleans Jazz and Heritage Festival,** 1205 N. Rampart St., New Orleans, LA 70116 (✆ **504/522-4786;** www. nojazzfest.com), to get the schedule for each weekend and information about other Jazz Fest–related shows around town.

JAZZ FEST POINTERS

A typical Jazz Fest day has you arriving sometime after the gates open at 11am and staying until you are pooped or until they close at around 7pm. Go back to where you are staying, get some dinner, and then hit the clubs. All night long, every club in the city has Jazz Fest–related bookings. Then you get up and start all over again. This is part of the reason we think Jazz Fest is so darn fun.

There are many nonmusical aspects of Jazz Fest to distract you, particularly the crafts. Local craftspeople and imported artisans fill a sizable section of the Fair Grounds with demonstrations and displays of their products during the festival. You might get to see Louisiana Native American basket making; Cajun accordion, fiddle, and triangle making; decoy carving; boat building; and Mardi Gras Indian beading and costume making.

And then there's the food. The heck with the music—when we dream of Jazz Fest, we are often thinking more about those 50-plus food booths filled with some of the best goodies we've ever tasted. The food ranges from local standbys—red beans and rice, jambalaya, étouffée, and gumbo—to more interesting choices such as oyster sacks, the hugely popular sausage bread, *cochon de lait* (a mouthwatering roast pig sandwich), alligator sausage po' boys, and quail and pheasant gumbo. There's plenty of cold beer, too, although you'll probably have to wait in some mighty long lines to get to it.

Try to purchase tickets as early as February if possible. They're available by mail through **TicketMaster** (© **504/522-5555**). To order tickets by phone or to get ticket information, call **New Orleans Jazz and Heritage Festival** (© **800/488-5252** outside Louisiana, or 504/522-4786; fax 504/379-3291). Admission for adults is $12 in advance and $16 at the gate; for children, $1.50 in advance and $2 at the gate. Evening events and concerts (order tickets in advance for these events as well) may be attended at an additional cost—usually between $20 and $30, depending on the concert.

JAZZ FEST PARKING & TRANSPORTATION   Parking at the Fair Grounds is next to impossible. The few available spaces cost $10 a day, but it's rare to get a space there. We strongly recommend that you take public transportation or one of the available shuttles.

The **Regional Transit Authority** operates bus routes from various pickup points to the Fair Grounds. Call © **504/248-3900.** Taxis, though probably scarce, will also take you to the Fair Grounds at a special event rate of $3 per person (or the meter reading if it's higher). We recommend **United Cabs** (© 504/524-9606).

PACKAGE DEALS If you want to go to Jazz Fest but would rather have someone else do all the planning, consider contacting **Festival Tours International,** 15237 Sunset Blvd., Suite 17, Pacific Palisades, CA 90272 (© 310/454-4080; Festtours@aol.com), which caters to music lovers who don't wish to wear name tags or do other hokey tour activities. Packages include accommodations, tickets, and also a visit to Cajun country for unique personal encounters with some of the finest local musicians. If you're flying to New Orleans specifically for the Jazz and Heritage Festival, consider calling **Continental Airlines** (© 800/525-0280 or 504/581-2965; www.flycontinental.com). It's the official airline of Jazz Fest and offers special fares during the event. You'll need the Jazz Fest promotional code, available from the festival's information line.

5 Tips for Travelers with Special Needs

FOR TRAVELERS WITH DISABILITIES

Be aware that while New Orleans facilities are mostly accessible (especially in the Quarter) with proprietors being most accommodating (opening narrow doors wider to fit wheelchairs and such), you are still dealing with older structures created before thoughts of ease for those with disabilities. Before you book a hotel, **ask questions** based on your needs. If you have mobility issues, you'll probably do best to stay in one of the city's newer hotels, which tend to be more spacious and accommodating. Sidewalks are often bumpy and uneven, and getting on the St. Charles streetcar might be too great a challenge.

For information about specialized transportation systems, call **LIFT** (© 504/827-7433).

You can join **The Society for Accessible Travel & Hospitality,** 347 Fifth Ave., Suite 610, New York, NY 10016 (© 212/447-7284; fax 212-725-8253; www.sath.org), to gain access to its vast network of connections in the travel industry. It provides information sheets on destinations and referrals to tour operators that specialize in traveling with disabilities. The society's quarterly magazine, *Open World,* is full of good information and resources.

The Moss Rehab Hospital (© 800/CALL-MOSS; 215/456-9600) has been providing friendly and helpful phone advice and referrals to travelers with disabilities for years through its **Travel Information Service** (© 215/456-9603). The website (**www. mossresourcenet.org**) is a great source for information, tips, and resources relating to accessible travel.

FOR GAY & LESBIAN TRAVELERS

This is a very gay-friendly town with a high-profile homosexual population that contributes much to the color and flavor of the city. You'll find an abundance of establishments serving gay and lesbian interests, from bars to restaurants to community services to certain businesses.

If you need help finding your way, you can stop by or call the **Gay and Lesbian Community Center,** 2114 Decatur St. (© 504/945-1103; fax 504/945-1102); hours vary, so call before stopping in.

Ambush Magazine, 828-A Bourbon St., New Orleans, LA 70116 (© **504/522-8047;** www.ambushmag.com), is a weekly entertainment and news publication for the Gulf South's gay, lesbian, bisexual, and transgender communities. *Impact Gulf South Gay News* is another popular area publication.

Grace Fellowship, 3151 Dauphine St. (© **504/944-9836**), and the **Vieux Carré Metropolitan Community Church,** 1128 St. Roch Ave. (© **504/945-5390**), are religious organizations that serve primarily gay congregations. Both invite visitors to attend services.

One useful website is **www.gayneworleans.com**, which provides information on lodging, dining, arts, and nightlife as well as links to other information on New Orleans gay life.

Above and Beyond Tours (© **800/397-2681**), is a travel agency that specializes in arranging tours for gay men mainly.

FOR SENIORS

Don't be shy about asking for discounts, but always carry some kind of identification, such as a driver's license, that shows your date of birth, especially if you've kept your youthful glow.

Also mention the fact that you're a senior when you first make your travel reservations. Both **Amtrak** (© **800/USA-RAIL;** www. amtrak.com) and **Greyhound** (© **800/231-2222;** www.greyhound. com) offer discounts to persons over 62, and most **major domestic airlines** offer discounts for senior travelers.

Members of the **American Association of Retired Persons (AARP),** 601 E St. NW, Washington, DC 20049 (© **800/424-3410;** www.aarp.org), get discounts on hotels, airfares, and car rentals. The AARP offers members a wide range of special benefits, including *Modern Maturity* magazine and a monthly newsletter. If you're not already a member, do yourself a favor and join.

6 Getting There

BY PLANE

Among the airlines serving the city's newly renamed **Louis Armstrong New Orleans International Airport** are: **America West** (*©* 800/235-9292; www.americawest.com), **American** (*©* 800/433-7300; www.im.aa.com), **Continental** (*©* 800/525-0280 or 504/581-2965; www.continental.com), **Delta** (*©* 800/221-1212; www.delta.com), **Northwest** (*©* 800/225-2525; www.nwa.com), **Southwest** (*©* 800/435-9792; www.iflyswa.com), **TWA** (*©* 800/221-2000; www.twa.com), **US Airways** (*©* 800/428-4322; www.usairways.com), and **United** (*©* 800/241-6522; www.ual.com). The airport is 15 miles west of the city, in Kenner.

BY CAR

You can drive to New Orleans via **I-10, I-55, U.S. 90, U.S. 61,** or across the Lake Pontchartrain Causeway on **La. 25.** From any direction, you'll see the city's distinctive and swampy outlying regions; if you can, try to drive in while you can enjoy the scenery in daylight. For the best roadside views, take U.S. 61 or La. 25, but only if you have time to spare. The larger roads are considerably faster.

It's a good idea to call before you leave home to ask directions to your hotel. Most hotels have parking facilities (for a fee); if they don't they'll give you the names and addresses of nearby parking lots.

Driving in New Orleans can be a hassle, and parking is a nightmare. Cabs are plentiful and not too pricey, so you really don't need a car in New Orleans unless you're planning several day trips.

Nevertheless, most major car-rental companies are at the airport including **Alamo** (*©* 800/327-9633; www.goalamo.com), **Avis** (*©* 800/331-1212; www.avis.com), **Budget** (*©* 800/527-0700; www.budgetrentacar.com), **Dollar** (*©* 800/800-4000; www.dollarcar.com), **Hertz** (*©* 800/654-3131; www.hertz.com), and **National** (*©* 800/227-7368; www.nationalcar.com).

BY TRAIN

The passenger rail lines cut through some beautiful scenery. **Amtrak** (*©* **800/USA-RAIL** or 504/528-1610; www.amtrak.com) trains serve the city's **Union Passenger Terminal,** 1001 Loyola Ave., from Los Angeles and intermediate points; from New York, Washington, and points in between; and from Chicago and intermediate points. The New Orleans train station is in the Central Business District. Taxis wait outside the main entrance to the passenger terminal. Hotels in the French Quarter and the Central Business District are a short ride away.

2

Getting to Know New Orleans

New Orleans is a very user-friendly city—that is, if you don't count the unusual directions and the nearly impossible-to-pronounce street names. It's a manageable size (only about 7 miles long), with most of what the average tourist would want to see concentrated in a few areas. This chapter contains some of the ins and outs of New Orleans navigation and gives you some local sources to contact for specialized information.

1 Orientation

ARRIVING

From the airport, you can get to your hotel on the Airport Shuttle (& 504/522-3500). For $10 per person (one way), the van will take you directly to your hotel. There are Airport Shuttle information desks (staffed 24 hr.) in the airport.

Note: If you plan to take the Airport Shuttle *to* the airport when you leave, call a day in advance and let them know what time your flight is leaving. They'll tell you what time they will pick you up.

A **taxi** from the airport to most hotels will cost about $21; if there are three or more passengers, the fare is $8 per person.

From the airport, you can reach the **Central Business District** by bus for $1.50 (exact change required). Buses run from 6am to 6:30pm. From 6 to 9am and 3 to 6pm, they leave the airport every 12 to 15 minutes and go to the downtown side of Tulane Avenue between Elks Place and South Saratoga Street; at other times, they leave every 23 minutes. For more information, call the **Louisiana Transit Company** (© **504/818-1077**).

VISITOR INFORMATION

The **New Orleans Metropolitan Convention and Visitors Bureau,** 1520 Sugar Bowl Dr., New Orleans, LA 70112 (© **800/672-6124** or 504/566-5003; www.neworleanscvb.com), is one of the most helpful tourist centers in any major city. Not only does it have a wide array of well-written brochures that cover everything from usual sightseeing questions to cultural history, the incredibly friendly and helpful staff can answer almost any random question you may have.

Once you've arrived in the city, you also might want to stop by the **Visitor Information Center,** 529 St. Ann St. (© **504/566-5031**), in the French Quarter. The center is open daily from 9am to 5pm and has walking- and driving-tour maps, and booklets on restaurants, accommodations, sightseeing, special tours, and pretty much anything else you might want to know about. The staff is friendly and knowledgeable about both the city and the state. You also might keep an eye out for the mobile **Info a la Cart** sites around town.

CITY LAYOUT

"Where y'at?" goes the traditional local greeting. "Where" is easy enough when you are in the French Quarter, the site of the original settlement. A 13-block-long grid between Canal Street and Esplanade Avenue, running from the Mississippi River to North Rampart Street, it's the closest the city comes to a geographic center.

After that, all bets are off. Because of the bend in the river, the streets are laid out at angles and curves that render north, south, east, and west useless. It's time to readjust your thinking: In New Orleans, the compass points are *riverside, lakeside, uptown,* and *downtown.* Keep in mind that North Rampart Street is the *lakeside* boundary of the Quarter and that St. Charles Avenue extends from the French Quarter, *downtown,* to Tulane University, *uptown.*

Canal Street forms the boundary between new and old New Orleans. Street names change when they cross Canal (Bourbon Street, for example, becomes Carondelet Street), and addresses begin at 100 on either side of Canal. In the Quarter, street numbers begin at 400 at the river because four blocks of numbered buildings were lost to the river before the levee was built).

THE NEIGHBORHOODS IN BRIEF

The French Quarter Made up of about 90 square blocks, this section is also known as the *Vieux Carré* ("Old Square") and is enclosed by Canal Street, North Rampart Street, the Mississippi River, and Esplanade Avenue. The Quarter is full of clubs, bars, stores, residences, and museums; its major public area is Jackson Square, bounded by Chartres, Decatur, St. Peter, and St. Ann streets. The most historic and best-preserved area in the city, it's likely to be the focal point of your stay.

Faubourg Marigny This area is east of the French Quarter (on the other side of Esplanade Avenue). Over the past decade, the Marigny has emerged as one of the city's vital centers of activity. You can still find the outlines of a small Creole suburb, and many old-time residents remain. Younger urban dwellers have moved into the area in significant numbers recently. Today, some of the best bars and nightspots in New Orleans are along Frenchmen Street, the Marigny's main drag. Along with the adjacent sections of the French Quarter, the Marigny is also a social center for the city's gay and lesbian communities.

Bywater This riverside neighborhood is past the Faubourg Marigny and is bounded on the east by an industrial canal. It is tempting to misspeak and call it "Backwater" because, at first glance, it seems like a wasteland of light industry and run-down homes. In fact, Bywater has plenty of nice, modest residential sections. It's home to the city's artists-in-hiding, and many local designers have shops among the urban decay. This is in keeping with the history of the area, which early on was home to artisans as well as communities of immigrants and free people of color.

Mid City/Esplanade Ridge Stretching north from the French Quarter to City Park, the Ridge hugs either side of Esplanade Avenue. This area encompasses a few distinct neighborhoods, all of which have certain things in common. In the 19th century, Esplanade was the grand avenue of New Orleans Creole society—the St. Charles Avenue of downriver. There is still evidence of those times, especially in the ancient oak trees forming a canopy above the road.

The oldest section of Esplanade Ridge, **Faubourg Treme,** is located directly across Rampart Street from the French Quarter. Like the Quarter, it was a dense 19th-century Creole community. Unlike the Quarter, Treme has remained almost untouched by preservationists and so has continued to be an organic residential community. Today, it is one of the most vibrant African-American neighborhoods in New Orleans, home to more than a few of the city's best brass bands. Unfortunately, Treme is also plagued by severe crime, so it's not advisable to walk through at night.

Central Business District Historically, **Canal Street** has been New Orleans's main street, and in the 19th century, it divided the French and American sections of the city. (By the way, there's no canal—the one that was planned for the spot never came off.)

The City at a Glance

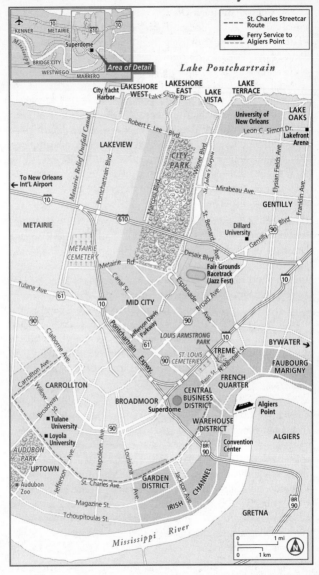

St. Charles Streetcar Route

Ferry Service to Algiers Point

Area of Detail

Lake Pontchartrain

Mississippi River

23

The **Central Business District (CBD)** is roughly bounded by Canal Street and the elevated Pontchartrain Expressway (Business Route U.S. 90) between Loyola Avenue and the Mississippi River. Some of the most elegant luxury hotels are in this area. Most of the district was known as Faubourg St. Mary when Americans began settling here after the Louisiana Purchase. Lafayette Square was the center of life here during the 19th century.

Within the CBD is the **Warehouse District.** More than 20 years ago, this area was full of abandoned warehouses and almost nothing else. With the efforts of some dedicated individuals and institutions, however, it's steadily evolving into a residential neighborhood with some commercial activity. Furthermore, this area also serves as the city's art gallery district, with many of the premier galleries concentrated along Julia Street.

Uptown/The Garden District Bounded by St. Charles Avenue (lakeside) and Magazine Street (riverside) between Jackson and Louisiana avenues, the Garden District remains one of the most picturesque areas in the city. Originally the site of a plantation, the area was subdivided and developed as a residential neighborhood for wealthy Americans. Throughout the middle of the 19th century, developers built the Victorian, Italianate, and Greek Revival homes that still line the streets. Most of the homes had elaborate lawns and gardens, but few of those still exist. The Garden District is located uptown (as opposed to the CBD, which is downtown); the neighborhood west of the Garden District is often called Uptown.

The Irish Channel The area bounded by Magazine Street and the Mississippi River, Louisiana Avenue, and the Central Business District got its name during the 1800s when more than 100,000 Irish immigrated to New Orleans. As was true elsewhere in the country, the Irish of New Orleans were often considered "expendable" labor. Many were killed while employed in dangerous labor. These days, the Channel is significantly less Irish, but it retains its lively spirit and distinctive neighborhood flavor. Much of the area is run-down, but just as much is filled with quiet residential neighborhoods. To get a glimpse of the Irish Channel, go to the antiques shop district on Magazine Street and stroll between Felicity Street and Jackson Avenue.

Algiers Point Directly across the Mississippi River from the Central Business District and the French Quarter and connected by the Canal Street Ferry, the point is the old town center of Algiers. It is another of the city's original Creole suburbs but probably the one that has changed the least over the decades. Today, you can see some of the best-preserved small gingerbread and Creole cottages in New Orleans. The neighborhood has recently begun to attract attention as a historic landmark, and it makes for one of the city's most pleasant strolls.

SAFETY

Although the city's high crime rate has made headlines over the past few years, an increased police force and vigilance have led to a decrease in crime. Problems still remain, however, and we want to help you avoid them as best you can.

The **French Quarter** is fairly safe, thanks to the number of people present at any given time, but some areas are better than others. On Bourbon Street, be careful when socializing with strangers and be alert to distractions by potential pickpocket teams. Dauphine and Burgundy are in quiet, lovely old parts of the Quarter, but as you near Esplanade, watch out for purse-snatchers. At night, stay in well-lighted areas with street and pedestrian traffic and take cabs down Esplanade and into the **Faubourg Marigny.** Conventional wisdom holds that one should not go much above Bourbon toward Rampart alone after dark, though the increased vigilance has meant a decrease in problems. Still, it might be best to stay in a group (or near one) if you can; and if you feel uncomfortable, consider taking a cab, even if it seems silly, for the (very) short ride. In the **Garden District,** as you get past Magazine toward the river, the neighborhoods can be rough, so exercise caution (more cabs, probably).

2 Getting Around

You really don't need to rent a car during your stay. Not only is the town just made for walking (thanks to being so flat—and so darn picturesque), most places you want to go are easily accessible on foot or by some form of the largely excellent public transportation system. Indeed, we find a streetcar ride to be as much entertainment as a practical means of getting around. At night, when you need them most, cabs are easy to come by. Meanwhile, driving and parking in the French Quarter bring grief. The streets are narrow and crowded, and many go one way only. Street parking is minimal (and likely to attract thieves), and parking lots are fiendishly expensive.

BY PUBLIC TRANSPORTATION

DISCOUNT PASSES   If you won't have a car in New Orleans, we strongly encourage you to invest in a **VisiTour** pass, which entitles you to an unlimited number of rides on all streetcar and bus lines. It costs $5 for 1 day, $12 for 3 days. Many visitors think this was the best tip they got about their New Orleans stay and the finest bargain in town. Passes are available from VisiTour vendors—to find the nearest one, ask at your hotel or guest house or call the **Regional Transit Authority** (℃ **504/248-3900**). You can call the RTA for information about any part of the city's public transportation system.

BUSES New Orleans has an excellent public bus system, so chances are there's a bus that runs exactly where you want to go. Local fares at press time are $1.25 (you must have exact change in bills or coins), transfers are an extra 25¢, and express buses are $1.25. You can get complete route information by calling the RTA (℃ **504/248-3900**) or by picking up one of the excellent city maps available at the Visitor Information Center, 529 St. Ann St. (℃ **504/566-5021**), in the French Quarter.

STREETCARS Besides being a national historic landmark, the **St. Charles Avenue streetcar** is also a convenient and fun way to get from downtown to Uptown and back. The trolleys run 24 hours a day at frequent intervals, and the fare is $1.25 each way (you must have exact change in bills or coins). It can get crowded at rush hour and when school is out for the day. Board at Canal and Carondelet streets (directly across Canal from Bourbon Street in the French Quarter) or anywhere along St. Charles, sit back, and look for landmarks or just enjoy the scenery.

The streetcar line extends beyond the point where St. Charles Avenue bends into Carrollton Avenue. The end of the line is at Palmer Park and Playground at Claiborne Avenue. It will cost you another $1 for the ride back to Canal Street. It costs 10¢ to transfer from the streetcar to a bus.

The **riverfront streetcar** runs from the Old Mint across Canal Street to Riverview, with stops along the way. It's a great step saver as you explore the riverfront. The fare is $1.25.

BY CAR

If you absolutely have to have a car, try one of the following car rental agencies: **Avis,** 2024 Canal St. (℃ **800/331-1212** or 504/523-4317; www.avis.com); **Budget Rent-A-Car,** 1317 Canal St. (℃ **800/527-0700** or 504/467-2277; www.budgetrentacar. com); **Dollar Rent-A-Car,** 1910 Airline Hwy., Kenner (℃ **800/ 800-4000** or 504/467-2285; www.dollarcar.com); **Hertz,** 901 Convention Center Blvd., No. 101 (℃ **800/654-3131** or 504/568-1645;

www.hertz.com); **Swifty Car Rental,** 2300 Canal St. (© **504/524-7368**); or **Alamo,** 1806 Airline Hwy., Kenner (© **800/GO-VALUE;** www.goalamo.com).

New Orleans drivers are often reckless, so drive defensively. The meter maids are an efficient bunch, so take no chances with parking meters, and carry quarters. It's probably best to use your car only for longer jaunts away from congested areas. Most hotels provide guest parking, often for a daily fee; smaller hotels or guesthouses (particularly in the French Quarter) may not have parking facilities but will be able to direct you to a nearby public garage.

The narrow streets and frequent congestion make driving in the French Quarter more difficult than elsewhere in the city. The streets are one way, and on weekdays during daylight hours, Royal and Bourbon streets between the 300 and 700 blocks are closed to automobiles. Also, the blocks of Chartres Street in front of St. Louis Cathedral are closed at all times. Driving is also trying in the Central Business District, where congestion and limited parking make life difficult for the motorist. Do yourself a favor: Park the car and use public transportation in both areas.

Once you get into more residential areas like the Garden District and off main drags like St. Charles Avenue, finding where you're going becomes quite the challenge. Street signs are often no bigger than a postcard and hard to read at that. At night they aren't even lit, so deciphering where you are can be next to impossible. If you must drive, we suggest counting the number of streets you have to cross to tell you when to make turns rather than relying on street signs.

BY TAXI

Taxis are plentiful in New Orleans. They can be hailed easily on the street in the French Quarter and in some parts of the Central Business District, and they are usually lined up at taxi stands at larger hotels. Otherwise, telephone and expect a cab to appear in 3 to 5 minutes. The rate is $2.10 when you enter the taxi and $1.20 per mile thereafter. During festival time, the rate is $3 per person (or the meter rate if it's greater) no matter where you go in the city. The city's most reliable company is **United Cabs** (© **504/524-9606**).

Most taxis can be hired for a special rate for up to five passengers. It's a hassle-free and economical way for a small group to tour far-flung areas of the city (the lakefront, for example). Within the city you pay an hourly rate; out-of-town trips cost double the amount on the meter.

ON FOOT

We can't stress this enough: Walking is by far the best way to see this town. There are too many unique and sometimes glorious sights to want to whiz past them. Sure, sometimes it's too darn hot or humid to make walking attractive, but there is always a cab or bus nearby. Drink lots of water if it's hot and pay close attention to your surroundings. If you enter an area that seems unsafe, retreat.

BY FERRY

The Canal Street ferry is one of the city's secrets—and it's free for pedestrians. The ride takes you across the Mississippi River from the foot of Canal to Algiers Point (25 min. round-trip), and it affords great views of downtown. Once in Algiers, you can take a walking tour of the old Algiers Point neighborhood and tour Mardi Gras World. At night, with the city's glowing skyline reflecting on the river, a ride on the ferry can be quite romantic. The ferry also does carry car traffic, in case you'd like to do some West Bank driving.

 FAST FACTS: New Orleans

American Express The local office (© 504/586-8201) is at 201 St. Charles Ave. in the Central Business District. It's open weekdays from 9am to 5pm.

Babysitters Ask at your hotel about babysitting services. If your hotel doesn't offer help finding childcare, try calling **Accent on Children's Arrangements** (© 504/524-1227) or **Dependable Kid Care** (© 504/486-4001).

Convention Center The **Ernest N. Morial Convention Center** (© 504/582-3000) is at 900 Convention Center Blvd.

Emergencies For fire, ambulance, and police, dial © **911.** This is a free call from pay phones.

Hospitals Most major hotels have in-house doctors on call 24 hours a day. If no one is available at your hotel or guesthouse, call or go to the emergency room at **Ochsner Medical Institutions,** 1516 Jefferson Hwy. (© **504/842-3460**), or the **Tulane University Medical Center,** 1415 Tulane Ave. (© 504/ 588-5800).

Internet Access The **Royal Access,** 621 Royal St. (© 504/525-0401) is open Monday through Thursday from 9am to 8pm; Friday through Saturday from 9am to 10pm; and Sunday from

9am to 6pm. Note, however, that in this changing world, cybercafes can come and go with the lifespan of a gnat, so call ahead before you go.

Liquor Laws The legal drinking age in Louisiana is 21, but don't be surprised if people much younger take a seat next to you at the bar. Alcoholic beverages are available around the clock, 7 days a week. You're allowed to drink on the street but not from a glass or bottle. Bars will often provide a plastic "go cup" so that you can transfer your drink as you leave (and some have walk-up windows for quick and easy refills). *One warning:* Although the police may look the other way if they see a pedestrian who's had a few too many (as long as he or she is peaceful and is not bothering anyone), they have no tolerance at all for those who are intoxicated behind the wheel.

Newspapers & Magazines To find out what's going on around town, you might want to pick up a copy of the daily *Times-Picayune* or *Offbeat,* a monthly guide (probably the most extensive one available) to the city's evening entertainment, art galleries, and special events. It can be found in most hotels, though it's often hard to locate toward the end of the month. The *Gambit Weekly* is the city's free alternative paper and has a good mix of news and entertainment information. It comes out every Thursday. The paper conducts an annual **"Best of New Orleans"** readers' poll; results are posted at www.bestofneworleans.com.

Pharmacies The 24-hour pharmacy closest to the French Quarter is **Walgreens**, 3311 Canal St., at Jefferson Davis (© **504/822-8072**). There is also a 24-hour **Rite-Aid** at 3401 St. Charles Ave. (© **504/896-4575**), which is more convenient if you're staying Uptown or in the Garden District.

Photographic Needs Two good options for 1-hour film processing are **Fox Photo Labs,** 414 Canal St. (© **504/568-0198**), and **French Quarter Camera,** 809 Decatur St. (© **504/529-2974**). Disposable and inexpensive cameras, film, and batteries can be found in any of the many corner grocery stores in the Quarter.

Post Office The main post office is at 701 Loyola Ave. There's also a post office in the World Trade Center. If you're in the Quarter, you'll find a post office at 1022 Iberville St. There's another one at 610 S. Maestri Place. If you have something large or fragile to send home and don't feel like hunting around for packing materials, go to **Royal Mail & Parcel,** 828 Royal St. (*②* **504/522-8523**) in the Quarter, or **Mail Box Pack & Ship,** 1201 St. Charles (*②* **504/524-5080**) uptown. The latter also has pickup service.

Radio WWOZ (FM 90.7) is *the* New Orleans radio station. They say they are the best in the world, and we aren't inclined to disagree. New Orleans jazz, R&B, brass bands, Mardi Gras Indians, gospel, Cajun, zydeco—it's all here. Don't miss music historian (and former White Panther activist, memorialized in a song by John Lennon) John Sinclair's shows (at press time, Wednesday from 11am to 2pm and Sunday from 2 to 5am), which got him named Best DJ in *OffBeat*'s annual poll. The city's NPR station is WWNO (FM 89.9). Also, Tulane's station, WTUL (FM 91.5), plays very interesting music.

Safety Be careful while visiting any unfamiliar city. In New Orleans, in particular, don't walk alone at night and don't go into the cemeteries alone at any time during the day or night. Ask around locally before you go anywhere; people will tell you if you should take a cab instead of walking or using public transportation. Most important, if someone holds you up and demands your wallet, purse, or other personal belongings, don't resist.

Taxes The sales tax in New Orleans is 9%. An additional 2% tax is added to hotel bills for a total of 11%.

Time Zone New Orleans observes central time, the same as Chicago. Between the first Sunday in April and the last Saturday in October, daylight saving time is in effect. During this period, clocks are set 1 hour ahead of standard time. Call *②* **504/828-4000** for the correct local time.

Transit Information Local bus routes and schedules can be obtained from the **RTA Ride Line** (*②* **504/248-3900**). **Union Passenger Terminal,** 1001 Loyola Ave., provides bus information (*②* **504/524-7571**) and train information (*②* **504/ 528-1610**).

Traveler's Aid Society You can reach the local branch of the society at *②* **504/525-8726**.

Weather For an update, call *②* **504/828-4000**.

3

Where to Stay

If you're doing your New Orleans trip right, you shouldn't be doing much sleeping. But you do have to put your change of clothes somewhere. New Orleans is bursting with hotels of every variety, so you should be able to find something that fits your preferences. However, during crowded times (Mardi Gras, for example), just finding anything might have to be good enough. After all, serious New Orleans visitors often book a year in advance for popular times.

Here, however, are a few tips. Don't stay on Bourbon Street unless you absolutely have to or don't mind getting no sleep. The open-air frat party that is this thoroughfare does mean a free show below your window, but it is hardly conducive to . . . well, just about anything other than participation in the same.

A first-time visitor might also strongly consider not staying in the Quarter at all. Try the beautiful Garden District instead. It's an easy streetcar ride away from the Quarter, and it's closer to a number of wonderful clubs and restaurants.

All of the guesthouses in this chapter are first rate. If you want more information, we highly recommend the **Bed and Breakfast, Inc. Reservation Service** ☆ (© **800/729-4640** or 504/488-4640; www.historiclodging.com), which represents around 50 establishments in every section of the city.

As a general rule, just to be on the safe side, always book ahead in spring, fall, and winter. And if your trip will coincide with Mardi Gras or Jazz Fest, book *way* ahead—up to a year in advance if you want to ensure a room. You should also be aware that rates frequently jump more than a notch or two for Mardi Gras and other festival times, and often have a 4- or 5-night minimum requirement.

The rates we've given in this chapter are for double rooms and do not include the city's 11% hotel tax. Realize that rates often shift according to demand. The high end of the range is for popular times like Mardi Gras and Jazz Fest, and the low end is for quieter periods like the month of December.

New Orleans Accommodations

Ashton Mechling Bed & Breakfast **36**	The Grand Victorian Bed & Breakfast **9**
B&W Courtyards Bed & Breakfast **39**	Hampton Inn **8**
Benachi House **34**	Hilton New Orleans Airport **1**
Chimes B&B **6**	Hilton New Orleans Riverside Hotel **21**
The Columns **5**	Holiday Inn Downtown—Superdome **33**
Courtyard by Marriott **20**	Holiday Inn New Orleans—Airport **2**
The Depot at Madame Julia's **17**	Hotel Inter-Continental **27**
Drury Inn & Suites **30**	The House on Bayou Road **35**
The Fairmont Hotel **32**	Hyatt Regency **16**
The Frenchmen **38**	International House **28**

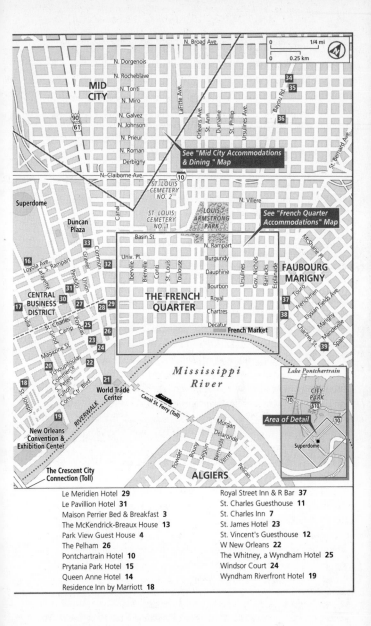

Le Meridien Hotel **29**		Royal Street Inn & R Bar **37**
Le Pavillion Hotel **31**		St. Charles Guesthouse **11**
Maison Perrier Bed & Breakfast **3**		St. Charles Inn **7**
The McKendrick-Breaux House **13**		St. James Hotel **23**
Park View Guest House **4**		St. Vincent's Guesthouse **12**
The Pelham **26**		W New Orleans **22**
Pontchartrain Hotel **10**		The Whitney, a Wyndham Hotel **25**
Prytania Park Hotel **15**		Windsor Court **24**
Queen Anne Hotel **14**		Wyndham Riverfront Hotel **19**
Residence Inn by Marriott **18**		

1 The French Quarter

VERY EXPENSIVE

Grenoble House   The Grenoble House, an old French Quarter town house built around a courtyard, is small, quiet, and close to everything. Rooms are all apartments with full kitchens, sitting/living areas, and bedrooms recently refitted with expensive new mattresses. Furnishings can be disappointingly modern—it clashes with the frequently exposed brick walls, if you ask us. Business-people like the apartment-like convenience. A special plus here is the personal, attentive service—they'll book theater tickets, restaurants, and sightseeing tours and will even arrange a gourmet dinner brought to your suite or a private cocktail party on the patio.

329 Dauphine St., New Orleans, LA 70112. © 800/722-1834 or 504/522-1331. Fax 504/524-4968. www.grenoblehouse.com. 17 suites. $199–$279 1-bedroom suite; $379–$459 2-bedroom suite. Rates include continental breakfast. Weekly rates available. AE, MC, V. No children under 12. **Amenities:** Small, unheated pool for dipping plus a Jacuzzi. *In room:* A/C, TV.

Hotel Maison de Ville 🐦🐦   On the list of *Best Small Hotels in the World,* the Maison de Ville is not cheap, but it's certainly an example of getting what you pay for. Tennessee Williams was a regular guest in room no. 9. Most of the rooms surround an utterly charming courtyard, where it's hard to imagine you're in the thick of the Quarter. Rooms (some of which have very tall ceilings and very tall—as in you need steps to reach them—beds) vary dramatically in size, however; some can be downright tiny, so ask when you reserve, as price is no indicator of size. Be careful you don't get a room overlooking the street—Bourbon is less than half a block away and makes its sorry presence known.

The far more spacious Audubon Cottages (larger than many apartments, some with their own private courtyards), located a few blocks away and including a small, inviting pool, can go for less than the cramped queen rooms in the main hotel. All rooms are thoroughly lush, and the service is stupendous. A wonderful romantic getaway—we just wish the continental breakfast wasn't so disappointing. Feel free to point this out to them, and gently explain that other, lesser establishments do that sort of thing much better.

727 Toulouse St., New Orleans, LA 70130. © 800/634-1600 or 504/561-5858. Fax 504/528-9939. www.maisondeville.com. 23 units, 5 cottages. $195–$225 double; $215–$235 queen; $225–$245 king; $325–$375 suite; $235–$325 1-bedroom cottage; $535–$725 2-bedroom cottage; $770–$1,005 3-bedroom cottage. AE, DC, MC, V. Valet parking $18. **Amenities:** Le Bistro restaurant; outdoor pool; access

French Quarter Accommodations

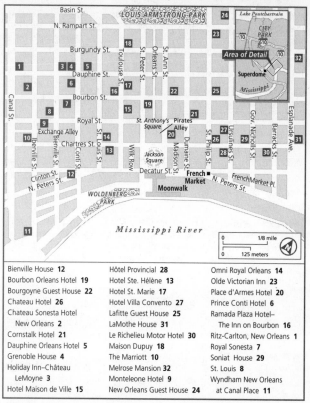

Bienville House **12**
Bourbon Orleans Hotel **19**
Bourgoyne Guest House **22**
Chateau Hotel **26**
Chateau Sonesta Hotel
  New Orleans **2**
Cornstalk Hotel **21**
Dauphine Orleans Hotel **5**
Grenoble House **4**
Holiday Inn–Château
  LeMoyne **3**
Hotel Maison de Ville **15**

Hôtel Provincial **28**
Hotel Ste. Hélène **13**
Hotel St. Marie **17**
Hotel Villa Convento **27**
Lafitte Guest House **25**
LaMothe House **31**
Le Richelieu Motor Hotel **30**
Maison Dupuy **18**
The Marriott **10**
Melrose Mansion **32**
Monteleone Hotel **9**
New Orleans Guest House **24**

Omni Royal Orleans **14**
Olde Victorian Inn **23**
Place d'Armes Hotel **20**
Prince Conti Hotel **6**
Ramada Plaza Hotel–
  The Inn on Bourbon **16**
Ritz-Carlton, New Orleans **1**
Royal Sonesta **7**
Soniat House **29**
St. Louis **8**
Wyndham New Orleans
  at Canal Place **11**

to nearby health club; concierge; room service (7am–10pm); massage; laundry and dry cleaning; shoe shine. *In room:* A/C, TV, dataport, minibar, hair dryer.

Melrose Mansion ☞ A standout even on a street full of envy-inducing mansions in a town full of pampering guesthouses, the Melrose Mansion has long combined luxury resort living with the best guesthouse offerings. Unfortunately, it seems lately to be resting on its laurels. Service, once impeccable, is less so, and the breakfasts, once handsome feasts, now tend toward the pre-packaged and ordinary. It still remains a charming old mansion, beautifully renovated, but it may no longer be totally justifying its high cost. The rooms vary from classic Victorian antiques to lighter country-style decor; bathrooms can be small, but plush bathrobes and linens help.

937 Esplanade Ave., New Orleans, LA 70116. ℂ **800/650-3323** or 504/944-2255. Fax 504/945-1794. www.melrosemansion.com. 20 units. $225–$250 double; $325–$425 suite. Rates include champagne breakfast and cocktail hour. AE, DISC, MC, V. Valet parking $15. **Amenities:** Pool. *In room:* A/C, TV, minibar.

Ramada Plaza Hotel–The Inn on Bourbon

This was formerly a Best Western, and it remains to be seen how the change in chain ownership will affect this hotel. One hopes it will help to bring the prices down, though that seems unlikely. The justification is the location: the former site of the 1859 French Opera House—the first opera house built in the United States (it burned down in 1919). Party animals should note that this means the hotel is right in the middle of the liveliest action on Bourbon. If you have a serious commitment to sleeping, though, choose another place to stay, or at least request an interior room. All rooms have Deep South decor.

541 Bourbon St., New Orleans, LA 70130. ℂ **800/535-7891** or 504/524-7611. Fax 504/568-9427. www.innonbourbon.com. 186 units. $205–$285 double. AE, DC, DISC, MC, V. Valet parking $13. **Amenities:** Bar; outdoor pool; fitness room; concierge; jewelry shop; gift shop; babysitting by arrangement; laundry and dry cleaning; express checkout. *In room:* A/C, TV, minibar.

Ritz-Carlton, New Orleans 🏵🏵

Sentimentalists that we are, we were deeply sad to see the venerable Maison Blanche department store go the way of Woolworth's, D. H. Holmes, and other Canal Street shopping landmarks. But for the city's sake, we are pleased to have a Ritz-Carlton take its place, preserving the classic glazed terra-cotta building and bringing a high-end luxury hotel to the Quarter. Again, being sentimentalists, we would rather find our luxury in a less—how shall we say—*generic* way, but we cannot deny that with name-brand recognition comes a reliable standard. And so the staff falls all over themselves to be friendly and helpful, rooms have lovely beds, king rooms are nicer than doubles, and the whole effect is very gracious and just a bit stuffy, an impression that deepens at night as cocktails are served in the lobby lounge where everything is very civil and jeans and other casual attire are frowned upon. (Indeed, there is supposed to be a dress code after 6pm, but we didn't see it enforced.) The spa is by far the nicest in town.

921 Canal St., New Orleans, LA 70112. ℂ **800/241-3333** or 504/524-1331. Fax 504/524-7233. www.ritzcarlton.com. 452 units. $395 double; from $480 and way, way up for suites. AE, DC, MC, V. Parking $25. Pets accepted. **Amenities:** Top-of-the-line spa and health club (with resistance pool, Jacuzzi, and personal trainers); concierge; shops; massage. *In room:* A/C, TV, dataport, minibar, hair dryer, iron, ironing board, safe, Nintendo.

Royal Sonesta 🏨🏨 One of the classiest hotels in the Quarter. The contrast between the hurly-burly of Bourbon Street and the Sonesta's chandeliered lobby couldn't be greater. Outside, it's raucous and boisterous and up all night. Inside, all is quiet and gracious, and if your room faces the courtyard (with a large pool), you are in another world altogether. Some people consider this the only acceptable, top-flight Bourbon Street hotel, though noise is still a problem in rooms that face Bourbon. But because the Sonesta is so large, unless you do have one of those rooms, you won't believe you are so close to such craziness. Rooms are undergoing a major renovation, and while the decor is likely to remain unmemorable, the hotel should be even prettier and more comfortable; the new bathrooms will gleam with marble and wood. *Note:* This is the best place in the Quarter to catch a cab; they line up at the corner.

300 Bourbon St., New Orleans, LA 70130. 📞 **800/766-3782** or 504/586-0300. Fax 504/586-0335. www.royalsonestano.com. 500 units. $245–$380 double; $445–$1,450 suite. AE, DC, DISC, MC, V. Parking $19. **Amenities:** Two restaurants, bar; pool; exercise room; concierge; business center; room service until 2am; massage. *In room:* A/C, TV, minibar.

Soniat House 🏨🏨🏨 The recipient of endless tributes from various prestigious travel journals, the Soniat House lives up to the hype. It's mighty wonderful. It's classic Creole—the treasures are hidden off the street in an oasis of calm that seems impossible in the Quarter. The beyond-efficient staff will spoil you, and the sweet courtyards, candlelit at night, will soothe you.

Rooms do vary, if not in quality then at least in distinction. All have antiques, but if you want, say, high ceilings and really grand furniture (room 23 has a 17th-century bed), you are better off in the main house or the suite-filled annex across the street. The rooms in the old kitchen and other buildings are not quite as smashing. On the main property, bathrooms are small. But across the street, they gain size, not to mention Jacuzzi bathtubs and antique furnishings.

1133 Chartres St., New Orleans, LA 70116. 📞 **800/544-8808** or 504/522-0570. Fax 504/522-7208. www.soniathouse.com. 33 units. $195–$285 double; $350–$650 suite; $655 2-bedroom suite. AE, MC, V. Valet parking $19. Children over 12 welcome only in rooms that accommodate 3. **Amenities:** Access to nearby health club and business center (for an additional charge); concierge; same-day dry cleaning and laundry. *In room:* A/C, TV, hair dryer, safe.

EXPENSIVE

Chateau Sonesta Hotel New Orleans 🏨 On the site of the former D. H. Holmes Canal Street Department Store (1849), the

Chateau Sonesta Hotel opened in 1995, making it one of the newer hotels in the French Quarter. While the building maintains the 1913 facade, inside is a generic high-end hotel, popular among business groups for its meeting rooms and location. At the Canal Street entrance is a newly erected statue of Ignatius Reilly, hero of *A Confederacy of Dunces,* whom we first met when he was waiting, as all of New Orleans once did, "under the clock"—the old Holmes clock now located in a bar, was for decades the favored rendezvous point for tout New Orleanians. Guest rooms are large, and many feature balconies overlooking Bourbon or Dauphine streets.

800 Iberville St., New Orleans, LA 70112. ℂ **800/SONESTA** or 504/586-0800. Fax 504/586-1987. www.chateausonesta.com. 251 units. $159–$289 double; $285–$798 suite. Extra person $40. AE, DC, DISC, MC, V. Valet parking $19. **Amenities:** Restaurant, bar; heated outdoor pool; exercise room; concierge; tour desk; gift shop; room service until at least midnight; babysitting; laundry and dry cleaning. *In room:* A/C, TV, minibar.

Dauphine Orleans Hotel 𝒢𝒢   On a relatively quiet and peaceful block of the Quarter, the Dauphine Orleans Hotel sports a casual elegance. It's just a block from the action on Bourbon Street, but you wouldn't know it if you were sitting in any of its three secluded courtyards. The license a former owner took out to make the place a bordello is proudly displayed in the bar, and its proprietors are happy to admit that ghosts have been sighted on the premises. The hotel's back buildings were once the studio of John James Audubon. All rooms have recently been upgraded.

415 Dauphine St., New Orleans, LA 70116. ℂ **800/521-7111** or 504/586-1800. Fax 504/586-1409. www.dauphineorleans.com. 111 units. $149–$269 double; $149–$289 patio room; $179–$399 suite. Rates include continental breakfast and afternoon tea. Extra person $15. Children under 17 stay free in parents' room. AE, DC, DISC, MC, V. Valet parking $12. **Amenities:** Bar; outdoor pool; small fitness room; Jacuzzi; concierge; complimentary French Quarter and downtown transportation; babysitting; laundry and dry cleaning; guest library. *In room:* A/C, TV, minibar, robes, hair dryer, iron and ironing board, marble bathrooms.

Holiday Inn–Chateau LeMoyne 𝒢   The Chateau LeMoyne is in a good location, just around the corner from Bourbon Street but away from the noise. It's a nice surprise to find a Holiday Inn housed in century-plus-old buildings, but the ambience stops at your room's threshold. Once inside, matters look pretty much like they do in every Holiday Inn. Too bad. One of these 19th-century buildings was designed by famed architect James Gallier, and you can still see bits of old brick, old ovens, and exposed cypress beams here and there, along with a graceful curving outdoor staircase. Even the spacious courtyard feels oddly sterile.

301 Dauphine St., New Orleans, LA 70112. © 800/447-2830 or 504/581-1303. Fax 504/525-8531. www.chateaulemoyne.com. 171 units. $159–$244 double; $259–$459 suite. Extra person $15. AE, DC, DISC, MC, V. Valet parking $18. **Amenities:** Bar; outdoor swimming pool; room service. *In room:* A/C, TV, coffeemaker, hair dryer, iron, ironing board.

Hotel Ste. Hélène ★★ *Finds*   Thanks to being in the shadow of the Omni Royal, its grand across-the-street neighbor, the Hotel Ste. Hélène could easily be overlooked. But in our opinion, this is what a slightly funky Quarter hotel should be. What it lacks in magnificence, it makes up for in character and location. Front rooms have balconies overlooking the street; others have beds set in alcoves (we find it romantic, though you might find it claustrophobic) with a sort of low-rent parlor sitting area. Bathrooms can be tiny but are clean and modern.

508 Chartres St., New Orleans, LA 70130. © 800/348-3888 or 504/522-5014. Fax 504/523-7140. www.stehelene.com. 26 units. $149–$265 double. AE, DC, DISC, MC, V. Parking (about $10) in nearby lot. **Amenities:** Continental champagne breakfast; pool; babysitting; laundry service. *In room:* A/C, TV.

Lafitte Guest House   Here you'll find the best of both worlds: antique living just blocks from Bourbon Street. The three-story brick building, with wrought-iron balconies on the second and third floors, was constructed in 1849 and has been completely restored. Thanks to new owners, there are ongoing upgrades plus better beds and new fixtures. Each room has its own Victorian flair (though rooms 5 and 40 have modern furnishings) with occasional memorable details like a cypress fireplace, plus touches like pralines on the pillow, sleeping masks, and sound machines with soothing (apparently) nature noises.

1003 Bourbon St., New Orleans, LA 70116. © 800/331-7971 or 504/581-2678. Fax 504/581-2677. www.lafitteguesthouse.com. 14 units. $149–$219 double. Extra person $25. AE, DISC, MC, V. Parking $10. *In room:* A/C, TV.

Maison Dupuy ★   A little out of the main French Quarter action and a tad closer than some might like to dicey Rampart (though the hotel is entirely safe), the Maison Dupuy, with its seven town houses surrounding a good-size courtyard (and a heated pool), is still warm and inviting. It's probably best for the business traveler who doesn't want a cookie-cutter chain hotel. Rooms are attractive (with mock French-provincial furniture). Floor space and balconies (with either courtyard or street views—the former is quieter) vary. Mattresses are very firm, and bathroom amenities are above average.

1001 Toulouse St., New Orleans, LA 70112. © 800/535-9177 or 504/586-8000. Fax 504/525-5334. www.maisondupuy.com. 200 units. $99–$269 superior double;

$149–$299 deluxe double with balcony; $329–$838 suite. AE, DC, DISC, MC, V. Valet parking $18 when available. **Amenities:** Restaurant, bar; heated outdoor pool; health club; concierge; room service (6am–midnight); babysitting; same-day laundry and dry cleaning. *In room:* A/C, TV, minibar.

Monteleone Hotel ★★

Opened in 1886, the Monteleone is the largest hotel in the French Quarter, and it seems to keep getting bigger without losing a trace of its trademark charm. Because of its size you can almost always get a reservation here, even when other places are booked. Everyone who stays here loves it, probably because its staff is among the most helpful in town. The big problem is the inconsistency among the rooms. Those freshly renovated are terrific, but older ones may only appeal to guests with film noir fantasies. Here's a guide: Rooms numbered in the 60s (260–269, 360–369, and so on) are lovely middle-size rooms with four-poster beds, posh bathrooms (some with oval Jacuzzi tubs), and river views. Rooms in the 50s are the largest but also have old, dinky bathrooms. Confused? Oh, just ask when making a reservation.

214 Royal St., New Orleans, LA 70130. ⓒ **800/535-9595** or 504/523-3341. Fax 504/528-1019. www.hotelmonteleone.com. 600 units. $150–$350 double; $360–$900 suite. Extra person $25. Children under 18 stay free in parents' room. Package rates available. AE, DC, DISC, MC, V. Valet parking $15 car, $17 van. **Amenities:** 3 restaurants, 2 bars; heated rooftop swimming pool (open year-round); fitness center (under-stocked but with fabulous views of the city and river); hot tub; sauna; concierge; room service (6am–11pm); babysitting; laundry. *In room:* A/C, TV, dataport, minibar, coffeemaker, hair dryer, iron, safe.

Omni Royal Orleans ★★

Despite being part of a chain, this is a most elegant hotel that, unlike others in its class, escapes feeling sterile and generic—only proper given that it is on the former site of the venerable 1836 St. Louis Exchange Hotel, one of the country's premier hostelries. The original building was destroyed by a 1915 hurricane, but the Omni, built in 1960, is a worthy successor. It enjoys a prime location in the center of the Quarter. Furnishings in the guest rooms are elegant, full of muted tones and plush furniture, with windows that let you look dreamily out over the Quarter.

621 St. Louis St., New Orleans, LA 70140. ⓒ **800/THE-OMNI** in the U.S. and Canada or 504/529-5333. Fax 504/529-7089. www.omniroyalorleans.com. 346 units. $199–$339 double; $339–$800 suite; $1,100 penthouse. Children under 18 stay free in parents' room. AE, DC, DISC, MC, V. Valet parking $19. **Amenities:** Restaurant, 2 bars; heated outdoor pool; health club; concierge; business center; florist; sundries shop and newsstand; beauty and barber shops; 24-hour room service; massage; babysitting; emergency mending and pressing; complimentary shoe shine. *In room:* A/C, TV, minibar, dataport, coffeemaker, iron and ironing board, terry robes, makeup mirror, umbrellas.

St. Louis 🎔   Right in the heart of the Quarter, the St. Louis is a small hotel that surrounds a lush courtyard with a fountain. But it's somewhat disappointingly dull for what ought to be a charming boutique hotel. Some rooms have private balconies overlooking Bienville Street, and all open onto the central courtyard. Rooms are undergoing a remodeling and getting new carpet, drapes, and furniture, which should freshen up a slightly stodgy decor by the time you read this. The otherwise uninteresting bathrooms do have bidets.

730 Bienville St., New Orleans, LA 70130. ℭ 800/537-8483 or 504/581-7300. Fax 504/679-5013. www.stlouishotel.com. 81 units. $145–$335 double; $345–$375 suite. Children under 16 stay free in parents' room. AE, DC, MC, V. Valet parking $16.50. **Amenities:** Louis XVI Restaurant; access to nearby health club; concierge; room service from restaurant at breakfast; babysitting; laundry. *In room:* A/C, TV.

Wyndham New Orleans at Canal Place 🎔   At the foot of Canal Street, the Wyndham is in the French Quarter—but not quite *of* it. It is literally *above* the Quarter: The grand-scale lobby, with its fine paintings and antiques, is on the 11th floor of the Canal Place tower, with expansive views of the river and the French Quarter. The lobby and guest rooms have been designed in a nicely muted neoclassical style. The rooms are on the floors above; each has a marble foyer and bathroom and fine furnishings (with good pillows).

100 Iberville St., New Orleans, LA 70130. ℭ 877/999-3223 or 504/566-7006. Fax 504/553-5120. www.wyndham.com. 437 units. $129–$339 double. Ask about packages and specials. AE, DC, DISC, MC, V. $25 valet parking; $15 self-parking. **Amenities:** Restaurant, bar; heated pool; privileges at a nearby 18-hole golf course; concierge; tour desk; 24-hour room service; laundry and dry cleaning; multilingual staff. Direct elevator access to Canal Place shopping center, where guests can use the health center free of charge. *In room:* A/C, TV, minibar.

MODERATE

Bienville House 🎔🎔   A nice little Quarter hotel, better than most (thanks to a combo of location, price, and room quality) though not as good as some (owing to a lack of specific personality). It's generally sedate, except perhaps during Mardi Gras when the mad gay revelers take over—as they do everywhere, truth be told. The friendly and helpful staff adds a lot of welcome spirit. Rooms mostly have high ceilings; kings have four-poster beds and slightly more interesting furniture than doubles. Some rooms have balconies overlooking the small courtyard that features a good pool for a dip. Note that the Iberville Suite is so large it actually made us laugh out loud—and we mean that in a good way.

320 Decatur St., New Orleans, LA 70130. © **800/535-7836** or 504/529-2345. Fax 504/525-6079. www.bienvillehouse.com. 83 units. $89–$300 double. Rates include continental breakfast. AE, DC, DISC, MC, V. Valet parking $11 cars, $15 sport-utility vehicles. **Amenities:** Gamay restaurant; outdoor pool; room service. *In room:* A/C, TV, dataport, coffeemaker, hair dryer, iron, fine toiletries.

Bourbon Orleans Hotel *⌖*   A lot of hotels claim to be centrally located in the French Quarter, but the Bourbon Orleans really is. The place takes up an entire block of prime real estate at the intersection of—guess where—Bourbon and Orleans streets.

A lot of hotels claim to have an interesting history, too, but this one really does. The oldest part of the hotel is the Orleans Ballroom, constructed in 1815 as a venue for the city's masquerade, carnival, and notorious quadroon balls. In 1881, the building was sold to the Sisters of the Holy Family, members of the South's first order of African-American nuns. The sisters converted the ballroom into a school and remained for 80 years until the building was sold to developers from Baton Rouge, who turned it into an apartment hotel.

Today, the hotel has recently undergone a $6-million renovation. You just wish it had more character to go along with its fascinating history. The public spaces are lavishly decorated, but their elegant interest doesn't quite extend to the standard guest rooms. Bigger than average, they will give no cause for complaint in either decor or comfort (we do like the Bath & Bodyworks amenities).

717 Orleans St., New Orleans, LA 70116. © **504/523-2222**. Fax 504/525-8166. www.bourbonorleans.com. 216 units. $119–$189 petite queen or twin; $139–$209 deluxe king or double; $179–$249 junior suite; $229–$379 town house suite; $259–$459 town house suite with balcony. Extra person $20. AE, DC, DISC, MC, V. Valet parking $24.64. **Amenities:** Restaurant, bar; good-size pool on the premises; room service during limited hours; same-day dry cleaning; nightly shoe shine. *In room:* A/C, TV, fax, dataport, optional voice mail, hair dryer.

Bourgoyne Guest House   This is an eccentric place with an owner to match. If you dislike stuffy hotels and will happily take things a little worn at the edges in exchange for a relaxed, hangout atmosphere, come here. Accommodations are arranged around a nicely cluttered courtyard. Studios are adequate little rooms with kitchens and bathrooms that appear grimy but are not (we saw the strong potions housekeeping uses; it's just a result of age). The Green Suite is as big and grand as one would like with huge tall rooms, a second smaller bedroom, a bigger bathroom, and a balcony overlooking Bourbon Street. For price and location it's a heck of a deal, maybe the best in the Quarter.

839 Bourbon St., New Orleans, LA 70116. ℂ **504/525-3983** or 504/524-3621. 5 apts. Studios $92 double; La Petite Suite $115 double, $140 triple, $155 quad; Green Suite $125 double, $150 triple, $175 quad. MC, V. *In room:* A/C, unstocked fridge, coffeemaker, iron.

Chateau Hotel   A bit removed from the well-traveled sections of the French Quarter, the Chateau is still only a short walk from wherever you're headed. You enter through an old carriageway into a large old Creole building. Oddly dark colors and fussy details unfortunately give you the mistaken first impression that you're in a seedy motel room, but it's better than that. Rooms are very clean, though mattresses are hard and bathrooms merely okay. The courtyard is very New Orleans (though it would benefit from more greenery) and features an oval-shaped swimming pool that cleverly looks like it might once have been a fountain.

1001 Chartres St., New Orleans, LA 70116. ℂ **504/524-9636.** Fax 504/525-2989. www.chateauhotel.com. 45 units. $109–$149 double. Rates include continental breakfast. 10% senior discount available. AE, DC, MC, V. Free parking. **Amenities:** Bar, continental breakfast; outdoor pool; concierge; breakfast room service (7am–11am). *In room:* A/C, TV, dataport, hair dryer, iron.

Cornstalk Hotel ✿   Thanks to the famous fence out front, this might be better known as a sightseeing stop than a place to stay, but consider staying here anyway. A gorgeous Victorian home on the National Register of Historic Places, it's nearly as pretty inside as out. It's located almost at the exact heart of the Quarter on a busy but not noisy section of Royal. If you want period charm, look no further. The high-ceilinged rooms have fireplaces or stained-glass windows, and some have ceiling medallions, scrolls, and cherubs from old plantations. The room with the largest bed is spectacular, while the rest are charming—you feel as if you have gone back 100 years.

Oh, the fence? Well, it's at least 130 years old, is made of cast iron, and looks like cornstalks painted in the appropriate colors.

915 Royal St., New Orleans, LA. 70116. ℂ **504/523-1515.** Fax 504/522-5558. www.travelguides.com/bb/cornstalk. 14 units. $75–$185 double. AE, MC, V. Limited parking $15. **Amenities:** Continental breakfast. *In room:* A/C, TV.

Hôtel Provincial ✿   Don't mention this to the owners, who are sensitive about it, but word from the ghost tours is that the Provincial is haunted, mostly by soldiers treated here when it was a Civil War hospital. It must not be too much of a problem, though, because guests rave about the hotel and never mention ghostly visitors. With flickering gas lamps, no fewer than five patios, and an overall tranquil setting, this feels less like a hotel than a guesthouse. Both the quiet and the terrific service belie its size, so it seems smaller and more intimate than it is. It's also in a good part of the Quarter on a quiet street off the beaten path. The rectangular pool is bigger than most in the Quarter.

1024 Chartres St., New Orleans, LA 70116. ☏ **800/535-7922** or 504/581-4995. Fax 504/581-1018. www.hotelprovincial.com. 94 units. $99–$289 double. Summer packages available. AE, DC, DISC, MC, V. Valet parking $11. **Amenities:** Restaurant, bar; pool. *In room:* A/C, TV, dataport, iron.

Hotel St. Marie   Location, location, location. Just a little above Bourbon Street on an otherwise quiet street, this hotel should be on your list of "clean and safe backup places to stay if my top choices are full." Surrounding a sterile courtyard with a drab pool, rooms are generic New Orleans in dark colors with standard-issue, mock-European hotel furniture. King rooms are more pleasant than doubles, and corner rooms are more spacious, which includes the otherwise dinky bathrooms (some with odd red lights that could really cause major ocular damage). Some rooms have balconies overlooking the street and courtyard. The unnumbered hallways can be dim, which could make a tipsy late-night return a challenge.

827 Toulouse St., New Orleans, LA 70112. ☏ **800/366-2743** or 504/561-8951. Fax 504/571-2802. www.hotelstmarie.com. 100 units. $150–$170 double. AE, DC, DISC, MC, V. Valet parking $15. **Amenities:** Restaurant, bar; room service (during dining room hours); laundry; dry cleaning. *In room:* A/C, TV.

Hotel Villa Convento ⭐   Local tour guides say this was the original House of the Rising Sun bordello, so if you have a sense of humor (or theater), be sure to pose in your bathrobe on your balcony so that you can be pointed out to passing tour groups. With its rather small public spaces and the personal attention that its owners and operators, the Campo family, give to their guests, the Villa Convento has the feel of a small European inn or guesthouse. It does a lot of repeat business. The building is a Creole town house; some rooms open onto the tropical patio, and many have balconies. Breakfast is served in the courtyard; guests may take a tray to their rooms.

616 Ursulines St., New Orleans, LA 70116. ☏ **800/887-2817** or 504/522-1793. Fax 504/524-1902. www.villaconvento.com. 25 units. $89–$105 double; $155 suite. Extra person $10. Rates include continental breakfast. AE, DC, DISC, MC, V. Parking $6. *In room:* A/C, TV, hair dryer.

Lamothe House ⭐   Somehow, a shiny new hotel doesn't seem quite right for New Orleans. More appropriate is slightly faded, somewhat threadbare elegance, and the Lamothe House neatly fits that bill. The Creole-style plain facade of the 1840s town house hides the atmosphere you are looking for—a mossy, brick-lined courtyard with a fish-filled fountain and rooms filled with antiques that are worn in the right places but not shabby. A continental breakfast is served in a second-floor dining room that just screams faded gentility. (As the, alas, sometimes cranky staff points out, it's not Victorian style; it *is* Victorian.) It's a short walk to the action in the Quarter. On a steamy night, sitting in the courtyard breathing the fragrant air, you can feel yourself slip out of time.

621 Esplanade Ave., New Orleans, LA 70116. (© **800/367-5858** or 504/947-1161. Fax 504/943-6536. www.new-orleans.org. 20 units. $64–$275 double. Rates include breakfast. AE, DISC, MC, V. Free parking, except special events. *In room:* A/C, TV.

Le Richelieu Motor Hotel ⊛   First a row mansion, then a macaroni factory, and now a hotel, this building has seen it all. It's at the Esplanade edge of the Quarter—a perfect spot from which to explore the Faubourg Marigny. Though slightly run-down these days, it's a welcoming spot for families, being out of the adult action. The McCartney family thought so; Paul, the late Linda, and their kids stayed here for months while Wings was recording an album. Besides an enormous VIP suite, rooms are standard high-end motel rooms, many with balconies. All overlook the French Quarter or the courtyard.

1234 Chartres St., New Orleans, LA 70116. (© **800/535-9653** or 504/529-2492. Fax 504/524-8179. 86 units. $95–$180 double; $200–$550 suite. Extra person or child $15. French Quarter Explorer and honeymoon packages available. AE, DC, DISC, MC, V. Free parking. **Amenities:** Restaurant, bar; outdoor pool; steam room; concierge; room service 7am–9pm. *In room:* A/C, TV, unstocked fridge, hair dryer, iron, ironing board.

Olde Victorian Inn ⊛⊛   While long-time clients might have been anxious when their beloved P.J. Holbrook retired and sold her business, they soon learned that current owners Keith and Andre West-Harrison took her legacy very seriously. "We changed nothing because the guests loved it, and it works." It certainly works for us. Decor (cutesy quaint and cluttered—expect doilies and teddy bears) remains untouched, as do P.J.'s legendary breakfasts, which the men make according to P.J.'s own recipes (on a recent visit, they stuffed us with Creole pancakes topped with peaches poached in homemade vanilla). Rooms at the back have bigger bathrooms. The owners brim over with joy for their job, and you quickly feel like a most welcome guest in their home. They also have three sweet, well-behaved dogs (not allowed in the rooms) that are equally gracious hosts.

914 N. Rampart St., New Orleans, LA 70116. ℭ **800/725-2446** or 504/522-2446. Fax 504/522-8643. www.oldevictorianinn.com. 6 units. $120–$175 double. Rates include full breakfast. Senior discount and weekly rates available. AE, DC, DISC, MC, V. Parking available on street. *In room:* A/C.

Place d'Armes Hotel ℛ   Parts of this hotel seem a bit grim and old, though its quite large courtyard and amoeba-shaped pool are ideal for hanging out. Plus, it's only half a block from the Café du Monde—very convenient when you need a beignet at 3am. This also makes it a favorite for families traveling with kids. Rooms are homey; however, 32 of them do not have windows and can be cell-like—ask for a room with a window when you reserve.

625 St. Ann St., New Orleans, LA 70116. ℭ **800/366-2743** or 504/524-4531. Fax 504/571-3803. www.frenchquarter.com. 80 units. $120–$190 double; $190 courtyard room. Rates include continental breakfast. AE, DC, DISC, MC, V. Parking (next door) $15. **Amenities:** Outdoor pool. *In room:* A/C, TV, hair dryer, iron.

Prince Conti Hotel ℛ   This tiny but friendly hotel with a marvelously helpful staff (some of whom are tour guides in their off hours) is in a great location off Bourbon and is not generally noisy. Second-floor rooms all have fresh striped wallpaper and antiques, but quality varies from big canopy beds to painted iron bedsteads. Bathrooms can be ultra-tiny, with the toilet virtually on top of the sink. Travelers with kids should stay at the hotel's sister location, the Place D'Armes, because it is farther from Bourbon and has a pool.

830 Conti St., New Orleans, LA 70112. ℭ **800/366-2743** or 504/529-4172. Fax 504/581-3802. hotels@frenchquarter.com. 53 units. $150 double; $215 suite. AE, DC, DISC, MC, V. Valet parking $15. **Amenities:** Restaurant, piano bar, breakfast cafe; breakfast room service 7am–10am. *In room:* A/C, TV, iron.

INEXPENSIVE

New Orleans Guest House   Run for more than 10 years by Ray Cronk and Alvin Payne, this guesthouse is a little off the beaten path (just outside the French Quarter across North Rampart Street), but it's painted a startling hot, Pepto-Bismol pink, so it's hard to miss.

Rooms, in the old Creole main house (1848) and in what used to be the slave quarters, are simple—call it motel Victorian, with small bathrooms that are more motel than Victorian. Each has a unique color scheme (not hot pink, in case you were worried). Room 7, with its own private balcony, is perhaps the nicest. The courtyard is a veritable tropical garden, with a couple of fluffy cats in residence.

1118 Ursulines St., New Orleans, LA 70116. ℭ **800/562-1177** or 504/566-1177. Fax 504/566-1179. www.neworleans.com/nogh/. 14 units. $79 double; $89 queen or twin; $99 king or 2 full beds. Rates include continental breakfast. Extra person $25. MC, V. Free parking. *In room:* A/C, TV, hair dryer, iron, safe.

2 The Faubourg Marigny

MODERATE

B&W Courtyards Bed & Breakfast 🏠🏠   The deceptively simple facade hides a sweet and very hospitable little B&B, complete with two small courtyards and a fountain. It's located in the Faubourg Marigny next to the bustling nighttime Frenchmen scene, a 10-minute walk or $5 cab ride (at most) to the Quarter. Owners Rob Boyd and Kevin Wu went to ingenious lengths to turn six oddly shaped spaces into comfortable rooms, of which no two are alike—you enter one through its bathroom. All are carefully and thoughtfully decorated. Rob and Kevin are adept at giving advice—and strong opinions—not just about the city but also about their own local favorites. Breakfast is light (fruit, homemade breads) but beautifully presented. Prepare to be pampered. They take good care of you here.

2425 Chartres St., New Orleans, LA 70117. ☏ 800/585-5731 or 504/945-9418. Fax 504/949-3483. www.bandwcourtyards.com. 5 units. $120–$175 double. Rates include breakfast. AE, DISC, MC, V. Parking available on street. **Amenities:** Jacuzzi. *In room:* A/C, TV, dataport, minibar, coffeemaker, hair dryer, iron, safe.

The Frenchmen 🏠🏠   This small, sweet, and slightly funky inn is very popular with in-the-know regular visitors. It's not for some, but others become loyal repeat customers. The inn feels out of the way, but in some respects, the location can't be beat. It's just across from the Quarter and a block away from the main drag of the Frenchmen section of the Faubourg Marigny, with its lively nightlife.

Housed in two 19th-century buildings that were once grand New Orleans homes, the individually decorated rooms vary in size considerably; some are very small indeed. Some have private balconies, and others have a loft bedroom with a sitting area. A small pool and Jacuzzi are in the inn's tropical courtyard.

417 Frenchmen St. (at Esplanade Avenue), New Orleans, LA 70116. ☏ 800/831-1781 or 504/948-2166. Fax 504/948-2258. www.french-quarter.org. 27 units. $79–$155 double. Rates include breakfast. AE, DISC, MC, V. Free parking, except special events. *In room:* A/C, TV.

INEXPENSIVE

Royal Street Inn & R Bar 🏠   This is a happening little establishment in a residential neighborhood with plenty of street parking and regular police patrols. It's a loose but not disorganized place, and there couldn't be a better choice for laid-back travelers. Breakfast isn't served here, but they still bill themselves as a B&B. That's for Bed and Beverage—the lobby is the highly enjoyable R Bar. You

check in with the bartender, and as a guest you get two complimentary cocktails at night. (As if you'll stop there.)

Regular rooms are small but cute, like a bedroom in a real house
but with doors that open directly to the street. Suites, the best value
near the Quarter, are well sized, accommodating up to four, and
feature kitchenettes as well as their own names and stories. The
Ghost in the Attic is a big room (complete with a mural of said
ghost) with sloping ceilings, pleasing for those with starving-artist
garret fantasies who don't like to give up good furniture.

1431 Royal St., New Orleans, LA 70116. ℂ 800/449-5535 or 504/948-7499.
Fax 504/943-9880. www.royalstreetinn.com. 5 units. $90 double; $130 suite. Price
includes tax; rates include bar beverage. AE, DISC, MC, V. **Amenities:** Bar. *In room:*
A/C, TV.

3 Mid City/Esplanade

EXPENSIVE

The House on Bayou Road ★★★   If you want to stay in a rural
plantation setting but still be near the French Quarter, try the
House on Bayou Road, quite probably the most smashing guesthouse in town. Just off Esplanade Avenue, this intimate Creole
plantation home, built in the late 1700s, has been restored by owner
Cynthia Reeves, who oversees an operation of virtual perfection.

Each room is individually decorated to a fare-thee-well—slightly
cluttered, not quite fussy, but still lovingly done. The Bayou St.
John Room (the old library) holds a queen-size four-poster bed and
has a working fireplace; the Bayou Delacroix has the same kind of
bed and a wonderfully large bathtub. The small Creole cottage is a
romantic getaway spot complete with a porch with a swing and
rocking chairs. The grounds are beautifully manicured, and there's
an outdoor pool, Jacuzzi, patio, and screened-in porch. Expect a
hearty plantation-style breakfast.

2275 Bayou Rd., New Orleans, LA 70119. ℂ 800/882-2968 or 504/945-0992.
Fax 504/945-0993. www.houseonbayouroad.com. 8 units, 2 cottages. $150–$310
double. Rates include full breakfast. AE, MC, V. Free parking. **Amenities:**
Restaurant; outdoor pool; Jacuzzi. *In room:* A/C, dataport, minibar, hair dryer, iron.

MODERATE

Ashton's Mechling Bed & Breakfast ★   This charming guesthouse has been undergoing some very fine renovations of late and is
a worthy alternative to some of its more costly compatriots. Decor
is a bit grandma-fussy, but we love the nice touch of seasonal decorations in the rooms. One room has a most inviting fluffy white
bed, but its bathroom is contained in a curtained-off corner, and

Mid City Accommodations & Dining

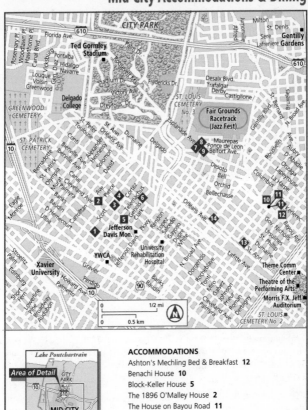

ACCOMMODATIONS
Ashton's Mechling Bed & Breakfast **12**
Benachi House **10**
Block-Keller House **5**
The 1896 O'Malley House **2**
The House on Bayou Road **11**

DINING
Cafe Degas **9**
Christian's **4**
Dooky Chase **13**
Gabrielle **8**
Indigo **11**
Liuzza's **6**
Lola's **7**
Mandina's **3**
Mona's Café & Deli **1**
Ruth's Chris Steak House **14**

another room has merely a partitioned area for the same. Those with personal-space issues might want to head to room 3, which is most grand—a four-poster bed and a nice bathroom with a claw-foot tub. Virtually all the rooms have wide wooden floorboards. Five new additional rooms are being built in the service wing. A full breakfast is served, featuring such local dishes as *pain perdu* and eggs Sardou.

2023 Esplanade Ave., New Orleans, LA 70116. (C) 800/725-4131 or 504/942-7048. Fax 504/947-9382. www.ashtonsbb.com. 5 units. $125–$155 double. Rates include full breakfast. AE, DISC, MC, V. Free parking. *In room:* A/C, TV, dataport, minibar, hair dryer, iron.

Benachi House   This place is a mixed bag. It's set in a grand old classic New Orleans house, but alas, the rooms are not nearly as dazzling as the public spaces, and they pale in comparison to others in town. The rooms are upstairs, along with the owner's bedroom, and are accessible only by stairs. Bathrooms are ordinary; this was once a family home, so think of your kids' bathrooms and you've got the idea. Suites, in a separate building across the street, have better furniture but are still disappointing, given the setting. Both buildings have patios with romantic fountains. A full breakfast featuring items like eggs Benedict is offered. *Note:* If the big black dog Magnus is there, it's best not to play with him. He can get overly rough.

2257 Bayou Rd., New Orleans, LA 70119. (C) 800/308-7040 or 504/525-7040. Fax 504/525-9760. www.nolabb.com. 4 units. $105–$135 double. Complimentary evening beverage. AE, DISC, MC, V. Free parking. *In room:* A/C, coffeemaker, hair dryer, iron.

Block-Keller House   One of two relatively new B&Bs in the up-and-coming Mid City area, the recently restored Block-Keller House has large, lovely rooms, but we barely noticed thanks to the gorgeous Victorian excess of the details found in the front rooms. Plaster curlicues! Archways! Mahogany mantelpieces with even weirder detailing! Sorry, we do get carried away, but only because the original architect did as well. It's located right on Canal Street, which makes the outside a tad noisy but also means that you are just blocks from several great neighborhood restaurants, and right on a bus line.

3620 Canal St., New Orleans, LA 70119 (C) 800/729-4640 or 504/488-4640. www.zhistoriclodging.com/block. 9 units. $100–$125. AE, MC, V. **Amenities:** Continental breakfast; Internet access. *In room:* A/C, TV.

The 1896 O'Malley House ⍟   This is another beautifully restored home turned B&B, in a building dating back to, you guessed it, 1896. Many of the original details, including marvelous tile on the various fireplaces in several of the rooms, are still intact. Second-floor rooms are larger, and most have Jacuzzi tubs. The third floor, with smaller, more garret-like rooms, is a clever use of design and space, with formerly dull wood walls turned most striking by pickling the wood to a lighter color (ask to see the photos of the mysterious science equations found scrawled on one wall).

120 S. Pierce St., New Orleans, LA 70119. ℂ 800/729-4640 or 504/488-4640. www.historiclodging.com/1896. 8 units. $99–$120. AE, MC, V. **Amenities:** Continental breakfast. *In room:* A/C, TV, hair dryers on request, Internet access.

4 Central Business District

VERY EXPENSIVE

Fairmont Hotel 𝒜𝒜   New Orleanians still sometimes think of this as the Roosevelt, and today's Fairmont Hotel upholds its predecessor's tradition of elegance. The marbled and columned lobby runs a full block and is famous for its over-the-top Christmas decorations. Rooms are done with pleasant if dull good taste—fine for business or if you don't demand much personality. Good mattresses, even better cotton sheets and down pillows, plus high ceilings make these much more comfortable and less stuffy than similar rooms at its peers. Some of the suites are positively enormous (and the hotel has so many that they often offer upgrades for a nominal fee).

123 Baronne St. (at University Place), New Orleans, LA 70112. ℂ 800/441-1414 or 504/529-7111. Fax 504/522-2303. www.fairmont.com. 700 units. $259–$329 double. Extra person $30. AE, DC, DISC, MC, V. Valet parking $15. **Amenities:** Restaurant, 2 bars; rooftop outdoor pool; tennis courts; rooftop health club (small but sporting enough machines); concierge; tour desk; activities desk; business center; gift shop; newsstand; currency exchange; beauty shop; 24-hour room service; massage, babysitting; laundry service; multilingual staff. *In room:* A/C, TV, dataport, hair dryer, iron.

Hilton New Orleans Riverside Hotel 𝒜 *Kids*   The Hilton is blessed with a central location—right at the riverfront near the World Trade Center of New Orleans, the New Orleans Convention Center, and the Aquarium. It's a self-contained complex of nearly a dozen restaurants, bistros, and bars; two gift shops; a full racquet and health club; and a huge exhibition space. In addition, Harrah's Casino and the Riverwalk Marketplace are accessible from the hotel's lobby, which contains a nine-story atrium. This is a top choice for families. Many of the spacious guest rooms have fabulous views of the river or the city.

2 Poydras St., New Orleans, LA 70140. ℂ **800/445-8667** or 504/561-0500. Fax 504/584-3979. www.neworleans.hilton.com. 1,600 units. $225–$475 double; $650–$2,000 suite. Special packages available. AE, DC, DISC, MC, V. Valet parking $25; self-parking $20. **Amenities:** 2 restaurants, 2 bars; concierge; airport transportation; 24-hour room service; laundry, dry cleaning and pressing service; shoe-shine service. Guests are eligible for membership ($27 for 3 days) in the hotel's Rivercenter Racquet and Health Club. *In room:* A/C, TV, minibar.

Hotel Inter-Continental ☆

The red granite Hotel Inter-Continental rises from the heart of the Central Business District within walking distance of the French Quarter and the Mississippi River attractions. It's a favorite of groups (including rock groups; the Stones stayed here two tours ago) and conventions. A strong, fresh decor features custom furniture; deep, rich colors; dark woods; lots of marble; better bathrooms; and many nice touches including "the best beds in town" (the mattresses are quite comfortable indeed). These handsome rooms feel quite luxurious. Some rooms have balconies that overlook the courtyard, although said courtyard is modern and industrial in appearance. The Governor's Floor (the 14th) has a VIP lounge and suites featuring period antiques and reproductions.

444 St. Charles Ave., New Orleans, LA 70130. ℂ **800/445-6563** or 504/525-5566. Fax 504/523-7310. www.interconti.com. 482 units. $305–$325 double; $500–$2,000 suite. AE, DC, DISC, MC, V. Valet parking $25. **Amenities:** Veranda Restaurant, Pete's Pub serving lunch daily, bar; pool; health club; concierge; business center; gift shop; 24-hour room service; barbershop and salon; massage; laundry and dry cleaning service; shoe-shine service. *In room:* A/C, TV, minibar.

Hyatt Regency ☆

If your trip to New Orleans revolves around an event at the Superdome, you should consider the Hyatt. The hotel occupies a 32-story building with guest rooms surrounding a seemingly bottomless central atrium. The public spaces are in grand corporate style, and so, as you'd expect, the lobby cafes generally attract a lunchtime crowd from the CBD. (If there's a Saints home game, however, expect to find a football crowd—the hotel's Hyttops Sports Bar & Grill is a popular hangout.) Guest rooms were clearly designed with the business traveler and the conventioneer in mind.

500 Poydras Plaza, New Orleans, LA 70113. ℂ **800/233-1234** or 504/561-1234. Fax 504/587-4141. www.hyatt.com. 1,184 units. $219–$244 double; $525–$625 suite. AE, DC, DISC, MC, V. Valet parking $18. **Amenities:** 2 restaurants, bar and grill; heated rooftop pool; whirlpool; exercise room; concierge; free shuttle service to the French Quarter; business center; gift shop; florist; salon; room service during limited hours; babysitting; currency exchange; multilingual staff. *In room:* A/C, TV.

Le Meridien Hotel ☆

This hotel is so committed to appearing classy that it covers the electrical cords of its lamps with shirred

> ## Spending the Night in Chains
> If you prefer the predictability of a chain hotel, there's a **Marriott** 𝓇 at 555 Canal St. at the edge of the Quarter (✆ **800/654-3990** or 504/581-1000). In the Central Business District, there is a **Residence Inn by Marriott** 𝓇, 345 St. Joseph St. (✆ **800/331-3131** or 504/522-1300), and a **Courtyard by Marriott** 𝓇, 300 Julia St. (✆ **504/598-9898**), both a couple of blocks from the Convention Center. The **Holiday Inn Downtown–Superdome** 𝓇 is, natch, right by the Superdome at 330 Loyola Ave. (✆ **800/HOLIDAY** or 504/581-1600).

designer fabric. You can't fault the location on Canal right across from the Quarter, but ultimately, it is anonymously ritzy with the public areas far more grand than the actual rooms. The latter are good-size with faux-luxe furniture. But the mattresses are overly stiff and closets are small, adding up to a comfortable but not particularly special experience. Bathrooms can be cramped, but the ergonomically designed amenities are eye-catching.

614 Canal St., New Orleans, LA 70130. ✆ 800/522-6963 or 504/525-6500. Fax 504/586-1543. www.meridienneworleans.com. 423 units. $355 double; $950–$2,000 suite. AE, DC, DISC, MC, V. Valet parking $21. **Amenities:** Restaurant; bar; heated outdoor pool; health club; sauna; concierge; business center; gift shop; jewelry store; art gallery; salon; 24-hour room service; massage; babysitting; laundry and dry cleaning; complimentary shoe shine. *In room:* A/C, TV, minibar.

Windsor Court 𝓇𝓇𝓇   *Condé Nast Traveler* voted the Windsor Court the Best Hotel in North America (and probably did it a disservice because who could ever live up to such hype?). In any case, there may be a finer hotel on the continent, but it can't be found in New Orleans. The unassuming, somewhat office-building exterior is camouflage for the quiet but posh delights within. Two corridors downstairs are mini-galleries that display original 17th-, 18th-, and 19th-century art, and there's a plush reading area with an international newspaper rack on the second floor. Everything is very, very chic and consequently just a little chilly. It's not too stiff for restless children, but it still feels more like a grownup hotel. The level of service is extraordinarily high.

The accommodations are exceptionally spacious with classy, not flashy, decor. All are suites featuring large bay windows or a private balcony overlooking the river (ask for a river view) or the city, a private foyer, a large living room, a bedroom with French doors, a large marble bathroom with particularly luxe amenities (plush robes, high-quality personal-care items, thick towels, a hamper, extra hair dryers), two dressing rooms, and a "petite kitchen."

300 Gravier St., New Orleans, LA 70130. ☎ **800/262-2662** or 504/523-6000. Fax 504/596-4749. www.windsorcourthotel.com. 324 units. $290–$400 standard double; $370–$505 junior suite; $400–$700 full suite; $700–$1,150 2-bedroom suite. Children under 12 stay free in parents' room. AE, DC, DISC, MC, V. Valet parking $20. **Amenities:** Grill Room Restaurant, Polo Club Lounge; health club with resort-size pool, sauna, and steam room; concierge; 24-hour suite service; in-room massage; laundry and dry cleaning. *In room:* A/C, TV, minibar, hair dryers.

W New Orleans 🏔🏔   While we have strong feelings indeed about staying in more New Orleans–appropriate, site-specific accommodations, we cheerfully admit that this is one fun hotel, and what is New Orleans about if not fun? There are certainly no more playful rooms in town, done up as they are in reds, blacks, and golds—frosty chic, to be sure, but oh, so comfortable, thanks to feather everything (pillows, comforters; and, for allergy sufferers, foam alternatives). Suites offer more space and, indeed, more of everything (two TVs, two VCRs, two bathrooms, one Oujia board). The rooms with views, especially those of the river, are outstanding. The ultra chic bar was designed by bar/club owner Rande "Mr. Cindy Crawford" Gerber. We do wish this whole experience wasn't so, well, New York, but then again, we find ourselves having so much fun it's kinda hard to get all that worked up about it.

333 Poydras St., New Orleans, LA 70130. ☎ **800/522-6963** or 504/525-9444. Fax 504/581-7179. www.whotels.com. 439 units. $359 double. AE, DC, DISC, MC, V. Valet parking $15. **Amenities:** Restaurant, bar; swimming pool; fitness center; concierge; business services; 24-hour room service; massage. *In room:* A/C, TV/VCR, CD player, minibar, coffeemaker, hair dryer, iron and ironing board, safe.

EXPENSIVE

International House 🏔🏔🏔   Everyone's favorite new hotel, the International House has set a standard with its creative design and meticulous attention to detail, and hotels in the area should be paying careful attention: The bar has been raised. Record-company and film execs should love it, but so should anyone who's had enough of Victorian sweetness and needs a palate cleanser. A wonderful old beaux-arts bank building has been transformed into a modern space that still pays tribute to its locale. In the graceful lobby, classical pilasters stand next to cool wrought-iron chandeliers.

Interiors are the embodiment of minimalist chic. Rooms are simple with muted, monochromatic (OK, beige) tones, tall ceilings and ceiling fans, up-to-the-minute bathroom fixtures, but also black-and-white photos of local musicians and characters, books about the city, and other clever touches that anchor the room in its New Orleans setting. Although the big bathrooms boast large tubs or space-age glassed-in showers, they do come off as a bit industrial. But compensations include cushy touches like fine towels, feather pillows, large TVs with movie channels, your own private phone number, dataports, CD players with CDs, and hair dryers.

221 Camp St., New Orleans, LA 70130. (©) 800/633-5770 or 504/553-9550. Fax 504/553-9560. www.ihhotel.com. 119 units. $149–$379 double; $369–$599 suite. AE, MC, V. Valet parking $17. **Amenities:** Lemon Grass Restaurant, bar; fitness center; concierge; gift shop; room service 8am–10pm; dry cleaning. *In room:* A/C, TV, dataport, minibar, hair dryer, iron.

The Pelham ★   This small hotel, in a renovated building that dates from the late 1800s, is one of the new wave of boutique hotels. From the outside and in its public areas, the Pelham feels like an upscale apartment building. Centrally located rooms are generally less bright than those on the exterior of the building; all have in-room safes. If you're not interested in staying right in the French Quarter or if you're looking for something with less public atmosphere than a hotel and more anonymity than a B&B, the Pelham is a good option.

444 Common St., New Orleans, LA 70130. (©) 888/211-3447 or 504/522-4444. Fax 504/539-9010. www.neworleanscollection.com/pelham. 60 units. $79–$399 double. AE, DC, DISC, MC, V. Parking $14.95 cars, $17.95 trucks plus tax. **Amenities:** Restaurant; concierge; room service; laundry service, express check-in. *In room:* A/C, TV, dataport, hair dryer, iron, safe.

Wyndham Riverfront Hotel ★   There couldn't be a better location if you're attending an event at the Convention Center: It's right across the street. But the rooms feel less like they're in a business hotel and more "use-convention-as-excuse-for–New Orleans–junket." Rooms are prefab elegant with stately wallpaper and armchairs, far more aesthetically pleasing than most big hotels. Bathrooms are nothing special but contain many fruity/flowery amenities from Bath & Bodyworks. Towels are thick but pillows rubbery. We did get a sense that the staff can be somewhat overwhelmed when a convention is staying there, but they were never less than gracious.

701 Convention Center Blvd., New Orleans, LA 70130. (©) 800/WYNDHAM or 504/524-8200. Fax 504/524-0600. www.wyndham.com. 202 units. $175–$220 double. AE, DC, DISC, MC, V. Valet parking $23. **Amenities:** Restaurant; bar; pool; exercise room; concierge; gift shop; room service until 11pm; laundry and dry cleaning; express checkout. *In room:* A/C, TV, minibar, coffeemaker, hair dryers, iron, safe.

MODERATE

Drury Inn & Suites This family-owned chain looks all too generic outside, but inside is a pleasant surprise, with grander-than-expected public spaces and rooms that are clean, new, and fancier than those in the average chain. All have high ceilings (except for ones on the 5th floor) and a decent amount of space, though bathrooms are small (with sinks in the dressing area). The beds are hard, but otherwise the furniture is good-quality generic-hotel average. A nice little heated rooftop pool, a small exercise room, and a generous comp breakfast make this not a bad little bargain for the area.

820 Poydras St., New Orleans, LA 700112-1016. ☎ **504/529-7800**. 156 units. $114 regular room; $149 suite. AE, DC, DISC, MC, V. $10 self-parking. **Amenities:** Daily full breakfast buffet, Mon–Thurs night complimentary cocktails; heated pool; exercise room; laundry and dry cleaning. *In room:* Coffeemaker, hair dryer, iron and ironing board, some suites have whirlpool tubs.

Le Pavillion Hotel Established in 1907 in a prime Central Business District location, Le Pavillion was the first hotel in New Orleans to have elevators. The lobby is stunning, just what you want in a big, grand hotel, with giant columns and chandeliers for days.

The standard guest rooms are all rather pretty and all have similar furnishings, but they differ in size. "Bay Rooms" are standard with two double beds and bay windows. Suites are actually hit or miss in terms of decor, with the nadir being the mind-bogglingly ugly Art Deco Suite. Much better is the Plantation Suite, decorated in antiques including pieces by Mallard, C. Lee (who, as a slave, studied under Mallard), Mitchell Rammelsberg, Belter, Badouine, and Marcotte.

833 Poydras St., New Orleans, LA 70140. ☎ **800/535-9095** or 504/581-3111. Fax 504/522-5543. www.lepavillion.com. 226 units. $125–$428 double; $595–$1,495 suite. AE, DC, DISC, MC, V. Valet parking $18. **Amenities:** Restaurant, bar; heated outdoor pool; fitness center and whirlpool spa; concierge; 24-hour room service, babysitting; laundry and dry cleaning; complimentary shoe shine. *In room:* A/C, TV, minibar.

St. James Hotel Once again, a fine preservation job, giving what could have been an eyesore derelict (if historic) building a new useful function. Actually, this is two different buildings, one of which used to be—get this!—the St. James Infirmary, sung about so memorably by many a mournful jazz musician. But because they had to make do with a non-uniform space, rooms vary in size and style, and a few lack windows. All rooms have marble bathrooms, and two suites and a room share a small, private brick courtyard with a fountain. There is a teeny-weeny pool—you might be forgiven for considering it really just a large puddle with nice tile. Overall, this is a good and friendly find, located just a block or two within the CBD.

330 Magazine St., New Orleans, LA 70130. © **800/273-1889** or 504/304-4000. www.decaturhouse.com 86 units. $99–$249. AE, DC, DISC, MC, V. $14.95–$17.95 valet parking. **Amenities:** Pool; health club; concierge; room-service breakfast only; babysitting; laundry and dry cleaning. *In room:* Coffeemaker, hair dryer, iron and ironing board, safe, bathrobe.

Whitney-Wyndham Historic Hotel 🅡 A grand old bank building has been cleverly converted into a fine modern hotel. The unique results include gawk-worthy public spaces; be sure to look up at all the fanciful, wedding-cake-decoration old plasterwork, and help us wonder how the heck safecrackers got past those thick slabs of doors. Best of all is the imposing lobby, full of stately pillars, now part restaurant but also, still part working bank—it puts other elegant establishments in town to shame. Rooms are a little too stately to classify as true business efficient, but also a little too generic to make this a romantic getaway. Having said that, we found the beds most comfortable and the bathrooms spacious. Overall, the Whitney has more character than your average upscale chain. If you are a hoity-toity businessman, you will probably like it a lot. And if you are preservationist, you will probably like it even more.

610 Poydras St., New Orleans, LA. © **504/581-4222.** 101 units. $159–$339. AE, DC, DISC, MC, V. **Amenities:** Restaurant, lobby bar, private dining room; fitness center; business services. *In room:* A/C, TV, dataport, CD player, minibar, coffee- and tea-making facilities, hair dryer, iron and ironing board, alarm clock, bathrobe, desk and ergonomic chair, Internet access, makeup mirror, Nintendo.

INEXPENSIVE

The Depot at Madame Julia's 🅡 *Finds* The Depot is an alternative to more commercial hotels in the CBD, and it takes up part of a whole complex of buildings dating from the 1800s. Low prices and a guesthouse environment mean a number of good things—including rooms with character and a proprietor who loves to help guests with all the details of their stay—but it also means shared bathrooms, rooms on the small and cozy side, and a location that, although quiet on the weekends, can get noisy in the mornings as the working neighborhood gets going. (Still being gentrified, the neighborhood is hit or miss, but more of the former than the latter thanks to arty Julia Street.) It's a quick walk or a short streetcar ride to the Quarter, which makes it an affordable alternative to the Quarter's much pricier accommodations. The budget-conscious and

those who prefer their hotels with personality will consider this a find.

748 O'Keefe St., New Orleans, LA 70113. © **504/529-2952**. Fax 504/529-1908. mmejuliadepothouse.com. 25 units, all with shared bathrooms. $65–$85 double. AE, personal checks (if paid in advance). *In room:* A/C.

5 Uptown/The Garden District

VERY EXPENSIVE

Pontchartrain Hotel 🏵🏵   If you have a weakness for faded grandeur and evocative atmosphere (and we do), here's your spot. If, on the other hand, you prefer antiseptic clean, you're in the wrong place. Newer hotels may make this local landmark seem slightly worn at the edges (though upgrades are fixing that), but to those who appreciate a certain shabby, old-world gentility, the Pontchartrain still feels like the most romantic and elegant hotel in the world, with a style no other hotel can match. Back in the day, it was the place for the likes of Rita Hayworth and Aly Kahn to tryst (courtesy of adjoining suites; Ms. Hayworth's still has the fanciful floral murals on walls). Its discreet ambience and pampering still make it a choice for celebrities (Tom Cruise and Nicole Kidman honeymooned here). Throughout, you can find some utterly fabulous furnishings (including Ming vases) that date from the hotel's early days.

The regular rooms, which are larger than most, have all gotten facelifts, including cedar-lined closets, cushy towels, and pedestal washbasins. The suites are named for prestigious guests of the past (Evelyn Waugh, Mary Martin, Cyd Charisse), but many may be turned into regular rooms during the ongoing renovations.

2031 St. Charles Ave., New Orleans, LA 70140. © **800/777-6193** or 504/524 0581. Fax 504/529-1165. www.pontchartrainhotel.com. 112 units. $95–$380 double. Extra person $10; during special events $25. Seasonal packages and special promotional rates available. AE, DC, DISC, MC, V. Parking $16. **Amenities:** Restaurant, bar; access to nearby spa with health club and outdoor pool; 24-hour room service; complimentary shoe shine. *In room:* A/C, TV.

EXPENSIVE

The Grand Victorian Bed & Breakfast 🏵🏵   Owner Bonnie Rabe confounded and delighted her new St. Charles neighbors when she took a crumbling Queen Anne–style Victorian mansion right on the corner of Washington (two blocks from Lafayette cemetery and Commander's Palace with a streetcar stop right in front) and, over the course of many arduous months, resurrected it into a

Uptown Accommodations, Dining & Nightlife

ACCOMMODATIONS ■
Chimes B&B **25**
The Columns **24**
Hampton Inn **22**
Maison Perrier Bed & Breakfast **26**
Park View Guest House **8**
St. Charles Inn **21**

NIGHTLIFE ●
Carrollton Station **2**
Dos Jefes Uptown
    Cigar Bar **13**
Ground Coffee House **15**
Madigan's **5**
Maple Leaf Bar **1**
Snake & Jake's Xmas
    Club Lounge **3**
St. Joe's Bar **9**
Tipitina's **29**

DINING ◆
Bluebird Cafe **23**
Brigtsen's **4**
Camellia Grill **6**
Casamento's **28**
Clancy's **11**
Dick & Jenny's **30**
Dunbar's Creole Cooking **14**
Franky & Johnny's **12**
Gautreau's **16**
Kelsey's **27**
La Crêpe Nanou **17**
Martin Wine Cellar and Delicatessen **20**
Martinique Bistro **10**
Pascal's Manale **19**
PJ's Coffee & Tea Company **7**
Upperline **18**

showcase B&B. The location makes its porches and balconies a most comfortable and convenient place to view Mardi Gras parades.

The stunning rooms are full of antiques (each has a four-poster or wood canopy bed) with the slightly fussy details demanded by big Victorian rooms. Linens, pillows, and towels are ultra plush, and some bathrooms have big Jacuzzi tubs. A generous continental breakfast is served, and friendly Bonnie is ready with suggestions on how to spend your time. Though Bonnie lives on the third floor, she is not always there, so as in any B&B, do not expect 24-hour service.

2727 St. Charles Ave., New Orleans, LA 70130. ⓒ **800/977-0008** or 504/895-1104. Fax 504/896-8688. www.gvbb.com. 8 units. $150–$350 double. Rates include breakfast. AE, DISC, MC, V. *In room:* A/C, TV, dataport, hair dryer, iron.

The Queen Anne ⭐ A somewhat different take on lodging, this was a one-family home for 130 years. The owners had to pass muster with the mayor, the governor, and the park service when they renovated it, and the result is perhaps the grandest building for a B&B in town. Furnishings are a bit sterile, however—hotel-room furniture masquerading as antique (though mattresses are top of the line). The inn, nicely located near the Mardi Gras parade route, is not our first choice for decor, but the stately rooms (each of which has some exquisite detail like tiled nonworking fireplaces) pull it off.

1625 Prytania St., New Orleans, LA 70130. ⓒ **800/862-1984** or 504/524-0427. Fax 504/522-2977. www.thequeenanne.com. 12 units. $159–$179 double. Rates include continental breakfast. AE, DC, DISC, MC, V. Self-parking $10. **Amenities:** Free shuttle to Convention Center, Harrah's Casino, and French Quarter; laundry services. *In room:* A/C, TV, unstocked fridge, microwave, hair dryer.

MODERATE

Chimes B&B ⭐⭐⭐ *(Finds)* This is a real hidden gem that truly allows you to experience the city away from the typical tourist experience. The Chimes is in a less fashionable but more neighborhood-like portion of the Garden District, just two blocks off St. Charles Avenue. Your hosts are the ever-charming and friendly Jill and Charles Abbyad, and the rooms are behind their house, surrounding a small, sweet, and yes, chime-filled courtyard.

Rooms vary in size from a generous L-shape to a two-story loft type to some that are downright cozy. All have antiques (including romantic old beds) but are so tastefully under-decorated, particularly in contrast to other B&Bs, that they are positively Zen. An ambitious continental breakfast is served in the hosts' house, and chatting with them can be so enjoyable you might get off to a late start. The hosts also speak French and Arabic. The Chimes is unfortunately not set up to accommodate guests with disabilities.

1146 Constantinople St., New Orleans, LA 70115. ℂ 800/729-4640 (for reservations only) or 504/488-4640. Fax 504/899-9858. www.historiclodging.com/chimes. html. 5 units. $99–$175 double; June to mid-Sept $65–$125 double. Rates include breakfast. Look for rates, availability, and featured specials online. AE, MC, V. Limited off-street free parking. Well-behaved pets accepted. *In room:* A/C, TV, dataport, coffeemaker, hair dryer, iron, bottled water.

The Columns 𝒢   New Orleans made a mistake when it tore down its famous bordellos. If somebody had turned one of the grander ones into a hotel, imagine how many people would stay there! The next best thing is the Columns, whose interior was used by Louis Malle for his film about Storyville, *Pretty Baby.* Please don't lounge around the lobby in your underwear, however, even if it is Victorian (the underwear, not the lobby). Built in 1883, the building is one of the greatest examples of a late-19th-century Louisiana residence. The grand, columned porch is a highly popular evening scene thanks to the bar inside. The immediate interior is utterly smashing; we challenge any other hotel to match this grand staircase and stained-glass-window combination.

Unfortunately, the magnificence of the setting is hurt by the relentlessly casual attitude toward the public areas. Cheesy furniture downstairs, an empty, neglected ballroom, and stale cigarette smoke in that gorgeous stairway (courtesy of the bar) detract mightily from the experience, making it perilously close to seedy in some spots. Too bad. This could be a deeply romantic hotel, ponderously Victorian, and we mean that in a good way. But bar revenue reigns supreme, so the smoke is probably there to stay. Low-end rooms are cozy with quilts and old bedsteads. High-end rooms are indeed that—it's the difference between the master's room and the servants' quarters. We particularly like room 16 with its grand furniture and floor-to-ceiling shutters that lead out to a private, second-story porch.

3811 St. Charles Ave., New Orleans, LA 70115. ℂ 800/445-9308 or 504/899-9308. Fax 504/899-8170. www.thecolumns.com. 20 units. $100–$170 double. Rates include full breakfast. AE, MC, V. Parking on street. **Amenities:** Bar. *In room:* A/C.

Hampton Inn   This is a top choice for a chain hotel, if you don't mind being a bit out of the way (we don't—it's quite nice up here on St. Charles in a grand section of town that is generally not overly touristed). The public areas are slightly more stylish than that found in other chains, and there are welcome touches like complimentary cheese and tea served daily from 6 to 7pm. The style does not extend to the rooms, however, which are pretty mundane. But they're not *that* bad: Hidden inside a bland color scheme are interesting details (decent photos for artwork, ever-so-slight Arts and Crafts detailing on furniture, and big TVs).

3626 St. Charles Ave., New Orleans, LA 70115. ℂ 800/426-7866 or 504/899-9990. Fax 504/899-9908. www.neworleanshamptoninns.com. 100 units. $129–$159 double. Rates include continental breakfast, free local calls, and free incoming faxes. AE, DC, DISC, MC, V. Free parking. **Amenities:** Complimentary coffee, cheese and tea happy hour daily; small lap pool; laundry and dry cleaning. *In room:* AC, TV.

Maison Perrier Bed & Breakfast ✿   This B&B is so new that it seems fresh out of the packaging; it hasn't quite mellowed like others in town. On the other hand, "mellowed" often means "shabby and threadbare," so this distinction may please you. This 1894 painted-lady Victorian has been restored to a gleaming fare-thee-well. It may or may not have been a turn-of-the-20th-century "gentlemen's club." Rooms now sport the names of the former landlady's "nieces," and each is themed—in color if nothing else (though we can do without Desiree, the wild animal–print room). And each has some special detail: a high four-poster bed, say, or fabulous old tile around a (nonworking) fireplace. Downstairs is a warm parlor and a rec room that is more modern than not, but the hosts ply you with drinks and evening hors d'oeuvres, and the vibe is convivial. Breakfast is fresh and filling and prepared by the resident cook—when was the last time you had a voodoo queen cook for you?

4117 Perrier St. (2 blocks riverside from St. Charles Ave., 3 blocks downtown from Napoleon Ave.), New Orleans, LA 70115. ℂ 888/610-1807 or 504/897-1807. Fax 504/897-1399. www.maisonperrier.com. $90–$250 double. Rates include breakfast. AE, DISC, MC, V. Parking available on street. **Amenities:** Complimentary bottled water and soft drinks; office supplies and machines; laundry service. *In room:* A/C, TV, private voice mail, dataport, minibar, hair dryer, iron and ironing board.

The McKendrick-Breaux House ✿✿   Owner Eddie Breaux saved this 1865 building just as it was about to fall down and turned it into one of the city's best B&Bs. The antiques-filled rooms are spacious (some of the bathrooms are downright huge), quaint, and meticulously decorated but not fussy. The public areas are simple, elegant, and comfortable. Really, the whole place couldn't be in better taste, and yet it's not intimidating, thanks to the warmth of Breaux and his staff. They are utterly hospitable and, like the best guesthouse hosts, quite knowledgeable about the city they love. The location is in the middle of the Lower Garden District, named the Most Trendy Neighborhood in America by *Utne Reader* magazine.

1474 Magazine St., New Orleans, LA 70130. ℂ **888/570-1700** or 504/586-1700. Fax 504/522-7138. www.mckendrick-breaux.com. 9 units. $125–$195 double. Rates include breakfast. AE, MC, V. Limited free off-street parking. **Amenities:** Jacuzzi. *In room:* A/C, TV, dataport, hair dryer, iron.

Prytania Park Hotel   This 1840s building (which once housed Huey Long's girlfriend) is now equal parts motel and funky simulated Quarter digs. Some rooms have been redone to the owner's pride (with darker wood tones and four-poster beds plus bathrooms that still have a Holiday Inn feel), but we kind of prefer the older section with its pine furniture, tall ceilings, and nonworking fireplaces.

1525 Prytania St. (enter off Terpsichore St.), New Orleans, LA 70130. ℂ **800/862-1984** or 504/524-0427. Fax 504/522-2977. www.prytaniaparkhotel.com. 74 units. $109 double; $119 suite. Extra person $10. Rates include continental breakfast. Children under 12 stay free in parents' room. Seasonal rates and special packages available. AE, DC, DISC, MC, V. Off-street parking available. **Amenities:** Free shuttle to Convention Center and French Quarter. *In room:* A/C, TV, minibar.

INEXPENSIVE

Park View Guest House   If you can't live without Bourbon Street mere steps away from your hotel entrance, then this is not the place for you. But if a true getaway to you means a step back in time, come to this way-uptown guesthouse that feels like an old-fashioned hotel (as well it should; it was built in 1881) and a glamorous Belle Epoque mansion with all the trimmings. Antiques-filled rooms are getting plusher every minute, benefiting from the addition of down comforters, good amenities, and hair dryers. All rooms have high ceilings; some have balconies overlooking Audubon Park.

7004 St. Charles Ave., New Orleans, LA 70118. ℂ **888/533-0746** or 504/861-7564. Fax 504/861-1225. www.parkviewguesthouse.com. 22 units, 17 with private bathroom. $95 double without bathroom, $115 double with bathroom. Rates include continental breakfast. Extra person $10. AE, DISC, MC, V. Parking on street. *In room:* A/C.

St. Charles Guesthouse   Very much worth checking out for those on a budget, the St. Charles Guesthouse—the first such accommodation in the Garden District and much copied over the last 20 years—is not fancy, but it's one of the friendliest hotels in town. Rooms are plain and run from low-end backpacker lodgings, which have no air-conditioning (even the management describes them as "small and spartan"), to larger chambers with air-conditioning and private bathrooms—nice enough but nothing special. That's OK. The place does have the required New Orleans–atmosphere elements: high ceilings, a long staircase, and antiques (there is such a fine line between "antique" and "old furniture"), not to mention the banana tree–ringed courtyard. It's only a short walk through the quiet and very pretty neighborhood to the St. Charles Avenue streetcar line.

1748 Prytania St., New Orleans, LA 70130. © **504/523-6556.** Fax 504/522-6340. www.stcharlesguesthouse.com. 35 units, 23 with private bathroom. $35–$95 double. Rates include continental breakfast. AE, MC, V. Parking available on street. **Amenities:** Pool.

St. Charles Inn

If you want to stay uptown and don't need or want the pampering of a fancy hotel or a precious guesthouse, you are probably looking for the St. Charles Inn. It's on the St. Charles streetcar line and is convenient to Tulane and Loyola universities and Audubon Park. Each room has two double beds or a king-size bed.

3636 St. Charles Ave., New Orleans, LA 70115. © **800/489-9908** or 504/899-8888. Fax 504/899-8892. 40 units. $65–$80 double. Rates include continental breakfast. AE, DC, DISC, MC, V. Free parking. **Amenities:** Restaurant, bar. *In room:* A/C, TV.

St. Vincent's Guesthouse

OK, now pay attention. This is not for anyone who hasn't stayed in a true European pension. It's not for well-heeled tourists. It's the kind of nonglitzy budget place so beloved by backpackers and, let's face it, ordinary Europeans. These are dorm-like, not ultra-comfortable rooms. Though they do have patchwork quilts on the beds, some of the units show serious wear and tear. The bathrooms, some of which show even more tear and wear, are all really plain. But the atmosphere is convivial. Breakfast ($6 "unless they are paying $79 in which case we just throw it in") is often whatever you want (well, not ostrich or the like); you just can't beat the price. But again, this isn't for everyone. If this description doesn't ring your bell, don't come here just for the bargain.

1507 Magazine St., New Orleans, LA. 70130. © **504/523-3411.** Fax 504/566-1518. www.stvincentsguesthouse.com. 75 units. $59–$89 double; $125 during Mardi Gras and Jazz Fest. AE, MC, V. Free parking. **Amenities:** Restaurant; outdoor pool. *In room:* A/C, TV.

4

Where to Dine

Within a short time during your trip to New Orleans, you will find yourself talking less about the sights and more about food—if not constantly about food. What you ate already, what you are going to be eating later, what you wish you had time to eat. We are going to take a stand and say to heck with New York and San Francisco: New Orleans has the best food in the United States.

There is, however, a reason why a 1997 study of U.S. eating habits proclaimed New Orleans the fattest city in the country (a fact the locals will cheerfully volunteer to you). At times, it might seem that everything is fried or served with a sauce, and sometimes both.

Some of you may fret about this. Some of you may be watching your waistlines. To which we say, with all due understanding and respect, "So what?" You're on vacation. Vow to make it up when you get home. If you are doing your trip properly, you will be walking and dancing so much that your scale might not be as unfriendly as you fear when you return home.

1 The French Quarter

EXPENSIVE

Antoine's ☆ CREOLE   Owned and operated by the same family for an astonishing 150 years, Antoine's is, unfortunately, beginning to show its age. With its 15 dining rooms and massive menu, it was once the ultimate in fine dining in New Orleans. But murmurs about a decline in quality have become open complaints. Still, it's hard to ignore a legend. Locals—loyal customers all, mind you—will advise you to focus on starters and dessert and skip the entrees. They are right; at best, the latter are bland but acceptable. The famous oysters Rockefeller (served hot in the shell, covered with a mysterious green sauce—Antoine's invented it ~~~~~ out the recipe) will live up to its rep, a~ and -shaped baked Alaska is surel~

713 St. Louis St. ℂ 504/581-442~
$56. AE, DC, MC, V. Mon–Sat ~

New Orleans Dining

To METAIRIE

Southern Baptist Hospital

BROADMOOR

Union Passenger Terminal (Amtrak)

UPTOWN

Lee Circle

GARDEN DISTRICT

See also "Uptown Accommodations & Dining" Map

New Orleans General Hospital

- - - St. Charles Streetcar Route
Ferry Service to Algiers Point
.... Riverwalk

Bizou **11**
Bluebird Café **3**
Bon Ton Café **18**
Commander's Palace **5**
Cuvee **20**
Dooky Chase **26**
Dunbar's Creole Cooking **1**
Elizabeth's **29**

Emeril's **24**
Emeril's Delmonico Restaurant & Bar **8**
Ernst's Café **22**
Feelings Café D'Aunoy **28**
56° **12**
The Grill Room **19**
The Harbor **29**
Herbsaint **10**

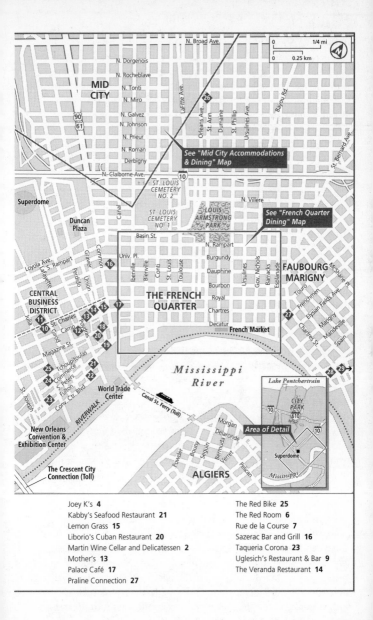

Joey K's **4**	The Red Bike **25**
Kabby's Seafood Restaurant **21**	The Red Room **6**
Lemon Grass **15**	Rue de la Course **7**
Liborio's Cuban Restaurant **20**	Sazerac Bar and Grill **16**
Martin Wine Cellar and Delicatessen **2**	Taqueria Corona **23**
Mother's **13**	Uglesich's Restaurant & Bar **9**
Palace Café **17**	The Veranda Restaurant **14**
Praline Connection **27**	

Arnaud's ⚸ CREOLE   Rave-producing fish dishes include snapper or trout Pontchartrain (topped with crabmeat), the spicy pompano Duarte, and the pompano David, a light fish dish that is the perfect choice for those attempting to watch waistlines. Any filet mignon entree is superb (the meat is often better than what's served in most steakhouses in town). Desserts aren't quite as magnificent, but the Chocolate Devastation is worth trying.

813 Bienville St. ⓒ **504/523-5433**. www.arnauds.com. Reservations recommended. Jackets required in main dining room. Main courses $17–$28. AE, DC, DISC, MC, V. Mon–Fri 11:30am–2:30pm; Sun Jazz brunch 10am–2:30pm; Sun–Thurs 6–10pm; Fri–Sat 6–10:30pm.

Bacco ⚸⚸ ITALIAN/CREOLE   Bacco is romantic and candlelit at night, more affordable and casual at lunchtime. Don't expect spaghetti and marinara sauce here. Instead, think rich, arresting creations such as *ravioli ripieni di formaggio,* featuring four creamy cheeses all melting into a sauce of olive oil, tomatoes, and browned garlic. Or try the *cannelloni con fungi,* stuffed with wild mushrooms and fresh herbs covered in a goat cheese and chive sauce. The menu changes regularly, but our latest trip featured an appetizer of truffled egg rolled in herbed bread crumbs with Gorgonzola cream sauce—rich, yes, but a combo you need to experience. Truffle pasta made us so happy we asked for the recipe.

310 Chartres St. ⓒ **504/522-2426**. www.bacco.com. Reservations recommended. Main courses $18–$31. AE, DC, MC, V. Daily 11:30am–2pm and 6–10pm.

Bayona ⚸⚸⚸ INTERNATIONAL   One of the city's top dining experiences, Bayona is beloved by savvy New Orleanians. In fact, two natives who were showing a visitor around the Quarter broke into spontaneous applause as they passed by. Chef Susan Spicer, who honed her considerable skills in France and at Le Bistro at the Maison de Ville, offers elegant, eclectic contemporary cuisine with Asian and Mediterranean flavors. You can sit inside the 200-year-old French Quarter Creole cottage or out in the courtyard.

Begin with one of the superb daily soups or the cream of garlic, a perennial favorite. Appetizers include grilled shrimp with cilantro sauce and black bean cakes, and flavorful veal sweetbreads sautéed with scallions and diced potatoes in a sherry vinaigrette. Knockout entrees have included medallions of lamb loin with a lavender honey aioli and zinfandel demi-glace, and a perfectly grilled pork chop with a stuffing of fontina cheese, fresh sage, and prosciutto. Heaven.

430 Dauphine St. ⓒ **504/525-4455**. www.bayona.com. Reservations required at dinner, recommended at lunch. Main courses $9–$12 at lunch, $14–$23 at dinner.

Acme Oyster House **2**	La Marquise **38**
Angeli On Decatur **50**	Le Bistro **33**
Antoine's **24**	Louis XVI **10**
Arnaud's **10**	Louisiana Pizza Kitchen **51**
Bacco **17**	Mama Rosa's **31**
Bayona **28**	Marisol **52**
Bella Luna **48**	Maximo's Italian Grill **49**
Brennan's **25**	Mr. B's Bistro **9**
Broussard's **27**	Mona Lisa **53**
Cafe au Lait **16**	Napoleon House **22**
Café Beignet **13**	Nola **19**
Café du Monde **41**	Old Dog NewTrick Cafe **14**
Café Giovanni **4**	Olde N'Awlins Cookery **26**
Café Maspero **40**	Pelican Club **15**
Cafe Sbisa **47**	Peristyle **32**
Central Grocery **45**	Petunia's **29**
Clover Grill **43**	Port of Call **55**
Court of Two Sisters **34**	Ralph & Kacoo's **39**
Dickie Brennan's Steakhouse **3**	Red Fish Grill **1**
Dominique's **30**	Rémoulade **12**
Felix's Restaurant & Oyster Bar **8**	Rib Room **23**
Galatoire's **7**	Royal Blend Coffee
Gamay **18**	& Tea House **35**
Gumbo Shop **37**	Royal Café **36**
Irene's **46**	Samurai Sushi **6**
Johnny's Po-Boys **21**	201 Restaurant & Bar **5**
K-Paul's Louisiana Kitchen **20**	Tujague's **44**
La Madeleine **42**	Verdi Marte **54**

AE, DC, DISC, MC, V. Mon–Fri 11:30am–1:30pm; Mon–Thurs 6–9:30pm; Fri–Sat 6–10:30pm.

Bella Luna ★ ECLECTIC/ITALIAN/CONTINENTAL With its sweeping view of the Mississippi, Bella Luna is considered the most romantic restaurant in town, but the food has both its fans and its detractors. We are coming down on the side of the former and not just because entrees are garnished with curious herbs from the chef/owner's garden. Definitely try the fettuccine appetizer, prepared tableside. It's happily quite light for a dish that can be gluey and heavy. A salmon tower with white truffle oil, cucumber, and red onion with Louisiana choupique caviar and capers—well, gee, doesn't that sound good? It is. Skip the meat entrees. Request a table close to the windows to better take in the view. Service can be uneven, so don't go unless you can linger—which you may well want to, hypnotized by Old Man River rolling along.

914 N. Peters St. ⓒ 504/529-1583. Reservations recommended. Main courses $16–$26. AE, DC, DISC, MC, V. Mon–Sat 6–10:30pm; Sun 6–9:30pm.

Brennan's ★ FRENCH/HAUTE CREOLE For more than 40 years, breakfast at Brennan's has been a New Orleans tradition, a feast that has surely kept many a heart surgeon busy. Expect no California health-conscious fruit-and-granola options here; this multicourse extravaganza is unashamedly sauce- and egg-intensive. It's also costly—it's not hard to drop $50 on breakfast—so you might be better off ordering the fixed-price meal. Breakfast at Brennan's has changed little over the years, and that is part of its charm, as is the building, constructed by Edgar Degas's great-grandfather. Enjoy dishes such as eggs Portuguese (poached on top of a tomato concoction, served in a puff pastry with hollandaise ladled over the whole) or the fine turtle soup. Even with a reservation, expect a wait.

417 Royal St. ⓒ 504/525-9711. Reservations recommended. Main courses $18–$22 at lunch, $28.50–$38.50 at dinner. AE, DC, DISC, MC, V. Daily 8am–2:30pm and 6–10pm. Closed Dec 25.

Broussard's ★ CREOLE Unfairly dismissed as a tourist trap (which, in truth, it was for some years), Broussard's is a perfectly fine alternative if your top choices are booked up. Chef Gunther Preuss and his wife, Evelyn, own the place, which includes an elegant, formal dining room and a lovely courtyard. "Gunther has a way with crab," claims his press material, and once we stopped giggling over that turn of phrase, we had to admit it was true. Try the appetizer of crabmeat Florentine, covered in a brie sauce. Order the baked filet of redfish Herbsaint (a local anise-flavored liqueur), clever and delicious in its components, which include impossibly sweet crabmeat and lemon risotto. Double chocolate Marquise Nelly Melba is as fun to eat as it is to say (it's a bittersweet chocolate parfait).

819 Conti St. © 504/581-3866. www.broussards.com. Reservations recommended. No jeans, shorts, sneakers, or T-shirts. Main courses $21.50–$36. AE, MC, V. Daily 5:30–10pm.

Café Giovanni ITALIAN Though Chef Duke LoCicero has been winning culinary awards right and left, Café Giovanni is kind of a mixed bag, thanks to a combo of admittedly entirely fine food, lackadaisical service, and—of course—the dreaded (or highly enjoyable, depending on your conversational needs during dinner and your love of schmaltz) singing waiters (to be found Wed, Fri, and Sat nights, singing opera with all their might). Still, any place that serves the gastronomic wonder that is fresh, buttery crescenza cheese on panettone *pain perdu* (Italian Christmas cake made as local French toast . . . kinda), smeared over foie gras and topped off with a reduction sauce that ought to be illegal, well, we can overlook a little operatic noise.

117 Decatur St. © 504/529-2154. Entrees $17.95–$27.95. Sun–Thurs 5:30–10pm; Fri–Sat 5:30–11pm. AE, DC, DISC, MC, V.

Court of Two Sisters CREOLE Thanks to a huge, foliage-filled courtyard, this is probably the prettiest restaurant in town, but even major ambience can't obscure lackluster food. Here you find the only daily jazz brunch in town, but it suffers from the typical buffet problem—too many dishes, none of which succeed except maybe the made-to-order items like eggs Benedict. Dinner may be improving, however, with the recent addition of a chef swiped from the highly regarded Christian's. You can't ask for a better setting, though.

613 Royal St. © 504/522-7261. www.courtoftwosisters.com. Reservations required at dinner. Main courses $15.50–$30; fixed-price menu $38; brunch $22. AE, DC, DISC, MC, V. Daily 9am–3pm and 5:30–10pm.

Dickie Brennan's Steakhouse 🐷🐷 STEAK Carnivores should be pleased with this latest Brennan family enterprise (Dickie's dad had long dreamed of opening a steakhouse), which has the feel of a contemporary clubhouse. All the meat is USDA Prime, and great care is taken to cook it just as the customer dictates. We like the tender, flavorful rib-eye, but do get that creamy spinach on the side. Start with the napoleon of tomato and Gorgonzola cheese topped with rémoulade sauce. Don't miss the bananas Foster bread pudding, which proves that there are still new twists on this old faithful dish.

716 Iberville St. ℂ 504/522-2467. www.dbrennanssteakhouse.com. Reservations recommended. Main courses $14.95–$32. AE, DC, DISC, MC, V. Mon–Fri 11:30am–2:30pm and 5:30–10pm; Sat–Sun 5:30–11pm.

Dominique's ℛ INTERNATIONAL   Here's yet another reason for the local restaurant scene to be grateful to Le Bistro at the Maison de Ville. Chef Dominique Macquet worked at Le Bistro before opening his eponymous restaurant. Named one of the seven best new restaurants in America by *Bon Appétit* in 1998, this medium-size bistro is well worth a little trot up the Rue Toulouse. Worth it, that is, as long as you want to try virtually cutting-edge dishes like duck pastrami or duck prosciutto—and trust us, you do. Don't miss the aquavit-citrus-cured salmon with crème fraîche appetizer Entrees can be a little less successful by comparison. For dessert, try the "cappamisu" (cappuccino-flavored tiramisu in a cup).

In the Maison Dupuy Hotel, 1001 Toulouse St. ℂ **504/522-8800.** Fax 504/595-2806. www.dominiquesrestaurant.com. Reservations recommended. Main courses $22–$28. AE, DC, DISC, MC, V. Daily 7–10:30am, 11:30am–1:30pm, and 6–10pm.

Galatoire's ℛℛ FRENCH   The venerable Galatoire's causes heated discussions these days among local foodies: Is it still the best restaurant in New Orleans or past its prime? Locals love it because they've gone for regular Sunday-evening dinners for years, and all the old waiters know their names. We love it because, in *A Streetcar Named Desire,* Stella took Blanche there to escape Stanley's poker game. It was Tennessee Williams' favorite restaurant (his table is the one right behind the word "RESTAURANT" on the window). Galatoire's has been run by the same family since 1905, and its traditions remain intact. They've also finished a spectacular renovation of the upstairs dining room, which had been closed since World War II, and this has brought much-needed additional seating.

Galatoire's is worth the trip, though you may not have the same experience as a knowledgeable local unless you get a waiter who can guide you (ask for John). We love the lump crabmeat appetizer (think coleslaw, only with all crab instead of cabbage), shrimp rémoulade, and oysters Rockefeller. Don't miss out on the terrific creamed spinach and the puffy potatoes with béarnaise sauce, which will make you swear off regular french fries forever.

Galatoire's doesn't accept reservations except for groups of eight or more, so expect a wait. Even the Duke and Duchess of Windsor had to wait in line.

209 Bourbon St. ℂ **504/525-2021.** Fax 504/525-5900. www.galatoires.com. Reservations accepted for groups of 8 or more. Jackets required after 5pm and all day Sun. Main courses $14–$27. AE, DC, DISC, MC, V. Sun noon–10pm; Tues–Sat 11:30am–10pm. Closed holidays.

Gamay 𝕽𝕽 CONTEMPORARY CREOLE   Here's a relatively new offering from the chef/owners of Gabrielle on Esplanade. By comparison, Gamay is a little bit more starched and formal than its predecessor, but the food is so darn good that we don't really care all that much. Try appetizers like barbecue shrimp pie and grilled mayhorn cheese with Beluga caviar and oysters. Among the entrees, the almond-crusted soft-shell crab with garlic shrimp and saffron pasta was too huge and rich to finish, though we did try gallantly. Dessert options include a heavenly strawberry shortcake.

In the Bienville House hotel, 320 Decatur St. ℂ **504/299-8800.** Fax 504/299-8802. Reservations recommended. Main courses $18–$28. AE, DC, DISC, MC, V. Fri 11:30am–2pm; Tues–Sat 6–10pm.

K-Paul's Louisiana Kitchen 𝕽 CAJUN   Paul Prudhomme was at the center of the revolution of the early 1980s when Cajun food became known throughout the world. His reputation and line of spices continue today, which is probably why there is constantly a line outside his restaurant. Unfortunately, although the food is still good, it's not spectacular and certainly is not worth the wait (upwards of 1½ hr.). The portions are Paul-size and as spicy as you might imagine, but nothing that special. Indeed, it feels as if the menu hasn't changed all that much in quite some time. More interesting food is available all over town, and at some places you can get (admittedly) Prudhomme-influenced food without the long wait.

416 Chartres St. ℂ **504/524-7394.** www.chefpaul.com. Reservations accepted for upstairs dining room only. Main courses $12.95–$16.95 at lunch, $22.95–$32.95 at dinner. AE, DC, DISC, MC, V. Tues–Sat 11:30am–2:30pm; Mon–Sat 5:30–10pm.

Le Bistro 𝕽𝕽 INTERNATIONAL   This tiny jewel of a bistro, part of the superb Hotel Maison de Ville, is easy to overlook among the higher-profile choices in the French Quarter. But it is a favorite among in-the-know locals, who think of it as a training ground for new chefs. Patrons also bask in the warm Gallic glow of hospitality emitted by long-time maitre d' Patrick, who will remember your name and your favorite dish. The menu changes regularly, but a recent visit produced uniformly marvelous dishes such as a Begger's Purse oyster appetizer, and generous entrees of wild boar and swordfish. It's also an excellent choice for lunch, with selections like the signature dish of mussels with thick french fries and homemade mayonnaise. Finish with the crème brûlée, and tell Patrick we said hi.

In the Hotel Maison de Ville, 733 Toulouse St. ℭ **504/528-9206.** www. maisondeville.com. Reservations recommended. Main courses $19.75–$24.75. AE, DC, DISC, MC, V. Mon–Sat 11:30am–2pm; Sun brunch 11:30am–2pm; daily 6–10pm.

Louis XVI *Overrated* FRENCH   For a long time considered one of the city's premier dining establishments, Louis XVI is unfortunately no longer truly worth recommending. It's not that the food is bad, by no means, but it isn't particularly special. It's classic French—beef Wellington, rack of lamb, appropriate sauces—but dull and costly. Dining is extremely formal; if you aren't gussied up enough, you will probably be hidden away in the bar section, where service can be most spotty. To be fair, it's probably a fine place if you are with—or indeed, are—traditional and/or unadventurous eaters.

In the St. Louis hotel, 730 Bienville St. ℭ **504/581-7000.** www.louisxvi.com. Reservations recommended. Jacket and tie optional; no jeans. Main courses $18–$34. AE, DISC, MC, V. Mon–Fri 7–11am; Sat–Sun 7am–noon; daily 6–10pm.

Marisol ℛ INTERNATIONAL   Restaurants have had bad luck in this space, so although this end of the Quarter (by the Frenchman section) badly needs a high-end restaurant, Marisol may be fighting a losing battle. It doesn't help that it's a little pricey for a place without a celebrity chef. With an overly ambitious menu that changes daily (with the exception of its signature Thai crab and coconut soup), dishes are hit or miss. But when they hit, you will really want them to stay around. On a recent visit, the roast double-cut pork chop was perfectly smoked. Red beet and white cheddar ice creams are worth a taste to say you did but not enough to warrant finishing them. The room is clean and dull and tries too hard to say "nouveau elegance," but the candlelit courtyard is as pretty as any higher-profile Quarter locale.

437 Esplanade Ave. ℭ **504/943-1912.** Fax 504/943-2028. www.marisolrestaurant. com. Reservations recommended. Main courses $18–$25. AE, DC, MC, V. Tues–Fri 11am–2pm and 6–10pm; Sun brunch 11am–2pm.

Nola ℛℛ CREOLE/NEW AMERICAN   This modern two-story building with a glass-enclosed elevator is the most casual and least expensive of chef Emeril Lagasse's three restaurants. The same problems that plague Emeril's, however, also surface here: fine food but often-horrible attitude and the potential for painfully slow service. Still, it's conveniently located in the Quarter. And then there's the food: an appetizer that's a sort of deconstructed roast beef sandwich and unique entrees like cedar-plank fish and Caribbean-style grilled free-range chicken (with a brown sugar–cayenne rub, served with sweet potato casserole, guacamole, and fried tortilla threads).

534 St. Louis St. ✆ **504/522-6652**. Fax 504/524-6178. www.emerils.com. Reservations recommended. Main courses $20–$30. AE, DC, DISC, MC, V. Mon–Sat 11:30am–2pm; Sun–Thurs 6–10pm; Fri–Sat 6pm–midnight.

The Pelican Club ⍟ NEW AMERICAN   It sometimes comes as a relief to eat at a fine New Orleans establishment that is not a variation on a Brennan. The Pelican Club is worth investigating, particularly for its reasonably priced three-course fixed-price meal. Everything is quite tasty. Escargots come in a tequila garlic butter sauce, topped with tiny puff pastries. Tender lamb arrives coated in rosemary-flavored bread crumbs with a spicy pepper jelly. For dessert, try the amazing profiteroles filled with coffee ice cream and topped with three sauces. The mostly young wait staff is sassy and opinionated in a good way. Take advantage of them.

312 Exchange Alley. ✆ **504/523-1504**. Fax 504/522-2331. Reservations recommended. Main courses $17–$28; fixed-price early dinner $25. AE, DC, DISC, MC, V. Daily 5–10pm.

Peristyle ⍟⍟⍟ FRENCH/AMERICAN/ITALIAN BISTRO NOLA foodies were devastated when Chef Anne Kearney's Peristyle was gutted by a fire in late 1999, and loud was the rejoicing when it was back up and running a few months later. But that was nothing compared with the clamor that followed when it became clear that somehow, the already highly regarded chef had topped herself; it seems impossible, but Peristyle is better than ever.

Though admittedly the space is now brighter and perhaps noisier than in its past incarnation, we are here to say we've eaten several meals since the reopening, and there hasn't been a clunker dish yet. We recently fought over which was more outstanding—farm-raised quail with roasted shallot–applewood bacon–pecan relish; sage-marinated pork chops with butternut squash gnocchi; or lemon-fennel tuna with crispy potato cake. It's just a delight, innovative without being threatening, and a near-perfect melding of flavors.

1041 Dumaine St. ✆ **504/593-9535**. Fax 504/529-6942. peristyle@earthlink.net. Reservations recommended. Main courses $20–$24. AE, DC, MC, V. Fri 11:30am–2pm; Tues–Thurs 6–9pm; Fri–Sat 6–10:30pm.

Rib Room ⍟ SEAFOOD/STEAK   Here is where New Orlean-ians come to eat beef. And who can fault their choice of surround-ings? The solid, cozy Old English ambience is complete with natural-brick ovens in back. But while the meat is good, it is not outstanding, and the acclaimed prime rib is a bit tough and more than lacking in flavor. Here also are filets, sirloins, brochettes, and tournedos. Carnivores, landlubbers, and ichthyophobes will be happier here than at one of the city's Creole restaurants, but it is not the must-do that its reputation would have you believe.

In the Omni Royal Orleans hotel, 621 St. Louis St. (C) **504/529-7045.** www.omniroyalorleans.com. Reservations recommended. Main courses $23.50–$34. AE, DC, DISC, MC, V. Daily 6:30–10:30am, 11:30–2:30pm (serving lunch Mon–Sat, brunch Sun), and 6–10pm.

MODERATE

Cafe Sbisa CREOLE   Right across from the French Market, Cafe Sbisa opened in 1899 and in the 1970s was one of the first restaurants to experiment with Creole cooking, and it's a local favorite. But here's one instance where you may not want to go where the locals go. We found the food decidedly mediocre. Barbecued shrimp came in a sauce something like heavy Worcestershire. A special of wild boar was tough and chewy and its preparation bland. A salad with Bibb lettuce, unusual zebra tomatoes, and a lemon vinaigrette, however, was quite special. You can't fault the atmosphere, which is classy and unpretentious with live piano music sometimes at night. The wait staff is almost smothering in their friendly, effusive care.

1011 Decatur St. (C) **504/522-5565.** Fax 504/523-8095. www.cafesbisa.com. Reservations recommended. Main courses $14.95–$24.95. AE, DC, DISC, MC, V. Sun–Thurs 5:30–10:30pm; Fri–Sat 5:30–11pm; Sun jazz brunch 10:30am–3pm.

Gumbo Shop CREOLE   This is the cheap and convenient way to get solid classic Creole food. The Gumbo Shop is a block off Jackson Square in a 1795 building. It's a bit touristy but not unappealing. Many folks love it here, while others (ourselves included) find it average at best. The menu reads like a textbook list of traditional local food: red beans and rice, shrimp Creole, crawfish étouffée. The seafood gumbo with okra is a meal in itself, and do try the jambalaya.

630 St. Peter St. (C) **504/525-1486.** www.gumboshop.com. Main courses $6.95–$15.95. AE, DC, DISC, MC, V. Daily 11am–11pm.

Irene's ⭐⭐ ITALIAN   Irene's is somewhat off the regular tourist dining path, and locals would probably prefer to keep it that way—it's hard enough getting into one of their favorite neighborhood bistros. In fact, in a constantly changing world, waiting upwards of 90 minutes for a table at Irene's is something you can count on. But those same locals feel it's worth it, and you may as well. Once you're lured in by the potent smell of garlic, you will find a cluttered, dark tavern, not unromantic (provided you don't mind a noise level a decibel or so above hushed), with ultra-friendly waiters who seem delighted you came. Soups can be intriguing fare such as sweet potato andouille sausage. On a recent visit, we were thrilled by soft-shell-crab pasta, an entirely successful Italian/New Orleans hybrid consisting of a whole fried crustacean atop a bed of pasta with a cream sauce of garlic, crawfish, tomatoes, and wads of whole basil leaves.

539 St. Phillip St. ℂ **504/529-8811.** Reservations accepted only for Christmas Eve, New Year's Eve, and Valentine's Day. Main courses $14–$18. AE, MC, V. Sun–Thurs 5:30–10:30pm; Fri–Sat 5:30–11pm. Closed all major holidays.

Maximo's Italian Grill ✿ ITALIAN Maximo's serves solid, if not particularly amazing, Italian food. A huge advantage is that it's open late for dining after an early show. There are usually more than a dozen pastas: some smothered with tomato sauce, some tossed with garlic and oil, and others dotted with clams. The house specialty is penne Rosa, topped with sun-dried tomatoes, garlic, arugula, and shrimp. The chef's signature item is veal T-bone *cattoche* (pan-roasted with garlic and fresh herbs).

1117 Decatur St. ℂ **504/586-8883.** Fax 504/586-8891. Reservations recommended. Main courses $8.95–$28.95. AE, DC, DISC, MC, V. Daily 6–11pm.

Mr. B's Bistro ✿✿ CONTEMPORARY CREOLE Run by Cindy Brennan, this deceptively simple place only helps solidify the Brennan reputation. It draws a steady group of regulars for lunch several days a week, always at their regular tables. The food, mostly modern interpretations of Creole classics, is simple but with spices that elevate the flavors into something your mouth really thanks you for. The crab cakes are about as good as that dish gets. Gumbo Ya Ya is a hearty, country-style rendition with chicken and sausage, perfect for a rainy day. The Cajun barbecued shrimp are huge and plump with a rich, thick, buttery sauce. It's so tasty it makes you greedy for every drop, completely oblivious to the silly bib they make you wear.

201 Royal St. ℂ **504/523-2078.** Fax 504/523-6815. www.mrbsbistro.com. Reservations recommended. Main courses $16–$25. AE, DC, DISC, MC, V. Mon–Sat 11:30am–3pm; Sun brunch 10:30am–3pm; Sun–Fri 5:30–10pm; Sat 5–10pm.

Olde N'Awlins Cookery ✿ CREOLE/CAJUN/SEAFOOD A decent standby if your first choices are full, this family-operated restaurant serves up reliably good traditional Cajun and Creole

favorites. Try the Cajun barbecued shrimp and don't forget to ask
for plenty of extra bread to sop up the rich, buttery, spicy sauce.
Oooh, fattening. Housed in an 1849 building that's been a private
house, a brothel, a bistro bar, and a disco, it makes use of the
original old brick and a charming courtyard to create a very pleasant and—dare we say it?—decidedly New Orleans atmosphere.
An extensive breakfast menu includes specialty egg dishes like
Atchafalaya (poached, with alligator sausage) and *des Allemandes*
(poached, on fried catfish).

729 Conti St. ✆ **504/529-3663.** www.oldenawlinscookery.com. Reservations
accepted only for parties of 5 or more. Breakfast items $7–$12; complete breakfast
$7; main courses $5.75–$14.75 at lunch, $14.50–$24.75 at dinner. AE, MC, V. Daily
8am–11pm. Breakfast served until 4pm.

Port of Call ✿ HAMBURGERS   Sometimes you just need a
burger—particularly when you've been eating many things with
sauce. Locals feel strongly that the half-pound monsters served at
the cozy (and we mean it) Port of Call are the best in town. We are
going to take a stand and say that, while they are certainly terrific,
all that meat may be too much of a good thing. The Port of Call
is just a half step above a dive, but it's a convivial place with a
staff that's attentive if somewhat harried during busy hours. The
hamburgers come with a baked potato (because you might not have
gotten enough food), and there also are pizzas and excellent filet
mignon. It's often jammed with business folks at regular eating
hours, so try it before 7pm, when people leaving work in the
Quarter begin to gather here.

838 Esplanade Ave. ✆ **504/523-0120.** Reservations not accepted. Main courses
$6–$19. AE, MC, V. Sun–Thurs 11am–1am; Fri–Sat 11am–2am.

Ralph & Kacoo's ✿ CREOLE/SEAFOOD   This is a satisfying,
reliable place for seafood, a decent backup place. The Creole dishes
are quite good, portions are more than ample, prices are reasonable,
and the high volume of business means everything is fresh. Start
with fried crawfish tails or the killer onion rings, and if you're adven-
turous, give the blackened alligator with hollandaise a try. Be sure to
try the satin pie for dessert—it's a creamy, mousse-like concoction
of peanut butter and a thin layer of chocolate that will please even
non–peanut butter fans.

519 Toulouse St. ✆ **504/522-5226.** Fax 504/522-5255. www.ralphandkacoos.com.
Reservations recommended. Main courses $6.95–$17.95. AE, DC, DISC, MC, V.
Mon–Thurs 11:30am–10pm; Fri–Sat 11:30am–11pm; Sun 11:30am–9:30pm.

Red Fish Grill ⚔ SEAFOOD   Red Fish is far better than anything else in its price range on Bourbon Street, and—surprise!—it's another Brennan restaurant. Ralph Brennan's place serves many New Orleans specialties with an emphasis on—surprise again—fish. Skip the dull salads in favor of appetizers like shrimp rémoulade napoleon (layered between fried green tomatoes). The fish entrees are light and flaky with flavors that complement one another, rich (it *is* New Orleans) but not overly so. The signature dish is a pan-seared catfish topped with sweet potato crust and an andouille cream drizzle. It's so outstanding, we asked for the recipe so we could try to re-create it at home. (We couldn't really, but it was fun trying.)

115 Bourbon St. ✆ **504/598-1200**. www.redfishgrill.com. Reservations limited. Main courses $8.75–$9.75 at lunch, $8.95–$17.75 at dinner. AE, MC, V. Daily 11am–3pm and 5–11pm.

Rémoulade CREOLE/AMERICAN   An informal cafe offshoot of the venerable Arnaud's, Rémoulade is certainly better than the otherwise most exceedingly tourist-trap restaurants on Bourbon Street, offering average but adequate local food at reasonable prices. You are best off ignoring the undistinguished jambalayas and gumbos in favor of trying some of the Arnaud's specialties featured here—particularly a fine turtle soup and shrimp rémoulade. *Note:* This is one of the few places in town that serves Brocatto's Italian ice cream. A visit for a taste of this fabulous local product (it's impossibly thick and creamy) is a mandatory pit stop on a hot day.

309 Bourbon St. ✆ **504/523-0377**. Reservations recommended. Main courses $4–$20. AE, MC, V. Daily 11:30am–midnight.

Royal Café ⚔ CREOLE   The Royal Café is felicitously located in perhaps the most photographed building in the Quarter—a corner edifice with multiple levels of intricate wrought-iron lacework on the balconies. Being suckers for setting, we wouldn't blame you if you chose to eat here strictly for the chance to sit on that same balcony, ferns overhead. Just don't blame us if the food is only average. Skip the disappointing shrimp rémoulade and merely okay salads and go for the hearty and just-right gumbo or the Louisiana french dip, which is more accurately described as a roast beef po' boy—it drips with gravy and will stick to your ribs.

700 Royal St. ✆ **504/528-9086**. www.royalcafe.com. Reservations recommended for parties of 6 or more. Main courses $6.75–$23.95. AE, MC, V. Mon–Fri 11am–3pm; Sat–Sun 10am–3pm; daily 5:30pm–10pm.

Samurai Sushi JAPANESE   Lord knows we love a cream sauce as much as, and probably more than, the next person, to say nothing of our deep commitment to deep-fried anything, but sometimes something's gotta give (like our waistbands), and that's why, if we can't get our hands on a plain green salad, we end up eating sushi. If you find yourself needing a similar break, you could do worse than to try out this French Quarter sushi spot. The Crunchy Roll (a California roll topped with tempura—see, we always come back to deep-fried) is worth checking out.

239 Decatur St. (✆) **504/525-9595.** Sushi $3.50–$7.50; lunch special $5.85–$9.95; dinner $12–$20. AE, DC, DISC, MC, V. Mon–Thurs 11:30am–10pm; Fri 11:30am–10:30pm; Sat 5–10:30pm; Sun 5–10pm.

Tujague's 🐾🐾 CREOLE   Dating back to 1856, Tujague's (pro-nounced *two*-jacks) is every bit as venerable and aged as the big-name New Orleans restaurants (heck, in the bar they've got a mirror that has been in place for 150 years!), and yet no one ever mentions it. We suspect it's because, unlike some of its peers, Tujague's has surprisingly good food, and locals want to keep it to themselves.

Tujague's does not have a menu; instead, each night they offer a set six-course meal. You will eat what they cook that night, and you will be glad. Don't expect fancy or nouvelle: This is real local food. The feast starts with a sinus-clearing shrimp rémoulade, heads to a fine gumbo (not as thick as some, but that's not a liability), then to a sample of their so-tender-you-cut-it-with-a-fork brisket, and then on to whatever is happening for an entree. Finish with the right-on-the-money bread pudding. Frankly, we can't wait to eat here again.

823 Decatur St. (✆) **504/525-8676.** Fax 504/525-8785. www.tujaguesrestaurant. com. Reservations recommended. Four-course lunch $8.50–$13.95; six-course dinner $28.95–$33.95. AE, DC, DISC, MC, V. Daily 11am–3pm and 5–10:30pm.

201 Restaurant & Bar 🐾 CONTEMPORARY LOUISIANA They do fish very nicely, with a decided Asian influence, at this casual but spiffy place. It made a big splash when it debuted, winning praise as one of the best new restaurants of the year. It's a simple space, a typical New Orleans high-ceilinged room, mercifully largely intact except for the addition of some modern and Depression-era lamps. At a recent meal, I was most pleased by shrimp-and-scallop potstickers with a spicy but sweet red-pepper dipping sauce, and a macadamia-crusted fish with a ginger soy butter.

201 Decatur St. (at Iberville St.). (✆) **504/561-0007.** www.201restaurant.com. Reservations recommended. Main courses $15–$23. AE, DC, DISC, MC, V. Mon–Fri 11am–3pm; Sun–Thurs 5–11pm; Fri–Sat 5pm–midnight.

INEXPENSIVE

Acme Oyster House *⋆⋆* SEAFOOD/SANDWICHES   This joint is always loud, often crowded, and the kind of place where you're likely to run into obnoxious fellow travelers. But if you need an oyster fix or you've never tried oyster shooting (taking a raw oyster, possibly doused in sauce, and letting it slide right down your throat), come here. There's nothing quite like standing at the oyster bar, eating a dozen or so freshly shucked bivalves on the half-shell. (You can have them at a table, but somehow they taste better at the bar.) Or try the oyster po' boy, with beer, of course.

724 Iberville St. ℂ **504/522-5973.** www.acmeoyster.com. Reservations for groups accepted. Oysters $3.99–$6.49; po' boys $5.49–$7.49; New Orleans specialties $5.99–$7.99; seafood $10.99–$13.99. AE, DC, DISC, MC, V. Sun–Thurs 11am–10pm; Fri–Sat 11am–11pm.

Angeli on Decatur *⋆⋆* ITALIAN/MEDITERRANEAN   This highly welcome addition to the Quarter features terrific food, and gets further praise for its nearly round-the-clock hours and local delivery service. Angeli's is a nice (and at night, dimly lit) space that doesn't overdo the angel theme. It's perfect for a light, even healthy meal, a break from some of the extravaganzas offered at more formal restaurants in town. Portions are substantial—splitting a Greek salad produced two full plates of fresh, lovely veggies and a couple of pieces of garlic bread. Add to that a small pizza (the Mystical—roasted garlic, goat cheese, onions, sun-dried tomatoes—is a top choice), and you've got a tasty, affordable meal for two, at any hour and even in your hotel room.

1141 Decatur St. (at Gov. Nicholls St.). ℂ **504/566-0077.** Main courses $6.95–$15. AE, MC, V. Mon–Thurs 10am–4am; Fri–Sat 24 hr.

Café Beignet *⋆* CAFE   This is a full-service, bistro-style cafe. At breakfast you can get Belgian waffles, an omelet soufflé, or bagels and lox. Items on the lunch menu include gumbo, crawfish pie, vegetable sandwiches, and salads. And, of course, beignets.

334B Royal St. ℂ **504/524-5530.** All items under $7. Daily 7am–5pm.

Café Maspero *⋆* SEAFOOD/SANDWICHES   Upon hearing complaints about the increasing presence in the Quarter of "foreign" restaurants such as Subway and the Hard Rock Cafe, one local commented, "Good. That must mean the line will be shorter at Café Maspero." Locals do indeed line up for burgers, deli sandwiches, seafood, grilled marinated chicken, and so on, in some of the largest portions you'll ever run into. And there's an impressive list of wines, beers, and cocktails, all delicious and all at low, low prices.

601 Decatur St. ✆ **504/523-6250.** Reservations not accepted. Main courses $4.25–$9. No credit cards. Sun–Thurs 11am–11pm; Fri–Sat 11am–midnight.

Clover Grill ⍟ COFFEE SHOP   We are cross lately with the Clover Grill. Once a place where the irreverent menu ("We're here to serve people and make them feel prettier than they are") competed with the even more outrageous staff for smart-aleck behavior, it has lost its luster. The menu has fewer jokes, and the once charmingly sassy staff is straying lately toward surly. But the burgers are still juicy and perfect and apparently still cooked under a hubcap (they say it seals in the juices). Breakfast is still served around the clock, and there are still often drag queens sitting at the counter. But too many times lately we've come in at night requesting a shake, only to be told "no shakes." Unacceptable for a 24-hour diner. Go—but tell them they are on probation until they reclaim their joie de vivre.

900 Bourbon St. ✆ **504/598-1010.** www.clovergrill.com. All items under $7. AE, MC, V. Daily 24 hours.

Felix's Restaurant & Oyster Bar ⍟⍟ SEAFOOD/CREOLE Like its neighbor the Acme Oyster House, Felix's is a crowded and noisy place, full of locals and tourists taking advantage of the late hours. It's more or less the same as the Acme. Each has its die-hard fans, convinced their particular choice is the superior one. Have your oysters raw, in a stew, in a soup, Rockefeller or Bienville style, in spaghetti, or even in an omelet. If oysters aren't your bag, the fried or grilled fish, chicken, steaks, spaghetti, omelets, and Creole cooking are mighty good, too.

739 Iberville St. ✆ **504/522-4440.** Fax 504/522-5002. www.felixs.com. Main courses $10–$19.75. AE, MC, V. Mon–Thurs 10am–midnight; Fri 10am–1am; Sat 10am–1:30am; Sun 10am–10pm.

Johnny's Po-Boys ⍟⍟ SANDWICHES   For location (right near a busy part of the Quarter) and menu simplicity (po' boys and more po' boys), you can't ask for much more than Johnny's. They put anything you could possibly imagine (and some things you couldn't) on huge hunks of French bread, including the archetypal fried seafood (add some Tabasco, we strongly advise), deli meats, cheese omelets, ham and eggs, and the starch-o-rama that is a French Fry Po' Boy. You need to try it. *Really.* Johnny boasts that "even my failures are edible," and that says it all. And they deliver!

511 St. Louis St. ✆ **504/524-8129.** Everything under $8. No credit cards. Mon–Fri 8am–4:30pm; Sat–Sun 9am–4pm.

Louisiana Pizza Kitchen PIZZA   This is a local favorite for its
creative pies and atmosphere. Individual-sized pizzas, baked in a
wood-fired oven, come with a wide variety of toppings (shrimp and
roasted garlic are two of the most popular). The best thing about the
pizza is that your toppings won't get lost in an overabundance of
cheese and tomato sauce.

95 French Market Place. ⓒ 504/522-9500. Pizzas $5.95–$8.25; pastas $4.50–
$10.95. AE, DC, DISC, MC, V. Sun–Thurs 11am–10pm; Fri–Sat 11am–11pm. There is
another branch at 615 S. Carrollton Ave. (ⓒ **504/866-5900**).

Mama Rosa's ⓡ ITALIAN/PIZZA   Done in by sauces and han-
kering for something plain? Get a big slice of pizza here. Although
the decor (typical red-and-white-checked tablecloths, a jukebox,
and a bar) is nothing to brag about, the pizzas are. You can get a
10- or 14-inch pie with a variety of toppings for a very reasonable
price. The crusts are thick—almost as thick as a pan pizza—and the
more you put on them, the better they are. The staff can be a bit
surly, but you're not here for the ambience.

616 N. Rampart St. ⓒ **504/523-5546.** Specials $5.50–$9.50; pizzas $9–$15.
AE, DC, DISC, MC, V. Sun–Thurs 11am–9pm; Fri–Sat 11am–10pm.

Napoleon House ⓡ CREOLE/ITALIAN   Folklore has it that
the name of this place derives from a bit of wishful thinking:
Around the time of Napoléon's death, a plot was hatched here
to snatch the Little Corporal from his island exile and bring him to
live in New Orleans. The third floor was added expressly for the
purpose of providing him with a home. Alas, it probably isn't true;
the building dates from a couple of years after Napoléon's death.
But let's not let the truth get in the way of a good story, or a good
hangout, which this is. Agreeably dark, it still seems like a place
where plots are being hatched in the corner. Go hatch some of
your own while nursing a drink or enjoying the only heated muf-
faletta in town.

500 Chartres St. ⓒ **504/524-9752.** Fax 504/525-2431. No reservations. Salads,
sandwiches, and seafood $3.25–$24.95. AE, DISC, MC, V. Mon–Thurs 11am–
midnight; Fri–Sat 11am–1am; Sun 11am–7pm.

Old Dog New Trick Café ⓡ VEGETARIAN   You'd think this
tiny cafe tucked away on equally tiny Exchange Alley would be lost,
but judging from the crowds, both local and tourist vegetarians have
managed to find it. They probably are hugely relieved when they do,
given how hard it is to find something they can eat in this town.
Large portions and small prices make this a pleasing, healthy stop.

The cafe calls itself "vegan friendly," but cheese and tuna do sneak onto the menu. The sandwiches, salads, and stuffed pitas, not to mention polenta and tofu dishes, have been voted Best Vegetarian by *Gambit* readers. Ben the Boston Terrier, who's featured on the sign, was 11 when this place opened; he's now ancient.

517 Frenchmen St. ℂ 504/522-4569. www.olddognewtrick.com. Main courses $6.95–$9.95. AE, MC, V. Daily 11:30am–9pm. They also have a new location at 517 Frenchmen St. in the Faubourg Marigny (ℂ 504/943-6337).

Petunia's ℛ CAJUN/CREOLE   Petunia's, in an 1830s town house, dishes up enormous portions of New Orleans specialties like shrimp Creole and Cajun pasta with shrimp and andouille, as well as a variety of fresh seafood. Breakfast and Sunday brunch are popular, with a broad selection of crepes that, at 14 inches, are billed as the world's largest. Options include the St. Marie, a blend of spinach, cheddar, chicken, and hollandaise; and the St. Francis, filled with shrimp, crab ratatouille, and Swiss cheese.

817 St. Louis St. (between Bourbon and Dauphine sts). ℂ 504/522-6440. Fax 504/528-9042. www.petuniasrestaurant.com. Reservations recommended at dinner. Main courses $5.95–$13.95 at breakfast and lunch, $8.95–$26.95 at dinner. AE, DC, DISC, MC, V. Daily 8am–11pm.

2 The Faubourg Marigny

MODERATE

Feelings Cafe D'Aunoy ℛ AMERICAN/CREOLE   This modest neighborhood joint is a short cab ride away from the French Quarter. Friendly and funky, it serves tasty, solid if not spectacular food. It feels like a true local find and can be a welcome break from the scene in the Quarter or from more intense dining. Try to get a table in the pretty courtyard or on the balcony overlooking it. The piano player is a neighborhood character; be sure to have a drink at the lively bar and chat with him. A recent visit produced a dressed red snapper topped with crab claw meat and crawfish dressing.

2600 Chartres St. ℂ 504/945-2222. Fax 504/945-7019. www.feelingscafe.com. Reservations recommended. Main courses $12.75–$23.75. AE, DC, DISC, MC, V. Sun and Fri 11am–2pm; Mon–Thurs 6–10pm; Fri–Sat 6–11pm.

INEXPENSIVE

Elizabeth's ℛℛ CREOLE   The average tourist may not head over to the Bywater because, well, because it's not the Quarter. That's too bad—not only will they miss a true N'Awlins neighbahood, but they will also miss places like Elizabeth's. Forget paying huge sums for average and goopy breakfast food. Here you eat, as they say, "real food done real good"—and, we add, real cheap. Food like Creole Rice Calas (sweet rice fritters), a classic breakfast dish that is nearly extinct from menus around town. Food calling for health advisories like stuffed French toast (*pain perdu* piled high with cream cheese flavored with strawberries), or their breakfast po' boy, a monster sandwich the size of the Sunday *Picayune* rolled up.

601 Gallier St. ② 504/944-9272. heiditr@bellsouth.net. No credit cards. Tues–Sat 7:30am–2:30pm.

The Harbor ⭐ SOUL FOOD   The Harbor has been a favorite of knowledgeable locals since 1949. This is the place to go for huge portions of authentic soul food, all for ridiculously low prices. (A combination plate will set you back $4.40.) You order at the counter, where all the women call you "Baby," set yourself down at a beat-up table, admire the zero decor, note that you are the only non-local, and dig in. Smothered pork chops, fried chicken, greens, red beans and rice—this is not gourmet, and we mean that as a compliment. Oh, and if you want their famous banana pudding—and you do, you really do—you must order it early in the day, with orders ready at 3pm.

2529 Dauphine St. ② 504/947-1819. All items under $6. No credit cards. Daily 6am–5pm.

Praline Connection *(Overrated* CREOLE/SOUL FOOD   To some NOLA residents, this might be heresy, but we think the Praline Connection is completely overrated. It's probably riding on sentiment and tradition, and so if this helps shake them up, well, then, good. It used to be the place to come for solid, reliable, and even marvelous Creole and soul food. The crowds still come, not noting that what they are getting is often dry and dull. Head to Dunbar's or, better still, the Harbor, where you can get the same type of food for less, with somewhat less crowding, more atmosphere, and cheaper prices.

542 Frenchmen St. ② 504/943-3934. www.pralineconnection.com. Reservations not accepted. Main courses $4–$13.95. AE, DC, DISC, MC, V. Sun–Thurs 11am–10:30pm; Fri–Sat 11am–midnight. **Praline Connection II**, 907 S. Peters St. (② 504/523-3973), offers the same menu and a larger dining room.

3 Mid City/Esplanade

EXPENSIVE

Ruth's Chris Steak House ⭐ STEAK   Even though branches of Ruth's Chris have popped up all over the country in the past few years, you won't get an argument locally if you pronounce this the best steak in town. If you're looking for prime beef—corn fed, custom aged, cut by hand, and beautifully prepared—this is the place. Cuts include filets, strips, rib-eyes, and porterhouses.

711 N. Broad St. ℂ 504/486-0810. www.ruthschris.com. Reservations recommended. Main courses $23.95–$58. AE, DC, DISC, MC, V. Mon–Wed 11:30am–10pm; Thurs 11:30am–10:30pm; Fri 11:30am–11pm; Sat 5–11pm; Sun noon–9:30pm.

MODERATE

Cafe Degas 𝕽𝕽 FRENCH   Just an adorable, friendly, charming French bistro—a delightful neighborhood restaurant, and one that doesn't emphasize fried food (trust us, that's a combo that's hard to find in this town!). Think quiches and real, live salads and simple but fun fish and meat dishes, all featuring big but simple flavors in generous portions. You can go light (a salad, a plate of patés and cheeses) or heavy (filet of beef tenderloin with a green peppercorn brandy sauce)—either way, you'll feel like you ate something worthwhile.

3127 Esplanade Ave. ℂ 504/945-5635. Fax 504/943-5255. www.cafedegas.com. Reservations recommended. Main courses $6.25–$18.50. AE, DC, DISC, MC, V. Mon–Fri 5:30–10pm; Sat 6–10:30pm; Sun 6–10pm; Sat 10:30am–2:30pm; Sun 10:30am–3pm.

Christian's 𝕽𝕽 CREOLE   Christian's is doubly well named. It's owned by Christian Ansel (whose culinary pedigree is strong; he's the grandson of a nephew of Jean Galatoire) and occupies a former church. Renovations preserved the architecture, including the high-beamed ceiling and (secular) stained-glass windows. The old altar is the waiters' station, and the sermon board out front lists the menu. This is one of the city's great French-Creole restaurants, with locals accounting for about 80 percent of its clientele. They come for appetizers like smoked soft-shell crabs, oysters Roland (baked in a garlic-butter sauce with mushrooms, parsley, bread crumbs, and Creole seasoning), and a strong rendition of oysters *en brochette.* The roasted duck is heavenly, as is the gumbo.

3835 Iberville St. ℂ 504/482-4924. Reservations recommended. Main courses $18–$30. AE, DC, MC, V. Tues–Fri 11:30am–2pm and 5:30–9:30 pm; Sat 5:30–9:30pm.

Dooky Chase 𝕽 SOUL FOOD/CREOLE   In the elegant dining rooms of Dooky Chase, classic soul food interacts gloriously with the city's French, Sicilian, and Italian traditions. Chef Leah Chase dishes up one of the city's best bowls of gumbo—no small achievement—along with more esoteric dishes such as shrimp Clemenceau, an unlikely but successful casserole of sautéed shellfish, mushrooms, peas, and potatoes. The fried chicken is exquisite as are the sautéed veal, grits, grillades, and court bouillon—a first cousin of gumbo in which okra is replaced by tomatoes, onions, and garlic, along with generous chunks of catfish. Prices are a bit high and service is less than brisk—though always friendly—but Dooky Chase offers very good food and a vintage New Orleans experience. Take a cab.

2301 Orleans Ave. © **504/821-0600** or 504/821-2294. Reservations recommended at dinner. Main courses $10–$25; fixed-price 4-course meal $25; Creole feast $37.50. AE, DC, DISC, MC, V. Sun–Thurs 11:30am–10pm; Fri–Sat 11:30am–11pm.

Gabrielle *☆☆* INTERNATIONAL   This rather small but casually elegant restaurant just outside the French Quarter is gaining a big reputation around town, thanks to superb food from a chef who studied under Paul Prudhomme and Frank Brigtsen. The foie gras with fig sauce appetizer features a generous portion that melts in your mouth. For a main course, you can't go wrong with any fish on the menu, from the pompano cooked in paper with garlic and tomatoes to the pan-fried trout with shrimp and roasted pecan butter. The Peppermint Patti dessert seems the most popular, a concoction made of chocolate cake, peppermint ice cream, and chocolate sauce.

3201 Esplanade Ave. © **504/948-6233.** Reservations recommended. Main courses $16–$28; early-evening special (Tues–Thurs 5:30–6:15pm) $15.95. AE, DC, DISC, MC, V. Oct–May Fri 11:30am–2pm; year-round Tues–Sat 5:30–10pm.

Indigo *☆* AMERICAN   Apparently it wasn't enough for Cynthia Reeves to own and operate arguably the best guesthouse in the city; she had to turn her sights to something else ambitious, and this lovely new restaurant is the result. Named for the product of the former plantation on which it in part rests (as does her B&B, the House on Bayou Road), Indigo is a romantic space already chockfull of savvy locals looking for a new dining experience. It's a tad expensive, but the food is generating nearly universal raves, thanks to clever and talented chef Randy Lewis. We swoon over the creamy crawfish vichyssoise (accompanied by a sweet little crawfish grilled-cheese sandwich). Fish—like the Romesco powder-dusted sea bass—is beyond just right. We were a bit sad that the molten chocolate cake dessert was not at all molten in the center, but the caramel ice cream on the side consoled us.

2285 Bayou Rd. ℂ **504/947-0123.** Reservations recommended. Main courses $24.50–$30. AE, DISC, MC, V. Tues–Sat 6–10pm.

Liuzza's 𝒜𝒜 CREOLE/ITALIAN   Actual moment from a recent Liuzza's visit: The crusty waitress hands a menu to a customer ("Here you go, Bay-bee") and then abruptly closes it. "Bay-bee," she instructs, gesticulating with a finger, "Numba One, or Numba Two—but *definitely* Numba One." Naturally, the Number One special was ordered (it proved to be a seafood lasagna, dripping with a white cream sauce) and devoured (despite its enormous size).

Yep, this is a neighborhood institution (since 1947; it's small and often crowded with regulars) and when the waitress talks, you betcha you listen. Presumably, she will also tell you to get the heavenly fried onion rings or the deep-fried dill pickle slices ("you people will batter and deep-fry anything that isn't nailed down!" remarked yet another astonished visitor). Try the Galboroni Pasta (spaghettini with spicy marinara sauce, pepperoni strips, and stuffed artichoke hearts). Great inexpensive food in an establishment dripping with New Orleans atmosphere—don't miss it, Bay-bee.

3636 Bienville St. ℂ **504/482-9120.** www.liuzzas.com. Main courses $4.95–$10.95. No credit cards (but there's an ATM on the premises). Mon–Sat 10:30am–10:30pm.

Lola's 𝒜𝒜𝒜 SPANISH/INTERNATIONAL   "Please, oh please, don't mention Lola's in the book!" beg our local foodie friends. Why? Because this small, special place doesn't take reservations, and the nightly wait is already long as it is. But we are going to spill the beans anyway while assuring you that this is worth waiting for, thanks to incredible Spanish dishes, from paellas to starters such as garlic shrimp tapas. Get there 15 to 30 minutes before opening time and wait in line. If there's a mob, don't be discouraged: Service is attentive and food comes quickly, so your wait shouldn't be long. Bring cash—and try not to get ahead of our friends in line!

3312 Esplanade Ave. ℂ **504/488-6946.** Reservations not accepted. Main courses $8.75–$14. No credit cards or out-of-town checks. Sun–Thurs 6–10pm; Fri–Sat 6–10:30pm.

Mandina's 𝒜𝒜 CREOLE/ITALIAN   In a city renowned for its small, funky, local joints as well as its fine-dining establishments, dis is da ultimate neighbahood New Awlins restaurant. Tommy Mandina's family has owned and operated this restaurant and bar since the late 1800s, and the menu hasn't changed much in the last 50 years or so. This is a good thing. Don't be afraid of your waiter— surly or gruff as he may be, his advice is always good.

Standouts among the appetizers are the greasy but yummy fried onion rings, the excellent tangy shrimp rémoulade, and the crawfish cakes. Soups are fine as well, especially seafood gumbo and turtle soup au sherry. Then go for the wonderful red beans and rice with Italian sausage, trout meunière, or our favorite comfort food, the sweet Italian sausage and spaghetti combo—exactly the way we remember it from childhood. Finish up with rum-soaked Creole bread pudding, and you'll feel like a native from da old neighbahood.

3800 Canal St. ℰ **504/482-9179.** Reservations not accepted. Main courses $7.50–$16.95. No credit cards. Mon–Sat 11am–10:30pm; Sun noon–9:30pm.

INEXPENSIVE

Mona's Café & Deli ✸✸ MIDDLE EASTERN   Unless you are already headed to Mid City, Mona's is out of your way; however, if you like Middle Eastern food and can't get real falafel, hummus, stuffed grape leaves, and baklava in your hometown, it's worth the trip. This restaurant and its attached grocery are in a building that must have once been a gas station, and the dining areas are very casual. Service is equally casual. Balancing the lack of elegance is great food at some of the lowest prices imaginable.

3901 Banks St. ℰ **504/482-7743** or 504/482-0661. Fax 504/482-0311. Sandwiches $2.75–$3.75; main courses $6–$11. AE, DISC, MC, V. Mon–Thurs 11am–9pm; Fri–Sat 11am–10pm; Sun noon–6pm. They also have locations Uptown (3151 Calhoun St.) and in the Faubourg Marigny (504 Frenchmen St.).

4 Central Business District

EXPENSIVE

Emeril's ✸✸ CREOLE/NEW AMERICAN   We are giving Emeril's first and still best restaurant two stars mostly on the firm belief that matters are still being properly overseen here, but given how thin the Chef is spreading himself these days (all those restaurants, plus the Food Network show—and now, an NBC sitcom!), we increasingly wish he would get himself off TV and back into the kitchen. And we are still cranky about how attitudinal the staff and service can be. Having said that, when this restaurant is on its game, doggonit, there isn't much better eating to be had.

Emeril's specialty is what he calls *New* New Orleans Cuisine, based on and using key ingredients of Creole classics but taking them in new and exciting directions. Everything in his bustling, noisy, warehouse-district restaurant is homemade, from the bacon to the Worcestershire sauce to the andouille sausage and home-cured tasso. Portions are gargantuan, each plate dances with color and texture, and side dishes are perfectly paired with entrees (such as grilled Creole-seasoned chicken with savory corn-and-andouille bread pudding). Among the daily specials are crawfish-and-morel-mushroom-stuffed artichoke bottoms with foie gras and roasted onion ragout and a drizzle of celery purée. The signature dessert, astonishingly rich banana cream pie with banana crust and caramel drizzle sauce, will leave you moaning and pounding on the table.

800 Tchoupitoulas St. (C) **504/528-9393.** www.emerils.com. Reservations required at dinner. Main courses $20–$35; menu degustation (tasting menu) $75. AE, DC, DISC, MC, V. Mon–Fri 11:30am–2pm; Mon–Thurs 6–10pm; Fri–Sat 6–11pm.

Emeril's Delmonico Restaurant and Bar ⋒ CREOLE Delmonico's was intended as less a chance for Emeril to show off the innovative cooking that has made him a star and more a chance to experiment with classic Creole dishes. Local opinions remain underwhelmed, however; though it does a brisk business (and boasts one of the loveliest interiors in New Orleans). This may be because it's so sauce-intensive and, also, costly. But it's fun to see what Emeril is up to in this context. Certainly, any complaints of ours are muffled by mouthfuls of the cream truffle angel hair pasta topped with crispy crab cakes. You can easily blow your budget on the tasting menu, and perhaps you should, when it features such delights as smoked salmon and wild-mushroom truffle stew with over-easy eggs, shaved black truffle, black truffle emulsion, crispy parsley, and a drizzle of white truffle oil. If Neal Shindler is still the chef de cuisine, you should eat very well—we think he's one to watch.

1300 St. Charles Ave. (C) **504/525-4937.** Fax 504/525-0506. www.emerils.com. Reservations required. Main courses $18–$32. AE, DC, DISC, MC, V. Mon–Fri 11:30am–2pm; Sun 10:30am–2pm; Sun–Thurs 6–10pm; Fri–Sat 6–11pm.

56° ⋒ ASIAN FUSION It's the prime temperature at which wine should be stored. Well, we figured you might ask. Anyway, this is a new restaurant by Chef Minh, the figure behind Lemon Grass. While there the menu is more heavily Vietnamese influenced, here (a lovely former bank space, in the Whitney Hotel) matters go a little more continental. We liked the tempura shrimp with sweet corn cake and the fried coconut shrimp with the Oriental slaw appetizer, but we loved the mussel noodle and broth dish, as well as the firm and earthy wild mushroom pasta. Truth be told, it is expensive, absolutely, and not as immediately memorable as Lemon Grass, but Minh's cooking is special no matter where it happens.

In the Whitney Hotel, 610 Poydras St. (C) **504/212-5656.** Reservations suggested. Lunch $11.50–$17.50; dinner $22.50–$32.75. AE, DC, MC, V. Mon–Fri 6–10am and 11am–2pm; Sun–Thurs 6–10pm; Fri–Sat 6pm–11pm.

The Grill Room ★★ NEW AMERICAN   This is a special-event place where the silverware is heavy, the linens thick, and all diners dressed to the nines. The Grill Room irokcs an elegant and stately place whose chefs constantly win culinary awards and whose cuisine, service, and wine list are all flawless. A recent debauch started with creamy terrine of foie gras on crunchy apricot-pecan brioche. For entrees, there was an impossibly rich roast goose with celeriac purée and foie gras croutons, and a lighter but no less divine Dover sole accompanied by *crosne,* rare vegetables from the south of France. Narrowing down a dessert selection is nearly impossible. One example: A ball of dense hazelnut mousse sits in a chocolate-covered filo cookie, rather like a giant piece of Godiva candy.

In the Windsor Court Hotel, 300 Gravier St. ✆ **504/522-1992.** Fax 504/596-4513. www.windsorcourthotel.com. Reservations recommended. Jacket and tie required. Main courses $16–$25 at lunch, $28–$39 at dinner. AE, DC, DISC, MC, V. Mon–Thurs 7–10:30am; Fri–Sat 7:30–10:30am; Sun 7–9am; Mon–Sat 11:30am–2pm; Sun brunch 9am–2pm; Sun–Thurs 6–10pm; Fri–Sat 6–10:30pm.

The Red Room ★ NEW AMERICAN   Sometimes—OK, often—we long for the days when civilized couples would go out for dinner and dancing. The Red Room supper club perfectly fills this need with delectable (albeit slightly pricey) meals that you can then work off on the dance floor, courtesy of the hip jazz/swing musical lineups. Don't be put off by the ugly but historically significant industrial exterior (it was apparently lifted from the Eiffel Tower, and no wonder they wanted to get rid of it). It gives way to an interior far more evocative of 1940s swank.

The nouvelle cuisine is excellent. We ate every bite of foie gras with sweet potato *galette* and a cranberry reduction, as well as a carpaccio salad with roasted garlic oil, and consequently couldn't finish the enormous crispy speckled trout with meunière sauce (easily enough for two people). Should you suffer a similar problem, try to rally for the sinful desserts; you can dance away the calories later.

2040 St. Charles Ave. ✆ **504/528-9759.** Reservations recommended. No jeans, T-shirts, tennis shoes, or shorts. Jackets for men suggested. Main courses $18–$32. AE, DC, DISC, MC, V. Wed–Sun 7–11pm.

Sazerac Bar and Grill ★ CONTINENTAL/CREOLE   A top-to-bottom renovation has so completely redesigned the venerable Sazerac that it is unrecognizable to bewildered locals. Once they get over the confusion, they are pleased to note that a once rather claustrophobic experience has been turned into a more airy one, with the room now open to the Fairmont's famous lobby. It's a good dining choice in the area; a recent meal found diners eating every bit of turtle soup, blackened red snapper with pecan-butter sauce, and sugar cane–glazed duck with a sweet potato andouille timbale.

In the Fairmont Hotel, 123 Baronne St. ℂ **504/529-4733.** Reservations recommended. Jackets recommended at dinner. Main courses $19.95–$29.95. AE, DC, DISC, MC, V. Mon–Sat 6am–2pm; Sun brunch 7am–2pm; daily 5:30–9pm.

MODERATE

Bon Ton Café ℛ CAJUN   At lunchtime, you'll find the Bon Ton Café absolutely mobbed with New Orleans businesspeople and their guests, but that's the best time to go. Its popularity is largely due to owner Al Pierce, his nephew Wayne, and Wayne's wife, Debbie. Al and Wayne grew up in bayou country, where Al learned Cajun cooking from his mother. He came to New Orleans in 1936, bought the Bon Ton in 1953, and since then has been serving up seafood gumbo, crawfish bisque, jambalaya, crawfish omelets, and other Cajun dishes in a manner that would make his mother proud.

401 Magazine St. ℂ **504/524-3386.** Reservations suggested. Main courses $12.50–$21.50 at lunch, $19.75–$28 at dinner. AE, DC, MC, V. Mon–Fri 11am–2pm and 5–9:30pm.

Cuvee ℛℛ CONTEMPORARY CREOLE   This new restaurant has been earning almost unanimous raves, and we strongly suggest you discover why for yourself. Should you indeed end up in this cozy, brick-lined room (suggesting a wine cellar, natch), try to order—assuming the seasonally changing menu allows—the lovely spicy merliton napoleon (with shrimp rémoulade) appetizer, though the pan-seared scallop with citrus *beurre blanc* isn't a bad second choice. We loved the pan-seared duck breast with duck comfit and foie gras, combined with a Roquefort risotto. The crunchy chocolate macadamia-nut torte is like the ultimate candy bar. An exquisite wine list helps you impress dates by providing phonetic pronunciations for all the wines.

322 Magazine St. ℂ **504/587-9001.** Reservations suggested. $7–$15 lunch; $18–$24 dinner. AE, DC, DISC, MC, V. Mon–Thurs 7–10am, 11:30am–2:30pm, and 6–10pm; Fri–Sat 6–11pm.

Herbsaint ℛℛ BISTRO   We've rhapsodized long and hard about Bayona, so it was nice of chef Susan Spicer to open a new restaurant so we can go on and on about *it.* French-American, as opposed to Bayona's more Mediterranean slant, Herbsaint (that would be the locally made pastis found in, among other places, the popular local cocktail, the Sazerac) hit the ground running in terms of immediate quality and the delight had thereof. Herbsaint immediately endears with its almost ridiculously low (for this level of restaurant) prices—even the entrees are comfortably under $20. Be sure to try the Herbsaint, tomato, and shrimp bisque—it sent us into rhapsodies, and we aren't even soup fans. For once, vegetarians will not feel left out; the herbed gnocchi with eggplant tomato sauce is a marvelous dish. OK, we aren't going to go on and on, only because that takes time away from when we all could be eating there.

701 St. Charles Ave. ℭ **504/524-4114.** Reservations suggested for lunch, and for 5 or more for dinner. Lunch $10–$14. Dinner $12–$18. AE, DC, DISC, MC, V. Mon–Fri 11:30am–3pm; Mon–Sat 5:30–10:30pm.

Lemon Grass 𝒢𝒢 VIETNAMESE   Chef Minh went directly from waiting tables at Emeril's to opening his own place—a bold move in such a competitive restaurant town. But in just a few short years, his modern Vietnamese cuisine has become a favorite among local foodies, and his success in his original Carrollton location (now sadly closed) has been capped with a new branch at the oh-so-hip International House hotel. This space—call it Asian cafe—is much more formal and deliberately designed than the original, the difference between hip and a neighborhood joint. Don't feel you are missing out on local cuisine by coming here. Crawfish can pop up in dishes, and Minh's take on shrimp mirliton is well worth trying. Try the flash-fried oysters crusted with nuts and served with wasabi leek confit. Among the entrees, we adore the spicy chicken roti.

In the International House, 217 Camp St. ℭ **504/523-1200.** Reservations recommended. Main courses $12.95–$18.95. AE, MC, V. Daily 7:30–9am and 11:30am–2:30pm; Sun–Thurs 6–10pm; Fri–Sat 6–11pm.

Liborio's Cuban Restaurant 𝒢 CUBAN   Nicely located in the CBD, this Cuban cafe attracts local business folk at lunchtime, when prices are very affordable (they do seem to be needlessly high at dinnertime). Plus, it's a fun space—the chartreuse sponged walls and pillowy parachute-fabric upholstering the ceiling make for a festive look. Lazy ceiling fans put you in mind of Hemingway's Havana. Order the day's special or be like us, partial to Cuban specialties like tender, garlicky roast pork, the flatbread Cuban sandwich, and sweet fried plantains.

321 Magazine St. ℭ **504/581-9680.** Reservations suggested. Lunch $6.50–$14; dinner $10.95–$20. AE, DC, DISC, MC, V. Mon–Fri 11am–2:45pm; Tues–Sat 5:45–9pm.

Palace Café 𝒢𝒢 CONTEMPORARY CREOLE   This is where to go for low-key, non-intimidating romantic dining. Housed—and most attractively—in the historic Werlein's for Music building, this popular Brennan family restaurant went through a bit of a slump but happily has resurged. Be sure to order the crabmeat cheesecake appetizer. They do fish especially well; dishes from a recent menu included andouille-crusted fish with a cayenne *beurre blanc* and chive aiolis, and Gulf shrimp Tchefuncte—that's toasted garlic and green onions in a Creole meunière sauce. For dessert, they invented the by-now ubiquitous white chocolate bread pudding, and no matter what others claim, they have the best.

605 Canal St. ✆ **504/523-1661.** Fax 504/523-1633. www.palacecafe.com. Reservations recommended. Main courses $10.95–$24.95. AE, DC, DISC, MC, V. Mon–Fri 11:30am–2:30pm; Sun brunch 10:30am–2:30pm; daily 5:30–10pm.

The Red Bike ⚘ NEW AMERICAN/ECLECTIC   Under new management, the Red Bike is a fine choice if you're looking for a healthy alternative to the endless array of sauces found elsewhere in the city. It's a handy place for a pit stop during gallery hopping in the Warehouse District. Inside the attractive cafe setting, you will find all sorts of yummy sandwiches on the house bread (for sale, along with other bakery delights, at the counter) including a recommended curried turkey salad. Most menu selections use interesting cheeses, herbs, and veggies. The prices here are so reasonable, the place teeters just on the edge of the "inexpensive" category.

746 Tchoupitoulas St. ✆ **504/529-BIKE.** Fax 504/529-2460. Main courses $7–$11 at lunch, $12–$23 at dinner. AE, DC, MC, V. Mon–Fri 11am–2:30pm; Sun 10am–2:30pm; Tues–Thurs 6–9:30pm; Fri–Sat 6–10pm.

The Veranda Restaurant ⚘ CONTINENTAL/CREOLE   This is one of the more unusual dining spaces in town, thanks to a glass-enclosed courtyard (one heck of a show during a thunderstorm). The chef, Willy Coln, is one of the most respected in New Orleans. Buffet buffs will think themselves in heaven with a lunch option of the same; you will find no gloppy macaroni and cheese here but rather all sorts of culinary wonders. Regular dining is less impressive but still tasty; consider Louisiana crab cakes in a light Creole mustard sauce for a starter, or braised duck or black linguine in a seafood saffron sauce. Leave room for one (or two) of several marvelous chocolate cakes.

In the Hotel Inter-Continental, 444 St. Charles Ave. ✆ **504/585-4383.** Reservations recommended. Main courses $16–$26. AE, DC, DISC, MC, V. Mon–Sun 6:30am–2pm and 5:30–10pm; Sun brunch 11am–2:30pm.

INEXPENSIVE

Ernst's Café CAJUN/CREOLE   The same family has run the restaurant and bar in this old brick building since 1902. Located right next to Harrah's casino and with live blues music Friday and Saturday night, it's a big local scene and serves sandwiches, hamburgers, fried shrimp, salads, red beans and rice, and po' boys.

600 S. Peters St. ℂ **504/525-8544.** Fax 504/527-0049. ernstcafe1902@aol.com. Main courses $6.50–$9.95. AE, DC, MC, V. Mon–Sat 11am–2am.

Mother's 🦞🦞 SANDWICHES/CREOLE   Perhaps the proudest of all restaurants when New Orleans was named Fattest City in the U.S. was Mother's, whose overstuffed, mountain-size po' boys absolutely helped contribute to the results. It has long lines and zero atmosphere, but who cares when faced with a Famous Ferdi Special—a giant roll filled with baked ham, roast beef, gravy, and debris (the bits of beef that fall off when the roast is carved)? Be sure to allow time to stand in line. It usually moves quickly, and there's always a seat when you get your food.

401 Poydras St. ℂ **504/523-9656.** Fax 504/525-7671. www.mothersrestaurant. com. Reservations not accepted. Menu items $1.75–$16.50. AE, M/C, V. Mon–Sat 5am–10pm; Sun 7am–10pm.

Taqueria Corona 🦞🦞 MEXICAN   It's hard to get good Mexican food outside of, well, Mexico and Southern California, and so when fans find a place like Taqueria Corona, they almost weep with gratitude. You'll find football-size burritos tasting just the right way (and that means not the generic fast-food way, thanks), grilled tacos, even gazpacho—and all of it for minimal prices. Be sure to order a side of *cebollitas,* grilled and seasoned green onions.

857 Fulton St. ℂ **504/524-9805.** Reservations not accepted. Most items under $10. AE, DISC, MC, V. Mon–Sat 11:30am–2pm; Sun–Thurs 5–9:30pm; Fri–Sat 5–10pm. There's also an Uptown location: 5900 Magazine St. (near Nashville; ℂ **504/897-3974**).

Uglesich's Restaurant & Bar 🦞🦞 SANDWICHES/SEAFOOD It's dangerous to call any one place "the best in New Orleans," but it's mighty tempting to make an exception for "Ugly's," a tiny, crowded, greasy neighborhood place that serves some of the most divine seafood in town. At lunchtime, especially during tourist seasons, you might have a very long wait before you order at the counter, another wait for a table, and a third wait for your food. But we swear it's worth it. Obviously, others who should know think so; you might well end up sitting next to some of the best chefs in town because this is where *they* go for lunch.

Among the musts are fried green tomatoes with shrimp rémoulade, shrimp in creamy sauce on a fried cake of grits, and voodoo shrimp (in a peppery butter sauce). Order extra bread to sop up sauce, but be sure to ask for it unbuttered. You'll be full, you might smell of grease, and you might well come back for more the next day.

1238 Baronne St. ✆ 504/523-8571 or 504-525-4925. Reservations not accepted. Menu items $9–$13. No credit cards. Mon–Fri 9am–4pm; open every other Sat. Closed July–Aug.

5 Uptown/The Garden District

EXPENSIVE

Brigtsen's ★★ CAJUN/CREOLE   In a setting both elegant and homey, chef Frank Brigsten serves some of the city's best contemporary Creole cuisine. Nestled in a converted 19th-century house at the Riverbend, Brigtsen's is warm, intimate, and romantic. The individual dining rooms are small and cozy. Brigsten has a special touch with rabbit; one of his most mouthwatering dishes is an appetizer of rabbit tenderloin on a tasso Parmesan grits cake with sautéed spinach and a Creole mustard sauce. The rabbit and andouille gumbo is intensely flavored. You can't miss with any of the soups, especially the lovely butternut squash shrimp bisque. One of the most popular dishes is roast duck with cornbread dressing and pecan gravy. Save room for dessert, perhaps the signature banana bread pudding with banana rum sauce. Brigtsen's offers one of the loveliest evenings you'll spend in a Crescent City restaurant. And the "Early Evening" dinner special is as good a bargain as you'll find.

723 Dante St. ✆ 504/861-7610. Reservations required (1–2 weeks in advance). Main courses $18–$26; 3-course "Early Evening" dinner (Tues–Thurs 5:30–6:30pm) $16.95. AE, DC, MC, V. Tues–Sat 5:30–10pm.

Clancy's ★★ CREOLE   Your friendly cab driver may insist that Clancy's is "out of town," so far uptown is this locals' favorite, but it's really not that much farther than going to the zoo. The food and neighborhood vibe alone are worth the trip. However, since this is not a tourist-oriented restaurant, the better service goes to the locals who nightly cram the smallish, oh-so–New Orleans room.

Said locals will make it up to you by passing along this bit of Clancy's wisdom: Order the night's specials rather than sticking to the menu (though on the menu resides a duck dish as good as duck gets). We did, and it resulted in a perfect grouper in a tomato *beurre blanc* sauce, topped with crawfish, and a memorable starter salad that included lump crabmeat and crawfish in homemade mayo and horseradish, with a deviled egg made with tasso on the side. Food too heavy? What the heck—make it even more so with a slice of mocha ice cream pie or lemon icebox pie. It's what the locals would do.

6100 Annunciation St. ☎ **504/895-1111**. Reservations recommended. Main courses $16.75–$26.75. AE, DC, MC, V. Tues–Thurs 11:30am–2pm; Mon–Thurs 5:30–10:30pm; Fri–Sat 5:30–11pm.

Commander's Palace ☆☆☆ CREOLE   Recently awarded the Lifetime Outstanding Restaurant Award by the James Beard Foundation, Commander's is one place that lives up to its reputation. It's not just the food—which is never less than good—it's the whole package. In a beautiful 1880s Victorian house, it consists of a nearly endless series of dining rooms from large to intimate, each more appealing and romantic than the last. On balmy nights, you can eat in the lovely courtyard. (Although the back garden room was recently remodeled, the original building remains our favorite place to dine.) The wait staff is incredibly attentive; several people pamper you throughout your meal. Each night features a multicourse fixed-price menu for around $35. It also allows you to mix and match off the regular menu—a good bargain and a great splurge.

The famous turtle soup with sherry is outstanding, so thick it's nearly a stew. Other marvelous appetizer choices include the shrimp and tasso with five-pepper jelly; carpaccio salad with roasted eggplant garlic; and the hearty crawfish bisque with homemade biscuits. Main-course selections change seasonally, but you are best off sticking with Creole-type offerings—such as the dreamy boned Mississippi roasted quail stuffed with Creole crawfish sausage.

Your serving team will tell you to try the famous bread pudding soufflé. Trust them. But chocolate lovers should not overlook the chocolate Sheba, a sort of solid chocolate mousse, ever so slightly chilled and covered in nuts. And everyone should consider the Creole cream cheesecake, which will make you rethink your position on cheesecakes. Then there is the gorgeous rendition of pecan pie a la mode and the not-on-the-menu-so-ask-for-it chocolate molten soufflé.

This is one must-do New Orleans restaurant, particularly appropriate for special occasions—but you can simply call your trip to New Orleans a special occasion, and we won't tell.

1403 Washington Ave. ☎ **504/899-8221**. www.commanderspalace.com. Reservations required. Jackets required at night and Sun brunch; no shorts, T-shirts, tennis shoes, or blue jeans. Main courses $29–$32; full brunch $20–$32; fixed-price $29–$36. AE, DC, DISC, MC, V. Mon–Fri 11:30am–1:30pm; Sat 11:30am–12:30pm; Sun brunch 10:30am–1:30pm; daily 6–9:30pm.

Martinique Bistro ☺☺ FRENCH   This place is just far enough Uptown to be off the regular tourist radar. Since it has only 44 seats when the courtyard is not open (100 with), you might have trouble getting a table. Nonetheless, this sweet little bistro, a private local favorite, is well worth the cab ride and potential wait. The yellow-squash soup is out of this world, and main courses such as the shrimp with sun-dried mango and curry, and seared boneless breast of duck are quite dazzling as well. Do try the sorbet sampler (flavors such as mango, bitter lemon, and even imported French currents). If the weather permits, be sure to sit in the jasmine-scented courtyard.

5908 Magazine St. ℂ **504/891-8495.** Reservations accepted only for parties of 5 or more. Main courses $15–$24. MC, V. Nov–May Sun–Thurs 5:30–9:30pm; Fri–Sat 5:30–10:30pm. June–Oct Sun–Thurs 6–10pm; Fri–Sat 6–11pm.

Upperline ☺☺☺ ECLECTIC/CREOLE   In a small, charming house in a largely residential area, the Upperline is more low-key than high-profile places such as Emeril's. In its own way, though, it's every bit as inventive. It's a great place to try imaginative food at reasonable (by fancy restaurant standards) prices. Owner JoAnn Clevenger and her staff are quite friendly, and their attitude is reflected in the part of the menu where they actually—gasp!—recommend dishes at *other* restaurants. Perhaps you can afford to be so generous when your own offerings are so strong. Standout appetizers include fried green tomatoes with shrimp rémoulade sauce (they invented this dish, now featured just about everywhere in town) and spicy shrimp on jalapeño cornbread. For entrees, there's moist, herb-crusted pork loin, roast duck with a sauce that tingles, and a fall-off-the-bone lamb shank. If you're lucky, there will be a special menu like the all-garlic meal, in which even dessert contains garlic.

1413 Upperline St. ℂ **504/891-9822.** www.upperline.com. Reservations required. Main courses $16.50–$24. AE, DC, MC, V. Sun brunch 11:30am–2pm; Wed–Sun 5:30–9:30pm.

MODERATE

Dick & Jenny's ☺☺ ECLECTIC/CREOLE   Dick was the chef at the Upperline for many years, and so his own place has been furiously busy since it opened, full of curious local foodies. (Actually, with only 12 or so tables, it's not hard for the room to fill up, so get there early or be prepared to wait most nights.) The menu (like so many others in town, truth be told) reads a bit fussy, a potential overdose of flavors, but in nearly all dishes, the combos work. The *pain perdu* appetizer—brie, duck comfit, and peach preserves—is like a grilled cheese sandwich from heaven, while the pepper-seared yellowfin tuna with a whole, dismantled artichoke dipped in red pepper aioli was delightful. As for dessert, we can't stop talking about the ice cream chocolate chip cookie sandwich sundae, but that mango-ginger crème brûlée hit a good spot as well.

4501 Tchoupitoulas St. (C) **504/894-9880.** Reservations not accepted. Main courses $12–$19. AE, MC, V. Tues–Sat 5:30–10:30pm.

Gautreau's (R) INTERNATIONAL   Those who knew the old Gautreau's (which closed in 1989 and reopened under new ownership) will be relieved to see that the restaurant has retained its warm and modest decor: The tin ceiling, the old New Orleans photographs, and the famous apothecary cabinet from the original drugstore have all been retained. The quality of the food has not changed either. Menus change seasonally; if you spot them on the menu, try the marinated shrimp and Dungeness crab served with sticky rice and orange-and-honey soy sauce, or warm crisped duck confit with sherried flageolets, mustard, and sage. The pastry chef does a fine honey-orange crème brûlée and a delightful triple-layer (chocolate, maple pecan, and almond) cheesecake.

1728 Soniat St. (C) **504/899-7397.** Fax 504/899-0154. Reservations recommended. Main courses $17–$32. DC, DISC, MC, V. Mon–Sat 6–10pm.

Kelsey's (R) CREOLE   For 8 years, chef Randy Barlow worked at K-Paul's with Paul Prudhomme, and the influence is apparent. The house specialty is eggplant Kelsey, a batter-fried eggplant pirogue (in the shape of a boat) stuffed with seafood seasoned with Parmesan and Romano cheeses, tomatoes, garlic, olive oil, parsley, and lemon juice. Fried green tomatoes sit atop spinach Florentine, while the Eggplant Delight (topped with barbecue shrimp) is another appetizer standout. If you order salad, ask them to go light on the dressing.

3923 Magazine St. (C) **504/897-6722.** Fax 504/897-6763. www.kelseysrestaurant. com. Reservations recommended. Main courses $8.95–$12.95 at lunch, $12.95–$24.95 at dinner. AE, DC, DISC, MC, V. Tues–Fri 11:30am–2pm; Tues–Thurs 5:30–9:30pm; Fri–Sat 5:30–10pm; Sun 5:30–9:30pm.

La Crêpe Nanou (R) FRENCH   Voted the top French bistro in New Orleans in the Zagat survey, La Crêpe Nanou is another not-so-secret local secret. It's always crowded. It's a romantic spot (windows angled into the ceiling let you gaze at the stars) that is simultaneously 19th century and quite modern. You can order crepes wrapped around a variety of stuffings, including crawfish. But you might want to save your crepe consumption for dessert (big and messy, full of chocolate and whipped cream) and concentrate instead on the big, healthy salads and moist, flaky fish.

1410 Robert St. ℂ **504/899-2670.** Fax 504/897-0697. Reservations not accepted. Main courses $8.95–$16.95. AE, DC, MC, V. Sun–Thurs 6–10pm; Fri–Sat 6–11pm.

Pascal's Manale ⍟ ITALIAN/STEAK/SEAFOOD   Barbecued shrimp. This restaurant has made its reputation with that one dish, and you should come here if only for that. The place is crowded and noisy and verges on expensive, but it grows on you. Don't expect fancy decor; the emphasis is on food and conviviality. Here you are going to get hearty, traditional N'Awlins fare, in a hearty, traditional N'Awlins setting. And there's nothing wrong with that, as long as you don't expect anything more. The barbecue shrimp sauce may no longer be the city's best (we are partial these days to the buttery wonder served at Mr. B's), but the shrimp within it—plump, sweet, kitten-size—are. Be sure to add sherry to the turtle soup, and be extra sure to skip the dull desserts. Try not to think about your arteries too much; lick your fingers, enjoy, and vow to walk your socks off tomorrow.

1838 Napoleon Ave. ℂ **504/895-4877.** Reservations recommended. Main courses $10.95–$23.95. AE, DC, DISC, MC, V. Mon–Fri 11:30am–10pm; Sat 4–10pm; Sun 4–9pm.

INEXPENSIVE

Bluebird Cafe ⍟⍟ AMERICAN   Employees here tell the story of a man who awoke from an extended coma with these two words: "huevos rancheros." As soon as possible, he returned to the Bluebird for his favorite dish. A similar scene repeats each weekend morning when locals wake up with Bluebird on the brain. Why? Because this place consistently offers breakfast and lunch food that can restore and sustain your vital functions. Try the buckwheat pecan waffle, cheese grits, or homemade sausage and corned beef hash, or see why the *huevos rancheros* enjoys its reputation. At midmorning on weekends, there is always a wait (up to 30 min.); it's worth it.

3625 Prytania St. ℂ **504/895-7166.** Reservations not accepted. All items under $7.95. No credit cards. Mon–Fri 7am–3pm; Sat–Sun 8am–3pm.

Camellia Grill ⍟⍟ HAMBURGERS/SANDWICHES   Even though it's *only* been a part of the city's food culture since 1946, the Camellia Grill seems to have always been there. Right off the St.

Charles Avenue streetcar, it's a fixture in many people's lives. As you sit on a stool at the counter, white-jacketed waiters pamper you while shouting cryptic orders to the chefs. There's often a wait because the Camellia serves some of the best breakfasts and burgers anywhere. It's famous for its omelets—heavy and fluffy at the same time. The pecan waffle is a work of art. The burgers are big and sloppy and among the best in town. Wash it all down with a chocolate freeze and then contemplate a slice of the celebrated pie for dessert.

626 S. Carrollton Ave. ℂ 504/866-9573. Reservations not accepted. All items under $10. No credit cards. Mon–Thurs 9am–1am; Fri 9am–3am; Sat 8am–3am; Sun 8am–1am.

Casamento's *ఛఛ* SEAFOOD   This restaurant takes oysters so seriously that it simply closes down when they're not in season. It pays off—this is *the* oyster place. You pay a bit more for a dozen, but your reward is a presentation that shows the care the staff puts in; the oysters are cleanly scrubbed and well selected. Take the plunge and order an oyster loaf: a big, fat loaf of bread fried in butter, filled with oysters (or shrimp), and fried again to seal it. Do your arteries a favor and only eat half. Casamento's also has terrific gumbo— perhaps the best in town. It's small, but the atmosphere is light, with the waitresses serving up jokes and poking good-natured fun at you, at each other, or at the guys behind the oyster bar.

4330 Magazine St. ℂ 504/895-9761. Reservations not accepted. Main courses $4.95–$11. No credit cards. Tues–Sun 11:30am–1:30pm and 5:30–9pm. Closed mid-June to mid-Sept.

Dunbar's Creole Cooking *ఛఛ* SOUL FOOD   For a genuine soul food experience, come to this small, super-friendly establishment run by the very charming Tina Dunbar. A no-decor, big-kitchen place, Dunbar's caters to blue-collar locals in search of breakfast (which can run as little as $1) or lunch. You'll feast on huge, soul-warming, and generally amazing dishes, including gumbo, cornbread, and bread pudding, with daily specials listed on a board. Even the health-conscious can be swayed by the red beans and rice. Service is down-home, and attire is definitely come-as-you-are.

4927 Freret St. ℂ 504/899-0734. Main courses $5–$10. AE, DISC, MC, V. Mon–Sat 7am–9pm.

Franky & Johnny's *ఛ* SEAFOOD   This is a favorite local hole-in-the-wall neighborhood joint with either zero atmosphere or enough for three restaurants, depending on how you view these things. And by "things" we mean plastic checked tablecloths, a ratty but friendly bar, and locals eating enormous soft-shell-crab po' boys with the crab legs hanging out of the bread and their mouths. You got your po' boys, your boiled or fried seafood platters with two kinds of salad, and goodness knows, you got your beer. Try that soft-shell-crab po' boy or the red beans and rice and other down-home dishes, and know you are somewhere that isn't for tourists.

321 Arabella St. (and Tchoupitoulas St.). ℂ **504/899-9146.** Main courses $5.95–$13.95. AE, DISC, MC, V. Daily 11am–10pm.

Joey K's 𝒢 CREOLE/SEAFOOD   This is just a little corner local hangout, though one that savvy tourists have long been hip to. Indeed, it was a tourist who told us to order the trout Tchoupitoulas, and we were glad—lovely pan-fried trout topped with grilled veggies and shrimp. Add to that daily blackboard specials like brisket, lamb shank and white beans with pork chop, or Creole jambalaya. You can order it all to go, and you'll be dining like a real uptown local.

3001 Magazine St. ℂ **504/891-0997.** Reservations not accepted. Main courses $5.95–$11.95. DC, MC, V. Mon–Fri 11am–10pm; Sat 8am–10pm.

Martin Wine Cellar and Delicatessen 𝒢𝒢 SANDWICHES Martin's saved us one busy pre–Mardi Gras weekend when crowds prevented us from hitting a sit-down restaurant for lunch. A gourmet liquor and food store, Martin's also has a full-service deli counter. In addition to the usual deli suspects, they offer about two dozen specialty sandwiches, concoctions like the Dave's Special: rare roast beef, coleslaw, paté de Campagne, and special mustard on rye. We ordered it on onion bread instead, and it made our list of the Ten Best Sandwiches of All Time. Weekdays feature daily specials (lamb shanks, barbecue shrimp, garlic soup). It's all inexpensive and delicious and the perfect Garden District spot for picnic makings, since it's just two blocks lakeside of St. Charles.

3827 Baronne St. ℂ **504/896-7380.** Fax 504/896-7340. www.martinwine.com. Everything under $10. AE, DC, DISC, MC, V. Mon–Sat 9am–6:30pm; Sun 10am–4pm.

Mystic Cafe 𝒢𝒢 MEDITERRANEAN   Local vegetarians flock here, though the cafe is technically Mediterranean, and some dishes include meat. The food is mostly butter-free and can be made without sugar upon request, but includes plenty of whole-grain, high-quality olive oil options. We've had some wonderful salads and sandwiches here. Some might find it a welcome relief from the usual full-throttle New Orleans fare (we plead guilty to this ourselves), but others might feel they are dining in California.

3244 Magazine St. ⓒ **504/891-1992**. Fax 504/897-9394. Main courses $5.75–$11.25. AE, DC, DISC, MC, V. Sun–Thurs 11am–11pm; Fri–Sat 11am–midnight.

6 Coffee, Tea & Sweets

Besides the selections below, we recommend **Café au Lait** ⓡ (307 Chartres St.; ⓒ **504/528-9933**), a good little coffeehouse space in an area of the Quarter sadly lacking much of the same (their freeze drinks are made for a hot day); **P.J.'s Coffee & Tea Company** ⓡ (5432 Magazine St.; ⓒ **504/895-0273**), a local institution with 17 locations around town offering a variety of teas and coffees; **Royal Blend Coffee & Tea House** ⓡ (621 Royal St.; ⓒ **504/523-2716;** www.royalblendcoffee.com), which has coffee, pastry, sandwiches, quiche, and salad; and **Rue de la Course** ⓡ (1500 Magazine St.; ⓒ **504/529-1455**), your basic comfy boho coffeehouse.

Café du Monde ⓡⓡⓡ COFFEE, TEA & SWEETS Excuse us while we wax rhapsodic. Since 1862, Café du Monde has been selling café au lait and beignets (and nothing but) on the edge of Jackson Square. Not only is it a must-stop on any trip to New Orleans, you may find yourself wandering back several times a day. What's a beignet? (Say ben-*yay*, by the way.) A square French dough-nut-type object, hot and covered in powdered sugar. You might be tempted to shake off some of the sugar. Don't. Trust us. Pour more on, even. Just don't wear black, or everyone will know what you've been eating. At 3 for about $1, they're a hell of a deal. Wash them down with chicory coffee, listen to the nearby buskers, ignore people trying to get your table, and try to figure out how many more stops you can squeeze in during your visit.

In the French Market, 813 Decatur St. ⓒ **504/581-2914**. Fax 504/587-0847. www.cafedumonde.com. Coffee, milk, hot chocolate, and beignets (3 for $1.00). No credit cards. Daily 24 hours. Closed Dec 25.

La Madeleine ⓡ FRENCH BAKERY/COFFEE, TEA & SWEETS La Madeleine is one of the French Quarter's most charming casual eateries, though it's nearly always crowded with tourists. Its wood-burning brick oven turns out a wide variety of breads, croissants, and brioches—and it is claimed that the skills for making the same come right from France, so it's all authentic.

547 St. Ann St. (at Chartres St.). ⓒ **504/568-0073**. Fax 504/525-1680. www.lamadeleine.com. Pastries $1.35–$2.59; main courses $3.90–$9.25. AE, DISC, MC, V. Daily 7am–9pm.

La Marquise ⚘ PASTRIES/COFFEE, TEA & SWEETS   Tiny La Marquise serves French pastries in the crowded front room and outside on a small but delightful patio. Maurice Delechelle is the master baker here; you'd be hard-pressed to find more delectable goodies.

625 Chartres St. ⓒ **504/524-0420**. Pastries $1.65–$5. No credit cards. Daily 7am–7pm.

5

Sights to See & Places to Be

Now, we admit that our favorite New Orleans activities involve walking, eating, listening to music, and dancing. If that's all you do while you're visiting, we won't complain. Still, some people feel guilty if they don't take in some culture or history on their vacation. New Orleans offers several fine museums and a world-class aquarium and zoo, all of which, in addition to being interesting in and of themselves, make marvelous refuges from the weather.

Frankly, New Orleans itself is one big sight. It's one of the most unusual-looking cities in America, and being nice and flat, it's just made for exploring on foot. Don't confine yourself to the French Quarter. Yes, it certainly is a seductive place, but to go to New Orleans and never leave the Quarter is like going to New York, remaining in Greenwich Village, and believing you've seen Manhattan. Stroll the lush Garden District or marvel at the oaks in City Park. Ride the streetcar down St. Charles Avenue and gape with jealousy at the gorgeous homes. Get really active and go visit some gators on a swamp tour. But if you only leave the Quarter to visit clubs and restaurants, we won't blame you a bit.

1 The French Quarter

There's a great deal to the French Quarter—history, architecture, cultural oddities—and to overlook all that in favor of T-shirt shops and the ubiquitous bars is a darn shame. Which is not to say we don't understand, and rather enjoy, the lure of the more playful angle. We just don't want you to end up like some tourists who never even get off Bourbon. (And when you do head there, please remember that you are walking by people's homes. You wouldn't like it if someone did something biologically disgusting on your doorstep. Afford French Quarter dwellers the same courtesy.)

The Quarter was laid out in 1718 by a French royal engineer named Adrien de Pauger, and today it's a great anomaly in contemporary America. Almost all other American cities have torn down or gutted their historic centers, but thanks to a strict preservation

New Orleans Attractions

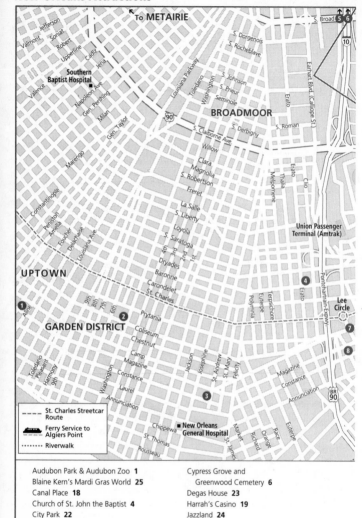

To METAIRIE

BROADMOOR

UPTOWN

GARDEN DISTRICT

Southern Baptist Hospital

Union Passenger Terminal (Amtrak)

Lee Circle

New Orleans General Hospital

--- St. Charles Streetcar Route
▬ Ferry Service to Algiers Point
···· Riverwalk

Audubon Park & Audubon Zoo **1**
Blaine Kern's Mardi Gras World **25**
Canal Place **18**
Church of St. John the Baptist **4**
City Park **22**
Confederate Memorial Museum **7**
Contemporary Arts Center **9**
Creole Queen **15**

Cypress Grove and
   Greenwood Cemetery **6**
Degas House **23**
Harrah's Casino **19**
Jazzland **24**
John James Audubon
   (boat to Audubon Zoo) **16**
Lafayette No. 1 Cemetery **2**

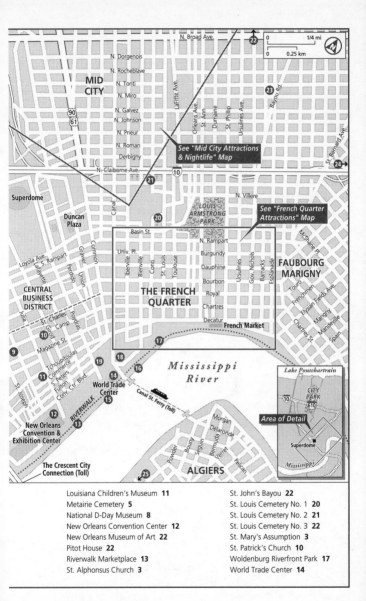

Louisiana Children's Museum **11**	St. John's Bayou **22**
Metairie Cemetery **5**	St. Louis Cemetery No. 1 **20**
National D-Day Museum **8**	St. Louis Cemetery No. 2 **21**
New Orleans Convention Center **12**	St. Louis Cemetery No. 3 **22**
New Orleans Museum of Art **22**	St. Mary's Assumption **3**
Pitot House **22**	St. Patrick's Church **10**
Riverwalk Marketplace **13**	Woldenburg Riverfront Park **17**
St. Alphonsus Church **3**	World Trade Center **14**

policy (and no thanks to the climate and a fire that destroyed the Quarter in the 1700s), the area looks exactly as it always has and is still the center of town.

Aside from Bourbon Street, you will find the most bustling activity at **Jackson Square,** where musicians, artists, fortunetellers, jugglers, and those peculiar "living statue" performance artists (a step below mime, and that's pretty pathetic) gather to sell their wares or entertain for change. **Royal Street** is home to numerous pricey antiques shops, with other interesting stores on **Chartres and Decatur streets** and the cross streets between.

The closer you get to **Esplanade Avenue** and toward **Rampart Street,** the more residential the Quarter becomes, and buildings are entirely homes. Walk through these areas, peeping in through any open gate; surprises wait behind them in the form of graceful brick and flagstone-lined courtyards filled with foliage and bubbling fountains.

The Quarter is particularly pedestrian-friendly. The streets are laid out in an almost perfect rectangle, so it's nearly impossible to get lost. It's also so well traveled that it is nearly always safe, particularly in the central parts. Again, as you get toward the fringes (especially near Rampart) and as night falls, you should exercise caution; stay in the more bustling parts and try not to walk alone.

Aquarium of the Americas ✰✰✰ (Kids   With all the other delights New Orleans offers, it's easy to overlook the Audubon Institute's Aquarium of the Americas—despite its million-gallon size. Who wants to look at fish when you could be eating them? But this is a world-class aquarium, highly entertaining and painlessly educational, with beautifully constructed exhibits.

The Aquarium is on the banks of the Mississippi River, a very easy walk from the main Quarter action. You can walk through the underwater tunnel in the Caribbean Reef exhibit and wave to finny friends swimming all around you, view a shark-filled re-creation of the Gulf of Mexico, or drop in to see the penguin exhibit. We particularly like the walk-through Waters of the Americas, where you wander in rain forests (complete with birds and piranhas) and see what goes on below the surface of swamps; one look will quash any thoughts of a dip in a bayou. The **IMAX theater** ✰✰ shows two or three films at regular intervals. The Audubon Institute also runs the city's zoo at Audubon Park uptown. **Combination tickets** for the Aquarium, the IMAX theater, the zoo, and a riverboat ride to the zoo are $26.50 for adults, $13.25 for children. You can also buy tickets for different combinations of the attractions.

Aquarium of the Americas **8**
Black Music Hall of Fame **23**
Beauregard-Keyes House **28**
The Cabildo **20**
The Cornstalk Fence **26**
1850 House **16**
French Market **14**
Gallier House Museum **27**
Germaine Wells
 Mardi Gras Museum **5**
Hermann-Grima House **4**
Historic New Orleans Collection **7**
Jackson Brewery **9**
Lafitte's Blacksmith Shop and Bar **24**
Madame John's Legacy **15**
Moonwalk **13**
Musée Conti Wax Museum **3**

Napoleon House **10**
New Orleans Historic
 Voodoo Museum **25**
New Orleans
 Pharmacy Museum **11**
Old Absinthe House **6**
Old Ursuline Convent **29**
Old U.S. Mint **30**
Our Lady of Guadeloupe Chapel–
 International Shrine of St. Jude **2**
The Presbytère **17**
St. Anthony's Garden **19**
St. Louis Cathedral **18**
St. Louis Cemetery No. 1 **1**
Spring Fiesta House **21**
Washington Artillery Park **12**
Voodoo Spiritual Temple **22**

1 Canal St., at Wells St. ℂ **800/774-7394** or 504/581-4629. Fax 504/565-3010. www.auduboninstitute.org. Aquarium $13 adults, $10 seniors, $6.50 children 2–12. IMAX $7.75 adults, $6.75 seniors, $5 children. Combination tickets $16.25 adults, $14 seniors, $10.50 children. Aquarium Sun–Thurs 9:30am–6pm; Fri–Sat 9:30am–7pm. IMAX daily 10am–6pm. Shows every hour on the hour. Last ticket sold 1 hour before closing. Closed Mardi Gras, Dec 25.

The Historic French Market 👫👫 (Kids) Legend has it that the site of the French Market was originally used by Native Americans as a bartering market. It began to grow into an official market in 1812. From around 1840 to 1870, it was part of Gallatin Street, an impossibly rough area so full of bars, drunken sailors, and criminals of every shape and size that it made Bourbon Street look like Disneyland. Today, it's a mixed bag (and not nearly as colorful as its past). The 24-hour Farmer's Market makes a fun amble as you admire everything from fresh produce to more tourist-oriented items like hot sauces and Cajun and Creole mixes. Snacks like gator on a stick (when was the last time you had that?) will amuse the kids. The Flea Market, just down from the Farmer's Market, is considered a must-shop place, but the reality is that the goods are kind of junky: T-shirts, jewelry, hats, crystals, toys, sunglasses, and that sort of thing. Still, some good deals can be had. The flea market is open daily.

On Decatur St., toward Esplanade Ave. from Jackson Sq.

St. Louis Cathedral 🏛   The St. Louis Cathedral prides itself on being the oldest continuously active cathedral in the United States. What usually doesn't get mentioned is that it is also one of the ugliest. The outside is all right, but the rather grim interior wouldn't give even a minor European church a run for its money.

Still, its history is impressive and somewhat dramatic. The cathedral formed the center of the original settlement, and it is still the major landmark of the French Quarter. This is the third building to stand on this spot. A hurricane destroyed the first in 1722. On Good Friday 1788, the bells of its replacement were kept silent for religious reasons rather than ringing out the alarm for a fire—which eventually went out of control and burned down more than 850 buildings, including the cathedral itself.

Rebuilt in 1794, the structure was remodeled and enlarged between 1845 and 1851 by J. N. B. de Pouilly. It's of Spanish design with a tower at each end and a higher central tower. The brick used in its construction was taken from the original town cemetery and was covered with stucco to protect the mortar from dampness. It's worth going in to catch one of the free docent tours; the knowledgeable guides are full of fun facts about the windows and murals and how the building nearly collapsed once from water table sinkage. Be sure to look at the slope of the floor; clever architectural design somehow keeps the building upright even as it continues to sink.

721 Chartres St. © **504/525-9585.** Fax 504/525-9583. Free admission. Free tours run continuously Mon–Sat 9am–5pm, Sun 2–5pm.

HISTORIC BUILDINGS
Old Absinthe House   The Old Absinthe House was built in 1806 by two Spaniards and is still owned by their descendants (who live in Spain and have nothing to do with running the place). The

building now houses the Old Absinthe House bar and two restaurants, Tony Moran's and Pasta e Vino. The drink for which the building and bar were named is now outlawed in this country (it caused blindness and madness). But you can sip a legal libation in the bar and feel at one with the famous types who came before you, listed on a plaque outside: William Makepeace Thackeray, Oscar Wilde, Sarah Bernhardt, Walt Whitman. Andrew Jackson and the Lafitte brothers plotted their desperate defense of New Orleans here in 1815.

The house was a speakeasy during Prohibition, and when federal officers closed it in 1924, the interior was mysteriously stripped of its antique fixtures—including the long marble-topped bar and the old water dripper that was used to infuse water into the absinthe. Just as mysteriously, they all reappeared down the street at a corner establishment called, oddly enough, the Old Absinthe House Bar (400 Bourbon St.). The latter recently closed, and a neon-bedecked daiquiri shack opened in its stead. Needless to say, the fixtures are nowhere in sight.

240 Bourbon St., between Iberville and Bienville sts. ✆ **504/523-3181**. www. oldabsinthehouse.com. Free admission. Daily from 9:30am.

Beauregard-Keyes House ✿ This "raised cottage," with its Doric columns and handsome twin staircases, was built as a residence by a wealthy New Orleans auctioneer, Joseph Le Carpentier, in 1826. Confederate Gen. P. G. T. Beauregard lived in the house with several members of his family for 18 months between 1865 and 1867, and from 1944 until 1970 it was the residence of Frances Parkinson Keyes (pronounced *Cause*), who wrote many novels about the region. Mrs. Keyes left her home to a foundation, and the house, rear buildings, and garden are open to the public. The gift shop has a wide selection of her novels.

1113 Chartres St., at Ursulines St. ✆ **504/523-7257**. Fax 504/523-7257. Admission $5 adults; $4 seniors, students, and AAA members; $2 children ages 6–13; free for children under 6. Mon–Sat 10am–3pm. Tours on the hour.

Old Ursuline Convent ✿✿ Forget tales of America being founded by brawny, brave, tough guys in buckskin and beards. The real pioneers—at least, in Louisiana—were well-educated French women clad in 40 pounds of black wool robes. That's right; you don't know tough until you know the Ursuline nuns, and this city would have been a very different place without them.

The Sisters of Ursula came to the mudhole that was New Orleans in 1727 after enduring a journey that several times nearly saw them lost at sea or to pirates or disease. Once in town, they provided the first decent medical care (saving countless lives) and later founded the local first school and orphanage for girls. They also helped raise girls shipped over from France as marriage material for local men, teaching the girls homemaking of the most exacting sort.

The convent dates from 1752 (the Sisters moved uptown in 1824, where they remain to this day), and it is the oldest building in the Mississippi River Valley and the only surviving building from the French Colonial period in the United States. Unfortunately, docents' histories ramble all over the place, rarely painting the full, thrilling picture of these extraordinary ladies to whom the city owes so much.

1112 Chartres St., at Ursulines St. © **504/529-2001.** Admission $5 adults, $4 seniors, $2 students, free for children under 8. Tours Tues–Fri 10am–3pm on the hour (closed for lunch at noon); Sat–Sun 11:15am, 1pm, 2pm.

The Old U.S. Mint 𝒜𝒜 𝒦𝒾𝒹𝓈 The Old U.S. Mint, a Louisiana State Museum complex, houses exhibits on New Orleans jazz and the city's Carnival celebrations. The first exhibit contains a collection of pictures, musical instruments, and other artifacts connected with jazz greats—Louis Armstrong's first trumpet is here. It tells of the development of the jazz tradition and New Orleans's place in that history. Across the hall is a stunning array of Carnival mementos.

400 Esplanade Ave., at N. Peters St. (enter on Esplanade Ave. or Barracks St.). © **800/568-6968** or 504/568-6968. Fax 504/568-4995. Admission $5 adults, $4 seniors and students, free for children under 12. Tues–Sun 9am–5pm.

The 1850 House 𝒜 James Gallier Sr. and his son designed the historic Pontalba Buildings for the Baroness Micaela Almonester de Pontalba. The rows of town houses on either side of Jackson Square were the largest private buildings in the country at the time. Legend has it that the Baroness, miffed that her friend Andrew Jackson wouldn't tip his hat to her, had his statue erected in the square, permanently doffing his chapeau toward her apartment on the top floor of the Upper Pontalba. It's probably not true, but we never stand in the way of a good story.

In this house, the Louisiana State Museum presents a demonstration of life in 1850, when the buildings opened for residential use. The self-guided tour explains in detail the uses of the rooms, which are filled with period furnishings. It vividly illustrates the difference between the "upstairs" portion of the house, where the upper-middle-class family lived in comfort, and the "downstairs," where the staff toiled in considerable drudgery. It's a surprisingly enjoyable look at life in the "good old days"; it might have you reconsidering just how good they were.

Lower Pontalba Building. 523 St. Ann St., Jackson Sq. © **800/568-6968** or 504/ 568-6968. Fax 504/568-4995. Admission $5 adults, $4 seniors and students, free for children under 13. Tues–Sun 9am–5pm. Closed state holidays.

Spring Fiesta Historic House ⓡ The New Orleans Spring Fiesta Association owns this historic mid-19th-century town house. It affords a peek back in time, furnished as it is with antiques of the Victorian era and many objets d'art from New Orleans's golden age of the 1800s. The association's fiesta, in March, coordinates tours of historic town houses, courtyards, and plantation homes around town.

826 St. Ann St., at Bourbon St. © **504/581-1367.** Fax 504/899-5633. $10 donation requested, groups of 10 or more only. By appointment only.

Our Lady of Guadeloupe Chapel—International Shrine of St. Jude ⓡ This is known as the "funeral chapel." It was erected (in 1826) conveniently near St. Louis Cemetery No. 1, specifically for funeral services, so as not to spread disease through the Quarter. We like it for three reasons: the catacomb-like devotional chapel with plaques thanking the Virgin Mary for favors granted, the gift shop full of religious medals including a number of obscure saints, and the statue of St. Expedite. He got his name, according to legend, when his crate arrived with no identification other than the word *expedite* stamped on the outside. Now he's the saint you pray to when you want things in a hurry. (We are not making this up.) Expedite has his cults in France and Spain and is also popular among the voodoo folks. He's just inside the door on the right—go say hi.

411 N. Rampart St., at Conti St. © 504/525-1551. www.saintjudeshrine.com.

MUSEUMS

In addition to the destinations listed here, you might be interested in the **Germaine Wells Mardi Gras Museum** (© **504/523-5433**), at 813 Bienville St., on the second floor of Arnaud's restaurant. You'll find a private collection of Mardi Gras costumes and ball gowns dating from around 1910 to 1960. Admission is free, and the museum is open during restaurant hours.

The **Ogden Museum of Southern Art** (which will feature everything from acrylics to sculpture to mixed media) is scheduled to open in January 2002. A temporary exhibit can be found at 603 Julia St. (© **504/539-9600**).

The Cabildo ⚜⚜⚜   Constructed from 1795 to 1799 as the Spanish government seat in New Orleans, the Cabildo was the site of the signing of the Louisiana Purchase transfer. It was severely damaged by fire in 1988 and closed for 5 years for reconstruction, which included total restoration of the roof by French artisans using 600-year-old timber-framing techniques. It is now the center of the Louisiana State Museum's facilities in the French Quarter. It's located right on Jackson Square and is quite worth your time.

A multiroom exhibition informatively, entertainingly, and exhaustively traces the history of Louisiana from exploration through Reconstruction from a multicultural perspective. It covers all aspects of life, not just the obvious discussions of slavery and the battle for statehood. Topics include antebellum music, mourning and burial customs (a big deal when much of your population is succumbing to yellow fever), immigrants and how they fared here. Throughout are fabulous artifacts, including Napoléon's death mask.

701 Chartres St. ℭ **800/568-6968** or 504/568-6968. Fax 504/568-4995. Admission $5 adults, $4 students and seniors, free for children under 13. Tues–Sun 9am–5pm.

Gallier House Museum ⚜   James Gallier Jr. designed and built the Gallier House Museum as his residence in 1857. Anne Rice fans will want to at least walk by—this is the house she was thinking of when she described Louis and Lestat's New Orleans residence in *Interview with the Vampire*. Gallier and his father were leading New Orleans architects—they designed the old French Opera House, the original St. Charles Exchange Hotel, Municipality Hall (now Gallier Hall), and the Pontalba Buildings. This carefully restored town house contains an early working bathroom, a passive ventilation system, and furnishings of the period. Leaders of local ghost tours swear that Gallier haunts the place. Look for seasonal special programs.

1118–1132 Royal St., between Governor Nicholls and Ursulines sts. ℭ **504/525-5661**. Admission $6 adults; $5 seniors, students, AAA members, and children ages 8–18; free for children under 8. Tours offered Mon–Fri at 10am, 11am, noon, 1:30pm, 2:30pm, 3:30pm.

Hermann-Grima House ⚜   The 1831 Hermann-Grima House is a symmetrical Federal-style building (perhaps the first in the Quarter) that's very different from its French surroundings. The knowledgeable docents who give the regular tours make this a satisfactory stop at any time, but keep an eye out for the frequent special tours. At Halloween, for example, the house is draped in typical 1800s mourning, and the docents explain mourning customs. The tour of the house, which has been meticulously restored, is one of the city's more historically accurate offerings.

820 St. Louis St. (℗ **504/525-5661**. Fax 504/568-9735. Admission $6 adults; $5 seniors, students, AAA members, and children ages 8–18; free for children under 8. Tours offered Mon–Fri at 10am, 11am, noon, 1:30pm, 2:30pm, 3:30pm.

Historic New Orleans Collection-Museum/Research Center 🕸🕸

The Historic New Orleans Collection's museum of local and regional history is almost hidden away within a complex of historic French Quarter buildings. The oldest, constructed in the late 18th century, was one of the few structures to escape the disastrous fire of 1794. These buildings were owned by the collection's founders, Gen. and Mrs. L. Kemper Williams. There are excellent tours of the Louisiana history galleries, which feature expertly preserved and displayed art, maps, and original documents like the transfer papers for the Louisiana Purchase of 1803. The collection is owned and managed by a private foundation, not a governmental organization, and therefore offers more historical perspective and artifacts than boosterism.

If you want to see another grandly restored French Quarter building, visit the **Williams Research Center,** 410 Chartres St. (℗ **504/598-7171**), which houses and displays the bulk of the collection's many thousands of items. Admission is free.

533 Royal St., between St. Louis and Toulouse sts. (℗ **504/523-4662**. www.hnoc. org. Free admission; tours $4. Tues–Sat 10am–4:30pm; tours Tues–Sat 10am, 11am, 2pm, 3pm. Closed major holidays, Mardi Gras.

Madame John's Legacy 🕸

The second-oldest building in the Mississippi Valley (after the Ursuline Convent) and a rare example of Creole architecture that miraculously survived the 1794 fire, Madame John's Legacy has finally been opened to the public.

Built around 1788 on the foundations of an earlier home destroyed in the fire of that year, the house has had a number of owners and renters, but none of them were named John. Or even Madame. It acquired its moniker courtesy of author George Washington Cable, who used the house as a setting for his short story "Tite Poulette." The protagonist was a quadroon named Madame John after her lover, who willed this house to her.

There are no tours, but you can enjoy two exhibits: one on the history and legends of the house and another of art by self-taught/primitive artists.

632 Dumaine St. ℂ **504/568-6968**. Fax 504/568-4995. Admission $3 adults, $2 students and seniors. Tues–Sun 9am–5pm.

Musée Conti Wax Museum ⓐ Kids

You might wonder about the advisability of a wax museum in a place as hot as New Orleans, but the Musée Conti is pretty neat—and downright spooky in spots. A large section is devoted to a sketch of Louisiana legends (Andrew Jackson, Napoléon, Jean Lafitte, Marie Laveau, Huey Long, a Mardi Gras Indian, Louis Armstrong, and Pete Fountain) and historical episodes. The descriptions, especially of the historical scenes, are surprisingly informative and witty.

917 Conti St. ℂ **504/525-2605**. www.get-waxed.com. Admission $6.75 adults, $5.50 seniors (over 62), $5.75 children ages 4–17, free for children under 4. Daily 10am–5:30pm. Closed Mardi Gras, Dec 25.

New Orleans Historic Voodoo Museum ⓐ

Some of the hard-core voodoo practitioners in town might scoff at the Voodoo Museum, and perhaps rightly so. It is largely designed for tourists, but it is also probably the best opportunity for tourists to get acquainted with the history and culture of voodoo. Don't expect high-quality, comprehensive exhibits—the place is dark, dusty, and musty. There are occult objects from all over the globe plus some articles that allegedly belonged to the legendary Marie Laveau. Unless someone on staff talks you through it—which they will, if you ask—you might come away with more confusion than facts. Still, it's an adequate introduction—and who wouldn't want to bring home a voodoo doll from here? There is generally a voodoo priestess on site, giving readings and making personal gris-gris bags. Again, it's voodoo for tourists, but for most tourists, it's probably the right amount. (Don't confuse this place with the Marie Laveau House of Voodoo on Bourbon Street.)

The museum also offers a **guided voodoo cemetery tour** of **St. Louis No. 1** to visit Marie Laveau's reputed grave. The tours might be light on verifiable facts, but they are usually entertaining. (Please don't scratch Xs on the graves; no matter what you've heard, it is not a real voodoo practice and it is destroying fragile tombs.)

Note: At press time, the museum was in the process of moving to a new location at 219 North Peters Street. The old address will remain open as a gift shop and the site of psychic readings. Please call the number below to see if the museum has moved.

724 Dumaine St., at Bourbon St. ℂ **504/523-7685**. www.voodoomuseum.com. Admission $7 adults, $5.50 students and seniors. Cemetery tour $16, Tour of the Undead $16. Daily 10am–8pm.

New Orleans Pharmacy Museum ⚘   Founded in 1950, the New Orleans Pharmacy Museum is just what the name implies. In 1823, the first licensed pharmacist in the United States, Louis J. Dufilho Jr., opened an apothecary shop here. The Creole-style town house doubled as his home, and he cultivated the herbs he needed for his medicines in the interior courtyard. Inside you'll find old apothecary bottles, voodoo potions, pill tile, and suppository molds.

514 Chartres St., at St. Louis St. ⓒ 504/565-8027. Fax 504/568-8028. www. pharmacymuseum.org. Admission $2 adults, $1 seniors and students, free for children under 12. Tues–Sun 10am–5pm.

The Presbytère ⚘⚘⚘   The Presbytère was planned as housing for the clergy but was never used for that purpose. Currently, it's part of the Louisiana State Museum, which has just turned the entire building into a smashing Mardi Gras museum. Five major themes (History, Masking, Parades, Balls, and the Courir du Mardi Gras) trace the history of this high-profile but frankly little-understood (outside of New Orleans) annual event. The exhibits are stunning and the attention to detail is startling, with everything from elaborate Mardi Gras Indian costumes to Rex Queen jewelry from the turn of the 20th century. A re-creation of a float allows you to pretend you are throwing beads to a crowd on a screen in front of you. Heck, even some of the restrooms masquerade (appropriately) as the ubiquitous Fat Tuesday port-a-potties! Check out the gift shop, the only place in town where you can buy those coveted Zulu beads.

751 Chartres St., Jackson Sq. ⓒ 800/568-6968 or 504/568-6968. Fax 504/568-4995. Admission $5 adults, $4 seniors and students, free for children under 13. Tues–Sun 9am–5pm.

Woldenberg Riverfront Park ⚘   Made up of just under 20 acres of newly repaired green space, Woldenberg Riverfront Park has historically been the city's promenade; now it's an oasis of greenery in the heart of the city. The park includes a large lawn with a brick promenade leading to the Mississippi. The Moonwalk has steps that let you go right down to Old Muddy—on foggy nights, you feel as if you are floating above the water. There are many benches from which to view the city's main industry—its busy port (second in the world only to Amsterdam in annual tonnage).

Along the Mississippi from the Moonwalk at the old Governor Nicholls Street wharf to the Aquarium of the Americas at Canal St. ⓒ 504/861-2537. Open daily dawn to dusk.

2 Outside the French Quarter

UPTOWN & THE GARDEN DISTRICT

If you can see just one thing outside the French Quarter, make it the Garden District. It has no significant historic buildings or, with one exception (see below), important museums. It's simply beautiful. In some ways, even more so than the Quarter, this is New Orleans. Authors as diverse as Truman Capote and Anne Rice have been enchanted by its spell. Gorgeous homes of superb design stand quietly amidst lush foliage, elegant but ever so slightly (or more) decayed. You can see why this is the setting for so many novels.

St. Elizabeth's Orphanage ☆☆ After 118 years as a girls' orphanage and boarding school, this grand mid-1800s building fell on hard times, only to be rescued by the city's favorite building benefactors, Anne and Stan Rice. It now holds Anne's doll collection and serves as the office for her Kith & Kin holding company.

Tours are some of the most entertaining in town. Even if you think you don't care about dolls, the displays (which also include some of the Rices' religious art collection) produce any number of good stories, particularly if the tour is being given by Bill Murphy, Anne's first cousin once removed, a longtime New Orleans newspaperman and historian. The building can also be rented for weddings.

1314 Napoleon Ave. © **504/899-6450.** www.annerice.com. Admission $7 adults, $5 children. Mon–Fri 1pm; Sat–Sun 11am, 1pm, 3pm. Guided tours only.

TROLLING ST. JOHN'S BAYOU & LAKE PONTCHARTRAIN ☆☆☆

St. John's Bayou is a body of water that originally extended from the outskirts of New Orleans to Lake Pontchartrain, and it's one of the most important reasons New Orleans is where it is today. Jean Baptiste Le Moyne, Sieur de Bienville, was commissioned to establish a settlement in Louisiana that would both make money and protect French holdings in the New World from British expansion. Bienville chose the spot where New Orleans now sits because he recognized the strategic importance of "back-door" access to the Gulf of Mexico provided by the bayou's linkage to the lake. Boats could enter the lake from the Gulf and then follow the bayou until they were within easy portage distance of the mouth of the Mississippi River. Area Native American tribes had used this route for years.

The early path from the city to the bayou is today's Bayou Road, an extension of Governor Nicholls Street in the French Quarter.

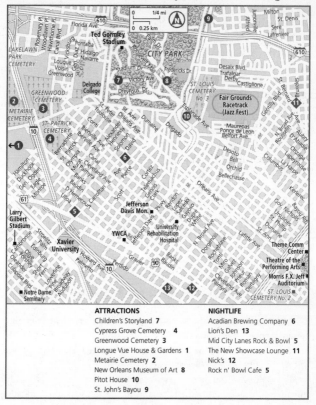

ATTRACTIONS	NIGHTLIFE
Children's Storyland **7**	Acadian Brewing Company **6**
Cypress Grove Cemetery **4**	Lion's Den **13**
Greenwood Cemetery **3**	Mid City Lanes Rock & Bowl **5**
Longue Vue House & Gardens **1**	The New Showcase Lounge **11**
Metairie Cemetery **2**	Nick's **12**
New Orleans Museum of Art **8**	Rock n' Bowl Cafe **5**
Pitot House **10**	
St. John's Bayou **9**	

Modern-day Gentilly Boulevard, which crosses the bayou, was another Native American trail.

New Orleans grew and prospered, and the bayou became a suburb as planters moved out along its shores. In the early 1800s, a canal was dug to connect the waterway with the city, reaching a basin at the edge of Congo Square. The basin became a popular recreation area with fine restaurants and dance halls (as well as meeting places for voodoo practitioners). Gradually, New Orleans reached beyond the French Quarter and enveloped the whole area.

The canal is gone, filled in long ago, and the bayou is a meek re-creation of itself. It is no longer navigable (even if it were, bridges were built too low to permit the passage of boats of any size), but residents still prize their waterfront sites, and rowboats and sailboats make use of the bayou's surface. It's one of the prettiest areas of New Orleans, full of the old houses tourists love to marvel at but without the hustle, bustle, and confusion of more high-profile locations. A walk along the banks and through the nearby neighborhoods is one of our favorite things to do on a nice afternoon.

GETTING THERE   The simplest way to reach St. John's Bayou from the French Quarter is to drive straight out Esplanade Avenue about 20 blocks. Right before you reach the bayou, you'll pass **St. Louis Cemetery No. 3** (just past Leda Street). It's the final resting place of many prominent New Orleanians, among them Thomy Lafon, the black philanthropist who bought the old Orleans Ballroom as an orphanage for African-American children and put an end to its infamous "quadroon balls." Just past the cemetery, turn left onto Moss Street, which runs along the banks of St. John's Bayou. If you want to see an example of an 18th-century West Indies–style plantation house, stop at the Pitot House, 1440 Moss St. (see later in this chapter).

To continue, drive along Wisner Boulevard, on the opposite bank of St. John's Bayou from Moss Street, and you'll pass some of New Orleans's grandest modern homes—a sharp contrast to those on Moss Street. If you want to go all the way to Lake Pontchartrain, here's a good route: Stay on Wisner to Robert E. Lee Boulevard, turn right, drive to Elysian Fields Avenue, and then turn left. That's the University of New Orleans campus on your left.

Turn left onto the broad concrete highway, Lake Shore Drive. It runs for 5½ miles along the lake, and in the summer, the parkway alongside its seawall is swarming with swimmers and picnickers. On the other side are more luxurious, modern residences.

Lake Pontchartrain is some 40 miles long and 25 miles wide. Native Americans once lived along both sides, and it was a major waterway long before white people were seen in this hemisphere. You can drive across it over the 23¾-mile Greater New Orleans Causeway, the longest bridge in the world.

When you cross the mouth of St. John's Bayou, you'll be where **the old Spanish Fort** was built in 1770. Its remains are now nestled amid modern homes. Look for the **Mardi Gras fountain** on your left. If you time your visit to coincide with sundown, you'll see the fountain beautifully lit in the Mardi Gras colors of purple (for justice), green (for faith), and gold (for power).

Tips Safety First

You will be warned against going to the cemeteries alone and urged to go with a scheduled tour group (see "Organized Tours," later in this chapter). It is true that, thanks to their location and layout—some are in dicey neighborhoods, and the crypts obscure threats to your safety—some cemeteries can be quite risky, making visitors prime pickings for muggers and so forth. Other cemeteries, those with better security and in better neighborhoods, not to mention with layouts that permit driving, are probably safe. Ironically, two of the most hazardous, St. Louis No. 1 and Lafayette No. 1, are often so full of tour groups that you could actually go there without one and be fairly safe. On the other hand, a good tour is fun and informative, so why not take the precaution?

If you're going to make a day of the cemeteries, you should also think about renting a car. You won't be driving through horrendous downtown traffic, you can visit tombs at your own pace, and you'll feel safer.

WHERE THE BODIES AREN'T BURIED ✦✦✦

Along with Spanish moss and lacy iron balconies, the cities of the dead are part of the indelible landscape of New Orleans. Their ghostly and inscrutable presence enthralls visitors, who are used to traditional methods of burial—in the ground or in mausoleums.

Why above ground? Well, it rains in New Orleans. A lot. And then it floods. Soon after the city was settled, it became apparent that Uncle Etienne had an unpleasant habit of bobbing back to the surface (doubtless no longer looking his best). Add to that cholera and yellow fever epidemics, which helped increase not only the number of bodies, but also the possibility of infection. Given that the cemetery of the time was in the Vieux Carré, it's all pretty disgusting to think about.

So in 1789, the city opened St. Louis No. 1, right outside the city walls on what is now Rampart Street. The "condo crypt" look—the dead are placed in vaults that look like miniature buildings—was inspired to a certain extent by the famous Père Lachaise cemetery in Paris. Crypts were laid out haphazardly in St. Louis No. 1, which quickly filled up even as the city outgrew the Vieux Carré and expanded around the cemetery. Other cemeteries followed. They have designated lanes, making for a more orderly appearance. The rows of tombs look like nothing so much as a city—a city where the dead inhabitants peer over the shoulders of the living.

For many years, New Orleans cemeteries were in shambles. Crypts lay open, exposing their pitiful contents—if they weren't robbed of them—bricks lay everywhere, marble tablets were shattered, and visitors might even trip over stray bones. Thanks to local civic efforts, several of the worst eyesores have been cleaned up, though some remain in deplorable shape.

THREE CEMETERIES YOU SHOULD SEE WITH A TOUR

St. Louis No. 1   This is the oldest extant cemetery (1789) and the most iconic. Here lie Marie Laveau, Bernard Marigny, and assorted other New Orleans characters. Louis the vampire from Anne Rice's *Vampire Chronicles* even has his (empty) tomb here. The acid-dropping scene from *Easy Rider* was shot here.

Basin St. between Conti and St. Louis sts.

St. Louis No. 2   Established in 1823, the city's next-oldest cemetery, unfortunately, is in such a terrible neighborhood (next to the so-called Storyville Projects) that regular cemetery tours don't usually bother with it. If there is a tour running when you are in town, go—it's worth it. Marie Laveau II, some Storyville characters, and others lie within its three blocks.

Note: As of this writing, there is no regular tour of St. Louis No. 2, which is absolutely unsafe. Do not go there, even in a large group, without an official tour.

N. Claiborne Ave. between Iberville and St. Louis sts.

Lafayette No. 1   Right across the street from Commander's Palace restaurant, this is the lush uptown cemetery. Once in horrible condition, it's been beautifully restored. Anne Rice's Mayfair witches have their family tomb here.

1427 Sixth St.

SOME CEMETERIES YOU COULD SEE ON YOUR OWN

But if you do, please exercise caution. Take a cab (albeit expensive) to and from or consider renting a car for the day. Most of these cemeteries (such as St. Louis No. 3 and Metairie) have offices that can sometimes provide maps; if they run out, they will give you directions to any grave location you like. All have sort-of-regular hours—figure 9am to 4pm is a safe bet.

St. Louis No. 3 Conveniently located next to the Fair Grounds racetrack (home of the Jazz Fest), St. Louis No. 3 was built on top of a former graveyard for lepers. Storyville photographer E. J. Bellocq lies here. The Esplanade Avenue bus will take you there.

3421 Esplanade Ave.

Metairie Cemetery Don't be fooled by the slightly more modern look—some of the most amazing tombs in New Orleans are here. Not to be missed is the pyramid-and-Sphinx Brunswig mausoleum and the "ruined castle" Egan family tomb, not to mention the former resting place of Storyville madam Josie Arlington.

5100 Pontchartrain Blvd. ⓒ 504/486-6331. By car, take Esplanade north to City Park Avenue, turn left until it becomes Metairie Avenue.

Cypress Grove and Greenwood Cemeteries Located across the street from each other, both were founded in the mid-1800s by the Firemen's Charitable and Benevolent Association. Each has some highly original tombs; keep your eyes open for the ones made entirely of iron. These two cemeteries are an easy bus ride up Canal Street from the Quarter.

120 City Park Ave. and 5242 Canal Blvd. By car, take Esplanade north to City Park Avenue, turn left until it becomes Metairie Avenue.

BUILDINGS WITH A HISTORY (& ONE WITH BULK)

Degas House ⓐ Legendary French Impressionist Edgar Degas felt very tender toward New Orleans; his mother and grandmother were born here, and he spent several months in 1872 and 1873 visiting his brother at this house. It was a trip that resulted in a number of paintings, and this is the only residence or studio associated with Degas anywhere in the world that is open to the public. One of his paintings showed the garden of the house behind his brother's. His brother liked that view, too; he later ran off with the wife of the judge who lived there. His wife and children later took back her maiden name, Musson. The Musson home, as it is formally known, was erected in 1854 and has since been sliced in two and redone in an Italianate manner. Currently, only the building on the right is open to the public (including a very nice B&B setup), but the owner is busy restoring the building on the left with plans to open it up as well and, even grander, plans to one day reunite the two.

2306 Esplanade Ave. (north of the Quarter, before you reach N. Broad Ave.). ⓒ **504/821-5009**. www.degashouse.com. $10 donation requested. Daily 10am–3pm.

Gallier Hall   This impressive Greek Revival building was the inspiration of James Gallier Sr. Erected between 1845 and 1853, it served as City Hall for just over a century and has been the site of many important events in the city's history. Several important figures lay in state in Gallier Hall, including Jefferson Davis and General Beauregard. More than 5,000 mourners came to Gallier Hall on July 14, 2001, to pay their respects to the flamboyant R&B legend Ernie K-Doe, who was laid out in a white costume and a silver crown and delivered to his final resting place in a big, brassy jazz procession.

545 St. Charles Ave.

Pitot House 𝕔   The Pitot House is a typical West Indies–style plantation home, restored and furnished with early-19th-century Louisiana and American antiques. Dating from 1799, it originally stood where the nearby modern Catholic school is. In 1810, it became the home of James Pitot, the first mayor of incorporated New Orleans (he served 1804–05).

1440 Moss St., near Esplanade Ave. at the southeast corner of City Park. 𝕔 **504/ 482-0312.** Admission $5 adults, $4 seniors and students, $2 children under 12. Parties of 10 or more $3 each. Wed–Sat 10am–3pm. Last tour begins at 2pm.

Jackson Barracks and Military Museum 𝕔   On an extension of Rampart Street downriver from the French Quarter is this series of fine old brick buildings with white columns. They were built in 1834 and 1835 for troops who were stationed at the river forts. Some say Andrew Jackson, who never quite trusted New Orleans Creoles, planned the barracks to be as secure against attack from the city as from outside forces. The barracks now serve as headquarters for the Louisiana National Guard, and there's an extensive military museum in the old powder magazine. Call before you go to confirm that the barracks and museum are open.

6400 St. Claude Ave. 𝕔 **504/278-8242.** Fax 504/278-8614. Free admission. Museum hours Mon–Fri 8am–4pm; Sat 9am–3pm.

The Superdome 𝕔   Completed in 1975 (at a cost of around $180 million), the Superdome is a landmark civic structure. It's a 27-story windowless building with a seating capacity of 76,000 and a computerized climate-control system that uses more than 9,000 tons of equipment. It's one of the largest buildings in the world in diameter (680 feet), and its grounds cover some 13 acres. Inside, no posts obstruct the spectator's view of sporting events, be they football, baseball, or basketball, while movable partitions and seats allow the building to be configured for almost any event. Most people think of the Superdome as a sports center only (the Super Bowl will be held there again in 2002), but this flying saucer of a building plays host to conventions, the Krewe of Endymion's annual massive Mardi Gras ball, and big theatrical and musical productions.

1500 block of Poydras St., near Rampart St. ✆ **504/587-3808** for tour information. Admission $6 adults, $5 seniors and students, $4 children 5–10, free for children under 5. Guided tours daily 10:30am, noon, 1:30pm (except during events). Group tours available on request. Tours subject to change and cancellation.

MUSEUMS & GALLERIES

Confederate Memorial Museum ★★
Not far from the French Quarter, the Confederate Museum was established in 1891 and currently houses the second-largest collection of Confederate memorabilia in the country. It opened so soon after the end of the war that many of the donated items are in excellent condition. Among these are 125 battle flags, 50 Confederate uniforms, guns, swords, photographs, and oil paintings. You'll see personal effects of Confederate Gen. P. G. T. Beauregard and Confederate President Jefferson Davis (including his evening clothes), and part of Robert E. Lee's silver camp service. It's somewhat cluttered and not that well laid out—for the most part, only buffs will find much of interest here, though they can have remarkable temporary exhibitions like a most moving one on Jefferson Davis's youngest daughter, Winnie.

929 Camp St., at St. Joseph's. ✆ **504/523-4522.** www.confederatemuseum.com. Admission $5 adults, $4 students and seniors, $2 children under 12. Mon–Sat 10am–4pm.

Contemporary Arts Center ★★
Redesigned in the early 1990s to much critical applause, the Contemporary Arts Center is a main anchor of the city's young arts district (once the city's old Warehouse District, it's now home to a handful of leading local galleries). Over the past 2 decades, the center has consistently exhibited influential and groundbreaking work by regional, national, and international artists in various mediums.

900 Camp St., at Joseph St. ✆ **504/528-3805.** Fax 504/528-3828. www.cacno.org. Admission $5 adults, $3 seniors and students, free for members; free to all on Thurs. Tickets $3–$25. Mon–Sat 10am–5pm; Sun 11am–5pm.

National D-Day Museum ★★★
Opened on D-Day, June 6, 2000, this is the creation of best-selling author (and *Saving Private Ryan* consultant) Stephen Ambrose, and it is the only museum of its kind in the country. It tells the story of all 19 U.S. amphibious operations worldwide on that fateful day of June 6, 1944. A rich

collection of artifacts (including some British Spitfire airplanes) coupled with top-of-the-line educational materials makes this new museum one of the highlights of New Orleans.

A panorama allows visitors to see just what it was like on those notorious beaches. There is also a copy of Eisenhower's contingency speech, in which he planned to apologize to the country for the failure of D-Day—thankfully, it was a speech that was never needed.

945 Magazine St., in the Central Business District. © **504/527-6012**. Admission $7 adults, $6 seniors, $5 children ages 5–17, free for children under 5. Daily 9am–5pm. Closed holidays.

New Orleans Museum of Art ★★   Often called NOMA, this museum is located in an idyllic section of City Park. The front portion of the museum is the original large, imposing neoclassical building ("sufficiently modified to give a subtropical appearance," said the architect Samuel Marx); the rear portion is a striking contrast of curves and contemporary styles.

The museum opened in 1911 after a gift to the City Park Commission from Isaac Delgado, a sugar broker and Jamaican immigrant. Today, it houses a 40,000-piece collection including pre-Columbian and Native American ethnographic art; 16th-through 20th-century European paintings, early American art; Asian art; and one of the six largest decorative glass collections in the United States.

The changing exhibits frequently have regional resonance, such as the one devoted to religious art and objects collected from local churches or the one—how's this for a complete change of pace—that focused on "dirty pictures" throughout the modern era!

1 Collins Diboll Circle, at City Park and Esplanade. © **504/488-2631**. Fax 504/488-6662. www.noma.org. Admission $6 adults, $5 seniors (over 64), $3 children 3–17, free to Louisiana residents Thurs 10am–noon. Tues–Sun 10am–5pm. Closed most major holidays.

Westgate ★   Death buffs and other morbid types will be thrilled to visit Westgate (also known as the "House of Death"), while others will come down with a serious case of the creeps. The hard-to-miss purple-and-black building is a gallery of "necromantic art" run by Leilah Wendell and Daniel Kemp, who inaugurated this project in 1979. Both are authors of metaphysical books about the personification of death, and the gallery is dedicated to Azrael, the embodiment of "what Western cultures refer to as the Angel of Death," says Wendell. The art, much of it by Wendell, uses plenty of death imagery with a heavy emphasis on its romance. The results are graphic and powerful. Some will find this deeply disturbing, but it certainly is one of the most unusual galleries in town and is worth a trip for the open-minded and curious.

5219 Magazine St. (at the corner of Bellecastle Street.), Uptown. ℭ **504/899-3077**. www.westgatenecromantic.com. Free admission; donations accepted. Tues–Sat noon–5pm.

FLOATING ACROSS THE RIVER TO ALGIERS POINT

Algiers, annexed by New Orleans in 1870, stretches along the western side of the Mississippi River and is easily accessible via the free ferry that runs from the base of Canal Street. *Take note:* The ferry is one of New Orleans's best-kept secrets. It's a great way to get out onto the river and see the skyline. With such easy access (a ferry leaves every 15–20 min.), who knows why the Point hasn't been better assimilated into the larger city, but it hasn't. Though it's only about a quarter-mile across the river from the French Quarter, it still has the feel of an undisturbed turn-of-the-20th-century suburb.

Strolling around here is a delightfully low-key way to spend an hour or two. The last ferry returns at around 11:15pm, but be sure to check the schedule before you set out, just in case. While you're there, stop in at **Blaine Kern's Mardi Gras World** ⋒⋒ (223 Newton St., Algiers Point; ℭ **800/362-8213** or 504/361-7821; www.mardigrasworld.com; open daily 9:30am–4:30pm; admission $13.50 adults, $10 seniors (over 62), $5.50 children 3–12, and free children under 3). Blaine Kern makes more than three-quarters of the floats used by the various krewes every Carnival season. Mardi Gras World offers tours of its collection of float sculptures and its studios, where you can see floats being made year-round. You can even try on some heavily bejeweled costumes. Bring your camera!

3 Parks & Gardens

PARKS

Audubon Park ⋒⋒   Across from Loyola and Tulane universities, Audubon Park and the adjacent Audubon Zoo (see "A Day at the Zoo," below) sprawl over 340 acres, extending from St. Charles Avenue all the way to the Mississippi River. This tract once belonged to city founder Jean-Baptiste Le Moyne. The city purchased it in 1871 and used much of the land for the World's Industrial and Cotton Centennial Exposition in 1884 and 1885. Despite having the (then) largest building in the world as its main exhibition hall (33 acres under one roof), the exposition was such a financial disaster that everything except the Horticultural Hall had to be sold off—and that hall fell victim to a hurricane a little later. After that, serious work to make this into a park began. Although John James Audubon lived only briefly in New Orleans, the city honored him by naming both the park and the zoo after him.

The huge trees with black bark are live oaks; some go back to plantation days, and more than 200 additional ones were recently planted here. With the exception of the trees, it's not the most visually interesting park in the world—it's just pretty and a nice place to be.

Without question, the most utilized feature of the park is the 1¾-mile paved traffic-free road that loops around the lagoon and golf course. Along the track are 18 exercise stations; tennis courts and horseback riding facilities can be found elsewhere in the park. Check out the pavilion on the riverbank for one of the most pleasant views of the Mississippi you'll find. The Audubon Zoo is toward the back of the park, across Magazine Street.

6500 Magazine St., between Broadway and Exposition Blvd. ✆ 504/581-4629. www.auduboninstitute.org. *Note:* The park opens daily at 6am. Even though it officially closes at 10pm, it's not advisable to be there any time after dark.

City Park 🎭🎭🎭   Once part of the Louis Allard plantation, City Park has been here a long time and has seen it all—including that favorite pastime among 18th-century New Orleans gentry: dueling. At the entrance, you'll see a statue of Gen. P. G. T. Beauregard, whose order to fire on Fort Sumter opened the Civil War and who New Orleanians fondly refer to as "the Great Creole." The extensive, beautifully landscaped grounds hold botanical gardens and a conservatory, four golf courses, picnic areas, a restaurant, lagoons for boating and fishing, tennis courts, horses for hire and lovely trails to ride them on, a bandstand, two miniature trains, and **Children's Storyland,** an amusement area with a carousel ride for children (see "Especially for Kids," below). At Christmastime, the mighty oaks, already dripping with Spanish moss, are strung with lights—quite a magical sight—and during Halloween, there is a fabulous haunted house. You'll also find the **New Orleans Museum of Art,** at Collins Diboll Circle, in a building that is itself a work of art (see "Museums & Galleries," above). The park's main office is in the casino building.

1 Palm Dr. ✆ 504/482-4888. Open daily 6am to 7pm.

GARDENS
Longue Vue House & Gardens 🎭🎭   The Longue Vue mansion is a unique expression of Greek Revival architecture set on an 8-acre

estate. It was constructed from 1939 to 1942 for Edgar Stern, who had interests in cotton, minerals, timber, and real estate and was also a noted philanthropist. Longue Vue House and Gardens is listed on the National Register of Historic Places and is accredited by the American Association of Museums. Styled in the manner of an English country house, the mansion was designed to foster a close rapport between indoors and outdoors, with vistas of formal terraces and pastoral woods. Some parts of the enchanting gardens were inspired by those of Generalife, the former summerhouse of the sultans in Granada, Spain.

7 Bamboo Rd., near Metairie. (C) **504/488-5488.** www.longuevue.com. Admission $10 adults, $9 seniors, $5 children and students. Mon–Sat 10am–4:30pm; Sun 1–5pm. Closed Jan 1, Mardi Gras, July 4, Labor Day, Thanksgiving, Dec 25.

A DAY AT THE ZOO

Audubon Zoo 🐾🐾🐾 *Kids*   It's been more than 20 years since the Audubon Zoo underwent a total renovation that turned it from one of the worst zoos in the country into one of the best. The result is a place of justifiable civic pride as well as a terrific destination for visitors with children. Here, in a setting of subtropical plants, waterfalls, and lagoons, some 1,800 animals (including rare and endangered species) live in natural habitats rather than cages. Don't miss the replica of a Louisiana swamp (complete with a rare white gator) or the new "Butterflies in Flight" exhibit, where more than 1,000 butterflies live among lush, colorful vegetation.

6500 Magazine St. (C) **504/581-4629.** www.auduboninstitute.org. Admission $9 adults, $5.75 seniors (over 64), $4.75 children 2–12. Daily 9:30am–5pm; 9:30am–6pm weekends in the summer. Last ticket sold 1 hour before closing. Closed holidays.

4 An Amusement Park

Jazzland 🐾 *Kids*   You know, with a name like that, you just can't help but hope for animatronic rides featuring Louis Armstrong and Ella Fitzgerald. But alas, this is just a standard theme park with a more adorable name. Only the window dressing should differentiate this from any Six Flags and the like. Big ol' roller coasters and a variety of other nausea-inducing rides are set in cutely monikered sections like Pontchartrain Beach, Gospel Garden, and Cajun Country ("just like the Louisiana bayou with boiled crawfish and high-spirited Cajun dancing!" promises the brochure—somehow, though, we don't recall thrill rides in the bayou unless you count swamp tours). Bring the kids and some aspirin for yourself.

12301 Lake Forest Blvd. (I-10 at I-510). (C) **504/253-8100.** Fax 504/253-8136. www.jazzlandthemepark.com. Admission $28 adults, $24 children ages 3–12, free for children under 3. Ask about special promotions. Parking $5. May–Oct Sun–Thurs 10am–10pm; Fri–Sat 10am–midnight (call to see if they extend the season).

5 Especially for Kids

The **French Quarter** in and of itself is fascinating to children over 7. A walkabout with a rest stop for beignets at **Café du Monde** will while away a pleasant morning and give you an opportunity to see the architecture and peek into the shops. Continue (or begin) their roots-music education with a visit to the **Jazz Museum** at the Old U.S. Mint and later to **Preservation Hall** (see chapter 7, "New Orleans After Dark") for a show. For those progeny who aren't terrifically self-conscious, a **horse-and-buggy ride** around the Quarter is very appealing—but save it for later when they start getting tired and you need a tiny bribe to keep them going. The **Musée Conti Wax Museum** (see "Museums," earlier in this chapter), which features effigies of local historical figures and holds guided tours at 11am and 2pm, is an acceptable pick if the weather turns on you. The **Canal Street ferry,** which crosses the Mississippi River to Algiers, is free to pedestrians and offers views of the harbor and skyline. Shuttle service is available from the Algiers ferry landing to **Blaine Kern's Mardi Gras World** (see listing above), where the floats and costumes alone should intrigue even adolescents—whether they'll admit it or not.

Returning to Canal Street, you'll find the **Aquarium of the Americas** (see listing near the beginning of this chapter) with lots of creatures from the deep and the not-so-deep. The *John James Audubon* riverboat (see "Organized Tours," below) chugs from the aquarium to lovely **Audubon Park** (see "Parks & Gardens," earlier in this chapter) and the highly regarded **Audubon Zoological Garden** (see "A Day at the Zoo," above).

And, of course, there is also **Jazzland,** detailed directly above.

The following destinations are particularly well suited for younger children.

Children's Storyland (*Kids*) The under-8 set will be delighted with this playground (rated one of the 10 best in the country by *Child* magazine), where well-known children's stories and rhymes have inspired the decor.

Kids and adults will enjoy the carousel, Ferris wheel, bumper cars, and other rides at the **Carousel Gardens,** also in City Park. It's open weekends only from 11am to 4:30pm. Admission is $1 for anyone over 2; $6 buys unlimited rides.

If you happen to be in New Orleans in December, be sure to take a **carriage ride** through City Park, when thousands of lights turn the landscape and trees into fairy-tale scenery.

City Park at Victory Avenue. © 504/483-9381. Admission $2 adults and children ages 2 and up, free for children under 2. Wed–Fri 10am–12:30pm; Sat–Sun 10am–4:30pm. Closed weekdays Dec–Feb.

Louisiana Children's Museum ★★★ (Kids)   This popular interactive museum is really a playground in disguise that will keep kids occupied for a good couple of hours. Along with changing exhibits, the museum offers an art shop with regularly scheduled projects, a mini grocery store, a chance to be a "star anchor" at a simulated television studio, and activities exploring music, fitness, water, and life itself. If you belong to your local science museum, check your membership card for entry privileges.

420 Julia St., at Tchoupitoulas St. © **504/523-1357.** Fax 504/529-3666. www.lcm.org. Admission $6. Mon–Sat 9:30am–4:30pm; Sun noon–4:30pm.

6 Organized Tours

IN THE FRENCH QUARTER

Historic New Orleans Walking Tours ★★★ (© **504/947-2120**) is the place to go for authenticity. Tour guides are carefully chosen for their combination of knowledge and entertaining manner. The daily French Quarter tours are the best, straightforward, nonspecialized walking tours of this neighborhood. Prices are $12 adults, $10 students and seniors. They also offer a Voodoo Tour and a Garden District Tour.

The Bienville Foundation ★★, run by Robert Batson (© **504/945-6789**), offers a Scandal Tour and a highly popular and recommended Gay Heritage Tour. The tours last roughly 2 hours and generally cost $20 per person. Times and departure locations also change seasonally, so call to find out what's happening when.

Kenneth Holdrich, a professor of American literature at the University of New Orleans, runs **Heritage Literary Tours** ★★, 732 Frenchmen St. (© **504/949-9805**). In addition to a general tour about the considerable literary legacy of the French Quarter, some tours, arranged in advance, can be designed around a specific author, like the Tennessee Williams tour. The narratives are full of facts both literary and historical, are loaded with anecdotes, and are often downright humorous. Tours, minimum 3 people ($20 for adults, $12 for student group rate) are "scheduled for your convenience."

BEYOND THE FRENCH QUARTER

Author Robert Florence (who has written two excellent books on New Orleans cemeteries) loves his work, and his **Historic New Orleans Walking Tours** ✿ (✆ 504/947-2120) are full of meticulously researched facts and more than a few good stories. A very thorough tour of the Garden District and Lafayette Cemetery (a section of town not many of the other companies go into) leaves daily at 11am and 1:45pm from the Garden District Book Shop (in the Rink, corner of Washington Avenue and Prytania Street). Rates are $14 adults, students and seniors $12, free for children under 12.

Tours by Isabelle ✿ (✆ 504/391-3544) conducts a 3-hour, 45-mile city tour for small groups in air-conditioned passenger vans. The fare is $39, and departure times are 9am and 2pm. Make reservations as far in advance as possible. For $46 you can join Isabelle's afternoon Combo Tour, which begins at 1pm and adds Longue Vue House and Gardens to all of the above.

SWAMP TOURS

Swamp tours can be a hoot, particularly if you get a guide who calls alligators to your boat for a little snack of chicken (please keep your hands inside the boat—they tend to look a lot like chicken to a gator). On all of the following tours you're likely to see alligators, bald eagles, waterfowl, egrets, owls, herons, ospreys, feral hogs, otters, beavers, frogs, turtles, raccoons, deer, and nutria (maybe even a black bear or a mink)—and a morning spent floating on the bayou can be mighty pleasant. Most tours last approximately two hours.

Among the companies we recommend are **Half Pint's Swamp Adventures** ✿ (✆ 318/280-5976 or 318/288-1544), **Lil' Cajun Swamp Tours** ✿ (✆ 800/725-3213 or 504/689-3213), **Dr. Wagner's Honey Island Swamp Tours** ✿✿ (✆ 504/641-1769 or 504/242-5877), **Cypress Swamp Tours** ✿✿ (✆ 800/633-0503 or 504/584-4501), and **Gator Swamp Tours** ✿ (✆ 800/875-4287 or 504/484-6100).

MYSTICAL & MYSTERIOUS TOURS

While most of the ghost tours are a bunch of hooey hokum, we are pleased that there is one we can send you to with a clear conscience: **Historic New Orleans Walking Tours** ✿✿✿ (✆ 504/947-2120) offers a Cemetery and Voodoo Tour, the only one that is fact- and not sensation-based, though it is no less entertaining for it. The trip goes through St. Louis Cemetery No. 1, Congo Square, and an active voodoo temple. It leaves Monday through Saturday at 10am and 1:15pm, Sunday at 10am only, from the courtyard at 334-B Royal St. Rates are $15 for adults, students and seniors $13, free for children under 12.

BOAT TOURS

For those interested in doing the Mark Twain thing, a number of operators offer riverboat cruises; some cruises have specific destinations like the zoo or Chalmette, while others just cruise the river and harbor without stopping. Docks are at the foot of Toulouse and Canal streets, and there's ample parking. Call for reservations, which are required for all these tours, and to confirm prices and schedules. Among the boats are the steamboat *Natchez,* 2 Canal St., Suite 1300 (© **800/233-BOAT** or 504/586-8777), the sternwheeler *John James Audubon,* 2 Canal St., Suite 1300 (© **800/233-BOAT** or 504/586-8777), a fun way to reach the Audubon Zoo, and the paddle-wheeler *Creole Queen,* Riverwalk Dock (© **800/445-4109** or 504/524-0814), which departs from the Poydras Street Wharf.

7 Gambling

After years of political and legal wrangling—much of which is still an ongoing source of fun in the daily paper—**Harrah's Casino** finally opened. "Oh, goody," we said, along with other even more sarcastic things, as we experienced severe disorientation stepping inside for the first time. It's exactly like a Vegas casino (100,000 sq. ft. of nearly 3,000 slot machines and 120 tables plus buffet and twice-nightly live "Mardi Gras parade" shows), which is mighty shocking to the system and also a bit peculiar since, like many a Vegas casino, it is Mardi Gras/New Orleans–themed—but exactly like a Vegas casino interpretation of same, which means it's almost exactly *not* like the real thing. We can't understand anyone coming here (and listen, we're fond of Vegas, so we're not anti-casino in general). But if you must go, it can be found on Canal Street at the river (© **504/533-6000**).

8 The Top Nearby Plantations

Laura: A Creole Plantation 🏰🏰🏰 *Tips*   If you see only one plantation, make it this one. Laura is the very model of a modern plantation—that is, when you figure that today's crop is tourism, not sugar cane or indigo. And it's all thanks to the vision of developer and general manager Norman Marmillion, who was determined to make this property rise above the average antebellum mansion. The hoopskirted tours found elsewhere are banished in favor of a comprehensive view of daily life on an 18th- and 19th-century plantation, a cultural history of Louisiana's Creole population, and a dramatic, entertaining, in-depth look at one extended Creole family.

This is a classic Creole house, simple on the outside but with real magic within. Unlike many other plantation homes, much is known about this house and the family that lived here, thanks to extensive records, particularly the detailed memoirs of Laura Locoul.

Basic tours of the main building and the property last about 55 minutes and are organized around true (albeit spiced-up) stories from the history of the home and its residents. (Of special note: The stories that eventually became the beloved Br'er Rabbit were first collected here by a folklorist in the 1870s.)

2247 La. 18, Vacherie, LA 70090. ℰ 225/265-7690. www.lauraplantation.com. Admission $10 adults, $4 students and children, free for children under 6. Closed major holidays.

Oak Alley Plantation ✮✮✮ This is precisely what comes to mind when most people think "plantation." A splendid white house, its porch lined with giant columns, approached by a magnificent drive lined with stately oak trees—yep, it's all here. Consequently, this is the most famous (and probably most photographed) plantation house in Louisiana. (Parts of *Interview with the Vampire* and *Primary Colors* were shot here.) It's also the slickest operation, with a large parking lot, an expensive lunch buffet (bring your own picnic), hoopskirted guides, and golf carts traversing the blacktopped lanes around the property.

The house was built in 1839 by Jacques Telesphore Roman III and was named Bon Séjour—but if you walk out to the levee and look back at the quarter-mile avenue of 300-year-old live oaks, you'll see why steamboat passengers dubbed it "Oak Alley." Roman was so enamored of the trees that he planned his house to have exactly as many columns—28 in all. Oak Alley lay disintegrating until 1914, when Mr. and Mrs. Jefferson Hardin of New Orleans bought it. In 1925, it passed to Mr. and Mrs. Andrew Stewart, whose loving restoration won it National Historic Landmark designation.

Overnight accommodations are available in five-century-old Creole cottages (complete with sitting rooms, porches, and air-conditioning). Rates are $105 to $135 and include breakfast but not a tour. The overpriced restaurant is open for breakfast and lunch daily from 9am to 3pm.

3645 La. 18 (60 miles from New Orleans), Vacherie, LA 70090. ✆ 800/44-ALLEY or 337/265-2151. www.oakalleyplantation.com. Admission $10 adults, $5 students, $3 children 6–12, free for children under 6. Mar–Oct daily 9am–5:30pm; Nov–Feb daily 9am–5pm. Closed Jan 1, Thanksgiving, Dec 25.

9 A Side Trip to Cajun Country

Its official name is Acadiana, and it consists of a rough triangle of Louisiana made up of 22 parishes (counties), from St. Landry Parish at the top of the triangle to the Gulf of Mexico at its base. Lafayette is its "capital," and it's dotted with such towns as St. Martinville, Abbeville, and Eunice. You won't find its boundaries on any map, nor the name "Acadiana" stamped across it. But those 22 parishes are Cajun country, and its history and culture are unique in America.

Contact the **Lafayette Parish Convention and Visitors Commission,** P.O. Box 52066, Lafayette, LA 70505 (✆ **800/346-1958** in the U.S., 800/543-5340 in Canada, or 337/232-3737; fax 337/232-0161; www.lafayettetravel.com). The office is open weekdays from 8:30am to 5pm and weekends from 9am to 5pm.

EUNICE

Founded in 1894 by C.C. Duson, who named the town for his wife, Eunice is a prairie town, not as picturesque as, say, Opelousas or Washington. Some of the most significant Cajun cultural happenings come out of this friendly town, however, including the Saturday morning jam sessions at the Savoy Music Center, the Liberty Theater's live radio broadcasts, and the Acadian Cultural Center.

Acadian Cultural Center 🟅🟅🟅 *Finds*   A terrific small museum, the Acadian Cultural Center is devoted to Cajun life and culture. Exhibits explain everything from the history of the Cajuns to how they worked, played, and got married. The graphics are lively and very readable, and most of the items on display were acquired from local families who have owned them for generations. The center has a collection of videos about Cajun life and will show any and all in the small theater (just ask). Anything by Les Blanc is a good choice, but you might also check out "Anything I Can Catch," a documentary about the nearly lost art of hand-fishing (you need to see someone catch a giant catfish with his bare hands).

250 West Park. © 337/262-6862. Free admission; donations accepted. Daily 8am–5pm.

Liberty Theater ✿✿✿ This classic 1927 theater has been lovingly restored and turned into a showcase for Cajun music. There's live music most nights, but Saturday attracts the big crowds for the "Rendezvous des Cajuns" radio show. From 6 to 8pm, Cajun historian and folklorist Barry Ancelet hosts a live program, simulcast on local radio, that features Cajun and zydeco bands. Oh, and it's all in French. Locals and tourists alike pack the seats and aisles, with dancing on the sloped floor by the stage. Don't understand what's being said? As Barry points out, turn to your neighbors—they will be happy to translate. This is the right way (actually, *the* way) to begin your Saturday night of music in Cajun country.

2nd and Park. © 337/457-6577. Admission $3 and up. www.dodat.whodat.net/eunice/liberty.

Savoy Music Center ✿✿✿ On weekdays, this is a working music store with instruments, accessories, and a small but essential selection of Cajun and zydeco CDs and tapes. In the back is the workshop where musician Marc Savoy lovingly crafts his Acadian accordions—not just fine musical instruments but works of art—amid cabinets bearing his observations and aphorisms. On most Saturday mornings, though, this nondescript Kelly-green building on the outskirts of Eunice is the spiritual center of Cajun music. Keeping alive a tradition that dates from way before electricity, Marc and his wife, Ann, host a jam session where you can watch the tunes being passed down from generation to generation. Here the older musicians are given their due respect, with septuagenarians and octogenarians such as Aldus Roger often leading the sessions while players as young as preteens glean all they can—if they can keep up. Meanwhile, nonmusical guests munch on hunks of boudin sausage and sip beer while listening or socializing. All comers are welcome. But don't come empty-handed—a pound of boudin or a six-pack of something is appropriate. And if you play guitar, fiddle, accordion, or triangle, bring one along and join in. Don't try to show off. Simply follow along with the locals, or you're sure to get a cold shoulder.

Hwy. 190 East (3 miles east of Eunice). © 337/457-9563. Tues–Sat 9am–noon; Tues–Fri 1:30–5pm.

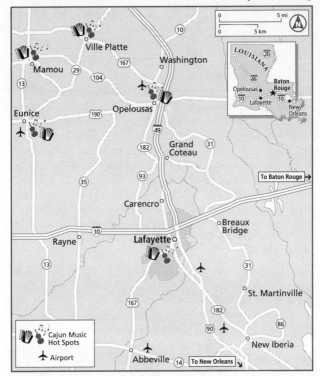

LAFAYETTE

Make your first stop the **Lafayette Parish Convention and Visitors Commission Center,** 1400 NW Evangeline Thruway (✆ **800/ 346-1958** in the U.S., 800/543-5340 in Canada, or 337/232-3808). Turn off I-10 at Exit 103A, go south for about a mile, and you'll find the office in the center of the median. It's open weekdays from 8:30am to 5pm and weekends from 9am to 5pm. Near the intersection of Willow Street and the thruway, the attractive offices are in Cajun-style homes set on landscaped grounds that hold a pond and benches.

We also highly recommend the **Festival International de Louisiane** ✿, a 6-day music and art festival that many find to be a good alternative to the increasingly crowded Jazz Fest. There's an interesting lineup each year, with an emphasis on music from other French-speaking lands. The festival takes place in the center of town with streets blocked off. It's low-key and a manageable size, and best of all, it's free! The festival is held at the end of April; call or write the Festival International de Louisiane, 735 Jefferson St., Lafayette, LA 70501 (℃ **337/232-8086;** www.festivalinternational.com).

SEEING THE SIGHTS

You shouldn't leave the area without exploring its bayous and swamps. Gliding through misty bayous dotted with gnarled cypress trees that drip Spanish moss, seeing native water creatures and birds in their natural habitat, and learning how Cajuns harvest their beloved crawfish is an experience not to be missed. To arrange a voyage, contact Terry Angelle at **Angelle's Atchafalaya Basin Swamp Tours,** Whiskey River Landing, P.O. Box 111, Cecilia, LA 70521 (℃ **337/228-8567**). His tour gives you nearly 2 hours in the third-largest swamp in the United States with Cajun guides who travel the mysterious waterways as easily as you and I walk city streets. The fares are $12 for adults, $10 for seniors, and $6 for children under 12.

Vermilionville ⟨⟨ This reconstruction of a Cajun-Creole settlement from the 1765 to 1890 era sits on the banks of the brooding Bayou Vermilion, adjacent to the airport on U.S. 90. While it may sound like a "Cajunland" theme park, it's actually quite a valid operation. Hundreds of skilled artisans labored to restore original Cajun homes and to reconstruct others that were typical of such a village. (It *must* be authentic; one Cajun we know refuses to go, not because he dislikes the place or finds it offensive but because "I already *live* in Vermilionville!")

1600 Surrey St. ℃ **800/99-BAYOU** or 337/233-4077. www.vermilionville.org. Admission $8 adults, $6.50 seniors, $5 students, free for children under 6. Tues–Sun 10am–4pm. Closed Jan 1, Dec 25. Take I-10 to Exit 103A. Take Evangeline Thruway south to Surrey St. and then follow signs.

ACCOMMODATIONS

Aaah! T'Frere's Bed & Breakfast ⟨⟨⟨ Everything about this place cracks us up, from the name (it's so they're first in any alphabetical listing) to the evening "T'Juleps" to the cheerful owners themselves, Pat and Maugie Pastor—the latter would be adorable even if she didn't daily preside over breakfast in red silk pajamas (she and Pat used to operate restaurants, and after years in chef's whites, she wanted as radical a change as possible). Oh, wait, did we mention the goofily named breakfasts? Daily extravaganzas, easily the best around, like the "Ooh-La-La, Mardi Gras" breakfast—eggs in white sauce on ham-topped biscuits, cheese and garlic grits, tomato grille, and chocolate muffins? The rooms (and grounds) are gorgeous, though the ones in the Garconniere in the back are a bit more Country Plain than Victorian Fancy. Look, they've been in business for years, they know how to do this right; just stay here, okay?

1905 Verot School Rd., Lafayette, LA 70508. ✆ **800/984-9347.** Fax 337/984-9347. www.tfreres.com. 6 units. $100 double; extra person $30. Rates include full breakfast. AE, DISC, MC, V. **Amenities:** Welcome drinks and Cajun canapés. *In room:* A/C, TV, dataport, coffeemaker, private bath, terrycloth robes.

DINING

Prejean's 🎯🎯 CAJUN   From the outside, Prejean's looks pretty much the way it always has, an unpretentious family restaurant with live Cajun music every night. But inside, chef James Graham has turned Prejean's from a fried seafood emporium to one of Acadiana's finest restaurants, showcasing the best ingredients and styles Cajun cuisine has to offer. Dance if there's room—but do whatever's necessary to sample the full range of excellent Cajun fare. Seafood is the specialty, with large menu sections devoted to fish, shrimp, oysters, crawfish, and crab dishes, and a few alligator dishes.

3480 I-49 North. ✆ **337/896-3247.** Fax 337/896-3278. www.prejeans.com. Reservations strongly recommended. Children's menu $3.50–$8.95; main courses $12–$24. AE, DC, DISC, MC, V. Sun–Thurs 11am–10pm; Fri–Sat 11am–11pm. Take I-10 to Exit 103B and then I-49 north to Exit 2/Gloria Switch.

Randol's Restaurant and Cajun Dance Hall 🎯 CAJUN   In addition to better-than-average Cajun food, Randol's offers a good-size, popular dance floor where dancers are likely to be locals enjoying their own *fais-do-do*. A house specialty is the seafood platter, which includes a cup of seafood gumbo, fried shrimp, oysters, and catfish, stuffed crab, crawfish étouffée, bread, and coleslaw.

2320 Kaliste Saloom Rd. ✆ **800/962-2586** or 337/981-7080. www.randols.com. Reservations accepted only for parties of 20 or more. Main courses $7.95–$17.95. MC, V. Sun–Thurs 5–10pm; Fri–Sat 5–11pm. Closed major holidays. From New Orleans, take I-10 west to Exit 103A. Follow Evangeline Thruway to Pinhook Rd., turn right, and follow Pinhook to Kaliste Saloom Rd. (right). Randol's is on your right.

VILLE PLATTE

If you want to take some Cajun music with you, you have a good reason to detour to the town of Ville Platte.

Floyd's Record Shop 🎯🎯   Floyd Soileau is in some ways the unofficial mayor of Acadiana. But he's meant much more to the region as one of the key entrepreneurs of bayou music. Long before Cajun and zydeco were known outside the region, he was recording and releasing the music, selling records by mail order and at this store. This is a must-stop locale with a fine selection of Floyd's releases by such artists as D. L. Menard (the Cajun Hank Williams) and Clifton Chenier (the King of Zydeco).

434 E. Main St. ✆ **337/363-2138**. Fax 337-363-5622. DISC, MC, V. Mon–Fri 8:30am–5:30pm; Sat 8:30am–5pm.

DINING

The Pig Stand ⭐⭐ PIG   A local institution, the Pig Stand is a little dump of a local hangout that serves divine barbecued chicken and other Southern specialties for cheap prices. It's a treat—don't miss it. And it's just down the street from Floyd's in case you worked up an appetite buying music.

318 E. Main St. ✆ **337/363-2883**. Main courses $11.99 and under. MC, V. Mon–Thurs 5am–10pm; Fri–Sat 5am–11pm; Sun 5am–2pm.

6

Shopping

Shopping in New Orleans is a highly evolved leisure activity with a shop for every strategy and a fix for every shopaholic—and every budget. The range is as good as it gets—many a clever person has come to New Orleans just to open up a quaint boutique filled with strange items gathered from all parts of the globe or produced by local, somewhat twisted, folk artists.

1 Major Hunting Grounds

CANAL PLACE At the foot of Canal Street (365 Canal St.) where it reaches the Mississippi River, this sophisticated shopping center holds more than 50 shops, many of them branches of the world's most elegant retailers: Brooks Brothers, Bally of Switzerland, Saks Fifth Avenue, Gucci, and Jaeger. Open Monday through Wednesday from 10am to 6pm, Thursday from 10am to 8pm, Friday and Saturday from 10am to 7pm, and Sunday from noon to 6pm.

THE FRENCH MARKET Shops in the Market begin on Decatur Street across from Jackson Square; offerings include candy, cookware, fashion, crafts, toys, New Orleans memorabilia, and candles. It's open from 10am to 6pm (and the Farmer's Market Café du Monde is open 24 hr.). Quite honestly, you'll find a lot of junk, but there are some good buys mixed in.

JACKSON BREWERY Just across from Jackson Square at 600–620 Decatur St., the old brewery building has been transformed into a jumble of shops, cafes, restaurants, and entertainment. Many shops in the Brewery close at 5:30 or 6pm, before the Brewery itself. Open Sunday through Thursday from 10am to 9pm, Friday and Saturday from 10am to 10pm.

JULIA STREET From Camp Street down to the river on Julia Street, you'll find many of the city's best contemporary art galleries. Of course, some of the works are a bit pricey, but there are good deals to be had if you're collecting and fine art to be seen if you're not. You'll find many of them listed below.

MAGAZINE STREET   This is the Garden District's premier shopping street. More than 140 shops (some of which are listed below) line the street in 19th-century brick storefronts and quaint cottage-like buildings. Among the offerings are antiques, art galleries, boutiques, crafts, and dolls. If you're so inclined, you could shop all the way from Washington Street to Audubon Park. Pick up a copy of *Shopper's Dream,* a free guide and map to most of the stores on 6 miles of Magazine, which is available all along the street.

NEW ORLEANS CENTRE   New Orleans's newest shopping center, at 1400 Poydras St., features a glass atrium and includes upscale stores like Lord & Taylor and Macy's. There are three levels of specialty shops and restaurants. Open Monday through Saturday from 10am to 8pm and Sunday from noon to 6pm.

RIVERBEND   The Riverbend district is in the Carrollton area. To reach it, ride the St. Charles Avenue streetcar to stop 44 and then walk down Maple Street 1 block to Dublin Park, the site of an old public market that was once lined with open stalls. Nowadays, renovated shops inhabit the old general store, a produce warehouse made of bargeboard, and the town surveyor's raised-cottage home.

RIVERWALK MARKETPLACE *Kids*   A mall is a mall is a mall, unless it has picture windows offering a Mississippi panorama. Even though you almost certainly have a mall at home, this is worth visiting. Besides, if you need T-shirts instead of sweaters or vice versa, this is the closest Gap to the Quarter. Note that the best river views are in the section of the mall closest to the Convention Center. It's the usual mall suspects: Victoria's Secret, Museum Store, Discovery Store, Banana Republic, Eddie Bauer. 1 Poydras St. Open Monday through Thursday from 10am to 9pm, Friday and Saturday from 10am to 10pm, and Sunday from 12:30 to 5:30pm.

2 Shopping A to Z

ANTIQUES

Audubon Antiques   Audubon has everything from collectible curios to authentic antique treasures at reasonable prices. There are two floors of goods, so be prepared to lose yourself. 2025 Magazine St. ℂ 504/581-5704. Mon–Sat 10:30am–5pm; Sun call first.

Boyer Antiques & Doll Shop   In addition to an assortment of antiques, you'll find an enchanting collection of old dolls, dollhouses and furniture, and toys. Most date from the 19th and early 20th century. 241 Chartres St. ℂ 504/522-4513. Mon–Sat 11am–5pm.

Bush Antiques and Beds Au Beau Reve This wonderful treasure trove features impressive European religious art and objects and a beautiful array of beds—sadly, the latter are out of most of our price ranges, but boy, are they fantastic. An extra treat is the collection of folk art on the rear patio. 2109–2111 Magazine St. ✆ **504/581-3518.** Fax 504/581-6889. www.bushantiques.com. Mon–Sat 10am–5pm.

Charbonnet & Charbonnet If country pine is what you're looking for, you'll find it here. Charbonnet & Charbonnet has some beautiful English and Irish pieces. In addition, custom furnishings are made on-site. 2728 Magazine St. ✆ **504/891-9948.** charbcharb@aol.com. Mon–Sat 9am–5pm.

Dixon & Dixon of Royal Dixon & Dixon features 18th- and 19th-century European fine art and antiques, jewelry, grandfather clocks, and Oriental rugs. The collection of tall-case clocks is one of the largest in the country. The Dixon & Dixon company is a long-standing family-run business; the firm has helped many younger collectors make some of their initial purchases. 237 Royal St. ✆ **800/848-5148** or 504/524-0282. Fax 504/524-7378. www.dixon-antiques.net. Mon–Sat 9am–5:30pm; Sun 10am–5pm.

Jack Sutton Antiques In some ways, the Suttons are to jewelry and antiques what the Brennans are to food: one family, different businesses. Of the number of Suttons around New Orleans, this one, our favorite, specializes in jewelry and objects. The selection of estate jewelry ("estate" meaning "older than yesterday but less than 100 years") is often better than that at other antiques stores—the author's engagement ring came from here—but due to the ebb and flow of the estate business, you can never be sure what may be offered. The store has a room devoted to "men's gift items" such as antique gambling, cigar, and drinking paraphernalia. 315 Royal St. ✆ **504/522-0555.** Fax 504/523-2762. Mon–Sat 10am–5:30pm; Sun 11am–5pm.

Keil's Antiques Kiel's, established in 1899 and currently run by the fourth generation of the founding family, has a considerable collection of 18th- and 19th-century French and English furniture, chandeliers, jewelry, and decorative items. 325 Royal St. ✆ **504/522-4552.** www.keilsantiques.com. Mon–Sat 9am–5pm.

Lucullus An unusual shop, Lucullus has a wonderful collection of culinary antiques as well as 17th-, 18th-, and 19th-century furnishings to "complement the grand pursuits of cooking, dining, and imbibing." They recently opened a second shop at 3932 Magazine St. 610 Chartres St. ✆ **504/528-9620.** Fax 504/561-8030. Mon–Sat 9:30am–5pm.

Magazine Arcade Antiques This large, fascinating shop once housed the Garden District's classiest merchant. Today, it holds an exceptional collection of 18th- and 19th-century European, Asian, and American furnishings as well as music boxes, dollhouse miniatures, cloisonné, lacquer, cameos, opera glasses, old medical equipment, windup phonographs, and antique toys. Allow yourself plenty of time to browse through it all. 3017 Magazine St. © 504/895-5451. Mon and Wed–Sat 10am–5pm.

Manheim Galleries At Manheim Galleries, you'll find an enormous collection of continental, English, and Oriental furnishings sharing space with porcelains, jade, silver, and fine paintings. Manheim Galleries is also the agent for Boehm Birds. 403–409 Royal St. © 504/568-1901. Mon–Sat 9am–5pm.

Miss Edna's Antiques Miss Edna's carries eclectic antiques—furniture, specialty items, curios—and paintings, with a focus on 19th-century works. Miss Edna recently moved a few feet up Magazine, doubling her inventory and expanding her art collection. 2035 Magazine St. © 504/524-1897. Mon–Sat 10am–5pm.

Rothschild's Antiques Rothschild's is a fourth-generation furniture merchandiser. Some of the most interesting things you'll find here are antique and custom-made jewelry (the store is also a full-service jeweler). There's a fine selection of antique silver, marble mantels, porcelains, and English and French furnishings. Rothschild's devotes tens of thousands of square feet to displaying and warehousing antiques. 241 and 321 Royal St. © 504/523-5816 or 504/523-2281. Mon–Sat 9:30am–5:30pm; Sun by appointment.

Sigle's Antiques & Metalcraft If you've fallen in love with the lacy ironwork that drips from French Quarter balconies, this is the place to pick out some pieces to take home. Sigle's has also converted some of the ironwork into useful household items. 935 Royal St. © 504/522-7647. Mon–Sat 10am–4pm.

Whisnant Galleries The quantity and variety of merchandise in this shop is mind-boggling. You'll find all sorts of unusual and unique antique collectibles including items from Ethiopia, Russia, Greece, South America, Morocco, and other parts of North Africa and the Middle East. 222 Chartres St. © 504/524-9766. www.whisnantantiques.com. Mon–Sat 9:30am–5:30pm; Sun 10am–5pm.

ART GALLERIES

With one major exception, galleries in New Orleans follow the landscape of antique shops: **Royal and Magazine streets.**

Ariodante A contemporary craft gallery, Ariodante features handcrafted furniture, glass, ceramics, jewelry, and decorative accessories by nationally acclaimed artists. Rotating shows offer a detailed look at works by various artists. 535 Julia St. ℂ **504/524-3233.** Tues–Sat 11am–5pm.

Arius Art Tiles Arius designs and sells art tiles of the sort you might have seen if you've ever been to Santa Fe, New Mexico. In fact, many of the tiles are made in Santa Fe, and Arius has a sister gallery in New Mexico. This is no trend-chasing or fly-by-night operation; the proprietors have been in the business for 25 years. Both Southwest and Louisiana designs are made here. You can also place a custom order. 504 St. Peter St. ℂ **504/529-1665.** Fax 504/529-1665. Daily 9:30am–5pm.

Arthur Roger Gallery Arthur Roger sets the pace for the city's fine-art galleries. Since opening in New Orleans 20 years ago, Roger has played a major role in developing the art community and in tying it to the art world in New York. Time and again, he has taken chances—moving early into the Warehouse District and briefly opening a second gallery in New York—and he continues to do so, scheduling shows that range from strongly regional work to the far-flung. The gallery represents many artists including Francis Pavy, Ida Kohlmeyer, Douglas Bourgeois, Paul Lucas, Clyde Connell, Willie Birch, Gene Koss, and George Dureau. 432 Julia St. ℂ **504/522-1999.** www.artroger.com. Mon–Sat 10am–5pm.

Bergen Galleries Bergen Galleries has the city's largest selection of posters and limited-edition graphics on such subjects as Mardi Gras, jazz, and the city itself and by such artists as Erté, Icart, Nagel, Maimon, and Tarkay. Bergen also features a large collection of works by sought-after African-American artists. The service by Margarita and her staff is friendly and extremely personable. 730 Royal St. ℂ **800/ 621-6179** or 504/523-7882. www.bergengalleries.com. Sun–Thurs 9am–9pm; Fri–Sat 9am–10pm.

Berta's and Mina's Antiquities In years past, Antiquities was just another place that bought and sold antiques and secondhand furniture and art. That all ended on the day in 1993 that Nilo Lanzas (Berta's husband and Mina's dad) began painting. Now you can barely see the furniture in the shop for all the new art. Dubbed "folk art" or "outsider art," Lanzas's works are colorful scenes from life in New Orleans or his native Latin America, stories out of the Bible, or images sprung from his imagination. His paintings are on wood with titles or commentaries painted on the frames. Don't be surprised to find Lanzas quietly painting away near the counter—he paints 10 to 12 hours a day. 4138 Magazine St. © **504/895-6201**. Mon–Sat 10am–6pm; Sun 11am–6pm.

Bryant Galleries This gallery represents renowned artists Ed Dwight, Fritzner Lamour, and Leonardo Nierman, among others. The varied work may include jazz bronzes, glasswork, and graphics. The staff is very helpful; if you can't get here during the hours listed, ask nicely and chances are they'll make arrangements for you. 316 Royal St. © **800/844-1994** or 504/525-5584. art@bryant.com. Sun–Thurs 10am–5:30pm; Fri–Sat 10am–9pm.

Carabaux Galleries This gallery's collection is built around the works of William Tolliver, an African-American artist from Mississippi whose untimely death at the age of 48 in 2000 received national coverage. Tolliver came to painting relatively late in his life and without formal training. Despite this, he quickly became an internationally recognized contemporary Impressionist painter. (He was chosen to create the official poster for the 1996 Summer Olympics.) At Carabaux Galleries, formally Galerie Royale, you can find a selection of Tolliver's museum-quality pieces as well as work by other artists. 3646 Magazine St. © **504/523-1588**. www.groyale.com. Daily 10am–6pm (11am–6pm on some Sun) or by appointment.

Cole Pratt Gallery, Ltd This gallery showcases the work of 35 Southern artists whose creations include abstract and realist paintings, sculptures, and ceramics. The art is of the highest quality and the prices surprisingly reasonable. 3800 Magazine St. © **504/891-6789**. Fax 504/891-6611. www.coleprattgallery.com. Tues–Sat 10am–5:30pm. July–Sept closes at 5pm.

The Davis Galleries One of two world-class galleries in New Orleans (the other being A Gallery for Fine Photography), this may be the best place in the world for Central and West African traditional art. The owner makes regular trips to Africa for collecting. Works on display might include sculpture, costuming, basketry, textiles, weapons, and jewelry. 904 Louisiana Ave. © **504/895-5206**. By appointment only.

Diane Genre Oriental Art and Antiques If all of the 18th- and 19th-century European antiques in the stores along Royal are starting to look the same, it's time to step into Diane Genre's shop. By comparison, the atmosphere in here seems as delicate as one of the ancient East Asian porcelains on display. Get an eyeful of furniture, 18th-century Japanese woodblock prints, and a world-class collection of Chinese and Japanese textiles. There are also scrolls, screens, engravings, and lacquers. 431 Royal St. ℂ **504/595-8945.** Fax 504-899-8651. www.dianegenreorientalart.com. By appointment only.

Dyansen Gallery A branch of the Dyansen family galleries (there are others in San Francisco and New York), this location features graphics, sculpture, and original gouaches by Erté. Other artists represented include Richard Estes, LeRoy Neiman, and Paul Wegner. 433 Royal St. ℂ **800/211-6984** or 504/523-2902. www.dyansengallery.com. Sun–Thurs 10am–6pm; Fri–Sat 10am–8pm; and by appointment.

Galerie Simonne Stern This gallery features paintings, drawings, and sculptures by contemporary artists. Recent shows have included the works of John Alexander, George Dunbar, and Simon Gunning. 518 Julia St. ℂ **504/529-1118.** www.sterngallery.com. Tues–Sat 10am–5pm; Mon by appointment.

A Gallery for Fine Photography It would be a mistake to skip this incredibly well stocked photography gallery. Even if you aren't in the market, it's worth looking around. Owner Joshua Mann Pailet (a photographer) calls this "the only museum in the world that's for sale." It really is like a museum of photography, with just about every period and style represented and frequent shows of contemporary artists. The staff is more than happy to show you some of the many photos in the files. The gallery emphasizes New Orleans and Southern history and contemporary culture (you can buy Ernest Bellocq's legendary Storyville photos) as well as black culture and music. There is something in just about every price range as well as a terrific collection of photography books if that better fits your budget. 322 Royal St. ℂ **504/568-1313.** Fax 504/568-1322. www.agallery.com. Mon–Sat 10am–6pm; Sun 11am–6pm.

Hanson Gallery Hanson Gallery shows paintings, sculpture, and limited-edition prints by contemporary artists such as Peter Max, Frederick Hart, Pradzynski, Anoro, Thysell, Deckbar, Zjawinska, Erickson, LeRoy Neiman, Richard MacDonald, and Behrens. 229 Royal St. ℂ **504/524-8211.** www.hansongallery-nola.com. Mon–Sat 10am–6pm; Sun 11am–5pm.

Hilderbrand Gallery Hilderbrand Gallery represents a number of international, national, and local artists including Ding Massimo Boccuni, Manfred Egender, Jim Sohr, Walter Rutkowski, Christian Stock, Cort Savage, Mark Westervelt, and Karl Heinz-Strohle. The gallery is a private showroom; call to get information about the artists and to schedule a visit. 4524 Magazine St. ℂ **504/895-3312** or 504/897-3905. By appointment only.

Kurt E. Schon, Ltd   Here you'll find the country's largest inventory of 19th-century European paintings. Works include French and British Impressionist and post-Impressionist paintings as well as art from the Royal Academy and the French Salon. Only a fraction of the paintings in the gallery's inventory are housed at this location, but if you're a serious collector, you can make an appointment to visit the St. Louis Street gallery at 510 St. Louis St. 523 Royal St. ℂ 504/524-5462. www.kurteschonltd.com. Mon–Sat 9am–5pm.

LeMieux Galleries   LeMieux represents contemporary artists and craftspeople from Louisiana and the Gulf Coast. They include Dr. Bob, Charles Barbier, Pat Bernard, Mary Lee Eggart, Leslie Elliottsmith, David Lambert, Shirley Rabe Masinter, Evelyn Menge, Dennis Perrin, Kathleen Sidwell, Leslie Staub, and Kate Trepagnier. 332 Julia St. ℂ 504/522-5988. Fax 504/522-5682. www.lemieuxgalleries.com. Mon–Sat 10am–6pm.

Marguerite Oestreicher Fine Arts   Like the other Julia Street galleries, this one concentrates on contemporary painting, sculpture, and photography. It also consistently shows work by emerging artists. The gallery's recent shows have included works by Drew Galloway and Raine Bedsole. 720 Julia St. ℂ 504/581-9253. Fax 504/566-1946. Tues–Sat 10am–5pm and by appointment.

Mario Villa   Mario Villa is New Orleans's undisputed king of design—or at least the city's most ubiquitous designer. You can see his hand (or mind, anyway) at work in the fancy Kevin Graham restaurant, Sapphire, and on the exterior columns of the Wyndham Riverfront Hotel. To get the full experience, drop into Villa's uptown showroom to get a good idea of his aesthetic. There are canvas rugs; plush sofas; wrought-iron chairs, lamps, and tables with organic twists and turns; and a liberal spray of photographs and paintings. It may not be to your taste, but Villa's work is certainly provocative and visually stimulating. Take a moment to look at one of the beds in the front rooms—if they won't enhance your dreams, for good or ill, nothing will. 3908 Magazine St. ℂ 504/895-8731. Fax 504/895-8167. mariovilla@earthlink.net. Tues–Sat 10am–5pm.

New Orleans School of Glassworks and Printmaking Studio   This institution serves multiple purposes. Here, within 20,000 square feet of studio space, are a 550-pound tank of hot molten glass and a pre–Civil War press. Established glasswork artists and master printmakers display their work in the on-site gallery and teach classes in glassblowing, kiln-fired glass, hand-engraved printmaking, papermaking, and bookbinding. Absolutely unique to the area, the place is worth a visit during gallery hours. Daily glassblowing, fusing, and slumping demonstrations are open for viewing. 727 Magazine St. ☎ **504/529-7277**. Mon–Sat 11am–5pm. Closed Sat June–Aug.

Peligro   A bit out of the way but worth checking out, Peligro is one of the best folk-art galleries in the city, with an emphasis on primitive and outsider art. The owners have a terrific eye for up-and-coming artists. Unfortunately, they seem to have de-emphasized the smaller items that made for marvelous, original gifts. 305 Decatur St. ☎ **504/581-1706**. Mon–Thurs 10am–6pm; Fri–Sat 10am–8pm; Sun noon–6pm.

Shadyside Pottery   Master potter Charles Bohn can be seen at his wheel all day Tuesday through Friday and until mid-afternoon on Saturday. He specializes in the Japanese tradition of *Raku*, a type of pottery that has a "cracked" look. 3823 Magazine St. ☎ **504/897-1710**. Mon–Sat 10am–5pm.

Wyndy Morehead Fine Arts   This gallery shows contemporary fine art in many media. It represents more than 75 local and national artists including Nofa Dixon, Robert Rector, William Lewis, Ron Richmond, and Joan Steiman. 3926 Magazine St. ☎ **504/ 269-8333**. www.wyndymoreheadfinearts.com. Mon–Sat 10am–5:30pm.

Zinsel Contemporary Fine Art   This fine-art gallery shows paintings, sculpture, photography, and works on paper by contemporary local, national, and international artists. If you're hopping along gallery row on Julia Street, be sure to hop in here; it regularly shows some of the best work on the strip. 624 Julia St. ☎ **504/588-9999**. Mon–Sat 10am–5pm.

BOOKS

Literary enthusiasts will find many destinations in New Orleans. **Maple Street Book Shop,** 7523 Maple St. (☎ **504/866-4916**), is an uptown mecca for bookworms; the **Maple Street Children's Book Shop** is next door at 7529 Maple St. (☎ **504/861-2105**); and **Beaucoup Books** is at 5414 Magazine St. (☎ **504/895-2663**).

Beckham's Bookshop   Beckham's has two entire floors of old editions, rare secondhand books, and thousands of classical LPs that will tie up your whole afternoon or morning if you don't tear yourself away. The owners also operate **Librairie Bookshop,** 823 Chartres St. (☎ **504/525-4837**), which has a big collection of secondhand books. 228 Decatur St. ☎ **504/522-9875**. Daily 10am–6pm.

Faubourg Marigny Bookstore   This well-stocked gay and lesbian bookstore also carries some local titles. It has a used section,

CDs, posters, cards, and gifts (all with a more or less gay or lesbian slant) and holds regular readings and signings. The staff makes this a fine resource center—you can call them for local gay and lesbian info. 600 Frenchmen St. (C) **504/943-9875**. Mon–Fri 10am–8pm; Sat–Sun 10am–6pm.

Faulkner House Books   This shop is on a lot of walking tours of the French Quarter because it's where Nobel Prize–winner William Faulkner lived while he was writing his early works *Mosquitoes* and *Soldiers' Pay.* Those who step inside instead of just snapping a photo and walking on will find something remarkable: possibly the best selection per square foot of any bookstore in the whole wide world, with every bit of shelf space occupied by a book that's both highly collectible and of literary value. The shop holds a large collection of Faulkner first editions and rare and first-edition classics by many other authors, and it has a particularly comprehensive collection of New Orleans–related work. Taking up one room and a hallway, Faulkner House feels like a portion of somebody's private home— which it is—but the selection of books here is almost magical. 624 Pirates Alley. (C) **504/524-2940**. www.faulknerbooks.com. Daily 10am–6pm.

Garden District Book Shop   Owner Britton Trice has stocked his medium-size shop with just about every regional book you can think of; if you want a New Orleans or Louisiana-specific book, no matter what the exact focus (interiors, exteriors, food, Creoles, you name it), you should be able to find it here. This is also where Anne Rice does book signings whenever she has a new release. They usually have autographed copies of her books plus fancy special editions of Rice titles that they publish themselves and a large selection of signed books by local and non-local authors (from Clive Barker to James Lee Burke). 2727 Prytania St. (in the Rink). (C) **504/895-2266**. Fax 504/895-0111. GDKreweaol.com. Mon–Sat 10am–6pm; Sun 11am–5pm.

George Herget Books   George Herget Books is another of New Orleans's great bookstores. More than 20,000 rare and used books covering absolutely every subject imaginable await browsers and collectors. If you're interested in a particular book on local subjects or by local artists, put this shop on your list—the local and regional selection may be limited, but some of the hardest-to-find books surface here. 3109 Magazine St. (C) **504/891-5595**. Mon–Sat 11am–6pm; Sun 11am–5pm.

Kaboom   On the edge of the Quarter, Kaboom is a bit off the beaten path, but bibliophiles should make the trek. This is a reader's bookstore, thanks to an owner whose knowledge of literature is almost scary. The stock (used books only) tends to lean heavily on fiction, but there is little you won't find here. 915 Barracks St. ℂ **504/ 529-5780.** kaboombks@aol.com. Daily 11am–6pm.

CANDIES & PRALINES

Aunt Sally's Praline Shop   At Aunt Sally's, you can watch skilled workers perform the 150-year-old process of cooking the original Creole pecan pralines right before your eyes. You'll know they're fresh. The large store also has a broad selection of regional cookbooks, Creole and Cajun foods, folk and souvenir dolls, and local memorabilia. In addition, Aunt Sally's has a collection of zydeco, Cajun, R&B, and jazz CDs and cassettes. They'll ship any purchase. In the French Market, 810 Decatur St. ℂ **800/642-7257** or 504/944-6090. www.auntsallys.com. Daily 8am–8pm.

Laura's Candies   Laura's is said to be the city's oldest candy store, established in 1913. It has fabulous pralines, but it also has rich, delectable golf-ball-size truffles—our personal favorite indulgence, although they've gotten a bit pricey. 600 Conti St; new location at 938 Royal St. ℂ **800/992-9699** or 504/525-3880. www.laurascandies.com. Daily 10am–7pm.

Leah's Candy Kitchen   After you've tried all of the city's Creole candy shops, you might very well come to the conclusion that Leah's tops the list. Everything here, from the candy fillings to the chocolate-covered pecan brittle, is made from scratch by second- and third-generation members of Leah Johnson's praline-cookin' family. 714 St. Louis St. ℂ **888/523-5324** or 504/523-5662. Daily 10am–6pm.

COSTUMES & MASKS

Costumery is big business in New Orleans, and not just in the days before Lent. In this city, you never know *when* you're going to want or need a costume. A number of shops in New Orleans specialize in props for Mardi Gras, Halloween, and other occasions. Here's a tip: New Orleanians often sell their costumes back to these shops after Ash Wednesday, and you can sometimes pick up a one-time-worn outfit at a small fraction of its original cost.

Little Shop of Fantasy   In the Little Shop of Fantasy, owners Mike Stark, Laura and Anne Guccione, and Jill Kellys sell the work of a number of local artists and more than 20 mask makers. Mike creates the feathered masks, Jill does the velvet hats and costumes, and Laura and Anne produce homemade toiletries. Some of the masks and hats are just fun and fanciful, but there are many fashionable ones as well. There are lots of clever voodoo items here, too, plus unusual toys and novelties. 523 Dumaine St. ℭ **504/529-4243.** Mon–Tues and Thurs–Sat 11am–6pm; Sun 1–6pm.

Mardi Gras Center   Mardi Gras Center carries sizes 2 to 50 and has a wide selection of new, ready-made costumes as well as used outfits. It also carries accessories such as beads, doubloons, wigs, masks, hats, makeup, jewelry, and Mardi Gras decorations. 831 Chartres St. ℭ **504/524-4384.** www.mardigrascenter.com. Mon–Sat 10am–5pm; Sun 10am–3pm.

Uptown Costume & Dance Company   The walls of this small store are covered with spooky monster masks, goofy arrow-through-the-head-type tricks, hats, wigs, makeup, and all other manner of playfulness. It draws a steady, yearlong stream of loyal customers: kids going to parties, dancers, clowns, actors. Conventioneers come here for rental disguises. The shop designs party uniforms for a number of Mardi Gras krewe members. Owner Cheeryll Berlier also creates a limited number of wacky Mardi Gras tuxedo jackets, which get gobbled up quickly. 4326 Magazine St. ℭ **504/895-7969.** Mon–Fri 10am–6pm; Sat 10am–5pm.

FASHION & VINTAGE CLOTHING

Billy Bob's   This is a clothing store featuring cool men's and women's contemporary clothing plus a fun atmosphere, thanks to hip music and Romeo the dog. Everything is under $100—Billy Bob's shoots for affordable but not cheesy. (T-shirts are funky and fun, not the "I've fallen and I can't reach my beer" kind found elsewhere in the Quarter.) 225 N. Peters St. ℭ **504/524-5578.** Mon–Sat 10am–6pm; Sun 11am–6pm.

Body Hangings   Cloaks have seen more favorable eras. Ever hopeful, though, this place is keeping the flame alive until the Sherlock Holmes look comes back in style. It has a good collection of capes, scarves, and cloaks. Men's and women's cloaks are available in wool, cotton, corduroy, and velveteen. 835 Decatur St. ℭ **800/574-1823** or 504/524-9856. Daily 10am–6pm.

The Grace Note   Primarily a clothing store, Grace Note also features some gifts. It's a bit pricey, but the clothes are stunning. The designers here work with vintage and new materials, and what they come up with is usually lush, memorable, and very touchable. If you want to swan around town, feeling as though you've stepped out of an 1800s novel, this is the place for you. The gift items come from "architectural or religious fragments"—think distressed wood and peeling paint—producing one-of-a-kind objects that evoke

turn-of-the-20th-century through 1940s styles. 900 Royal St. © 504/
522-1513. Mon–Sat 10am–6pm; Sun 11am–5pm.

Jazz Rags   This store is stuffed full of stylish, upscale, but reasonably priced men's and women's vintage clothes. You can find locals
combing the racks here for Mardi Gras and Halloween costumes.
The snazzily dressed owner, usually accompanied by Ardvis the
friendly hound (who hangs out at several nearby stores), is clearly a
fashion plate—ask her advice for picking out an outfit. 1215 Decatur
St. © 504/523-2942. Thurs–Mon noon–6pm.

Jim Smiley Fine Vintage Clothing   Jim Smiley has attracted
national media recognition as one of the best shops in the world. It
features exceptional men's and women's attire, accessories, linens,
and textiles from the 19th and 20th centuries. 2001 Magazine St.
© 504/528-9449. mondochuck@aol.com. Daily 11am–5pm.

Mariposa   Our favorite vintage clothing shop on Magazine Street
has the right ratio of selection to cost (high for the former, low—or
at least low-ish—for the latter) plus a very helpful and fun sales staff.
2038 Magazine St. © 504/523-3037. Mon–Sat 11am–6pm; Sun noon–5pm.

Trashy Diva   Despite the name, there is nothing trashy about the
vintage clothes found here. They are absolute treasures, not the
usual haphazard bulk found at other vintage shops, and in terrific
shape, dating from the turn of the 20th century to the 1960s. The
drawback is that you will pay through the nose for them. Many
items are at least three figures—indeed, there was one showpiece
1920s flapper dress on display behind the counter recently, made
of pure gold cloth, all yours for a mere $700. You can also admire
garments from divas like Bette Davis and Joan Crawford that are
on display. 829 Chartres St. © 504/581-4555. www.trashydiva.com. Daily
noon–6pm.

Violet's   Our greatest temptation among French Quarter shops,
given how we feel about romantic, Edwardian, and 1920s-inspired
clothes in lush fabrics like velvet and satin. There are some dazzling
creations here, plus accessories (jewelry, hats, scarves). A second
location is at 507 St. Ann St. (© **504/588-9894**). 808 Chartres St.
© 504/569-0088. Fax 504/569-0089. Daily 10am–8pm.

Yvonne LaFleur—New Orleans   Yvonne LaFleur, a confessed
incurable romantic, is the creator of beautifully feminine original
designs. Her custom millinery, silk dresses, evening gowns, lingerie,
and sportswear are surprisingly affordable, and all are enhanced
by her signature perfume. Her store is in the Riverbend district.

8131 Hampson St. ⓒ **504/866-9666.** www.yvonnelafleur.com. Mon–Wed and Fri–Sat 10am–6pm; Thurs 10am–8pm.

GIFTS

Accent Annex Mardi Gras Headquarters This is one of the biggest suppliers of Mardi Gras beads, masks, and other accoutrements, and it has just about everything you need to properly celebrate Mardi Gras in New Orleans or to stock up for that party you want to throw back home. Note the reasonably priced bags of used beads. Riverwalk. ⓒ **504/568-9000.** Daily 10am–6pm.

Angele Parlange Design Angele Parlange is a textile and interior designer of national renown, and she has been featured in countless magazines such as *Elle* and *Vogue*. She gleans much of her inspiration from her illustrious ancestors, who built Parlange Plantation in New Roads, Louisiana. The shop features Parlange's collection of interior furnishings, including hand-printed pillows, fabrics, furniture, bedding, and imaginative items for entertaining. 5419 Magazine St. ⓒ **504/897-6511.** Mon–Fri 10am–5:30pm; Sat 10am–5pm.

The Anne Rice Collection Want to dress like Lestat? Want to buy vampire- or ghost-related tchotchkes? This is a must-stop for the faithful, as Rice brings you all manner of Gothic-related items, from clothes to knickknacks including her old shoes, costumes, and jewelry, plus T-shirts with her personal slogans on them (taken in all at once, it seems she careens between taking matters all too seriously and being completely in on the joke), not to mention skeletons, vampire dolls, and crosses. What did you expect, Hummel figures and flowery pottery? Lately, Rice has been handwriting all the info cards on the sales items, so you get an autograph with purchase. 2727 Prytania St. (in the Rink). ⓒ **504/899-5996.** Fax 504/895-8168. www.annerice.com. Mon–Sat 10am–6pm; Sun 11am–4pm.

Janet Molero The eponymous owner is an interior designer, but we like her shop for its assortment of fragrant candles and other gifts. 3935 Magazine St. ⓒ **504/269-8305.** Fax 504/269-0872. www.janetmolero.com. Mon–Sat 10am–5pm.

Living Room The friendly owner here has done a fine job assembling the wares at her original folk-craft store, almost making up for the loss of the site's former occupant, the beloved Olive Book Store. The Living Room holds an eclectic assortment of old and new furnishings, knickknacks (think frames made of wood from old plantations, old spoons, and other recycled materials), fine art, and antiques. Be sure to say hi to the store dogs, Louise and Oil ("Earl" with an accent), who are neighborhood characters (Earl is featured as Mr. Louisiana in a recent book called *Dog Bless America*). 927 Royal St. ℂ **888/598-8860** or 504/595-8860. www.livingroom4u.com. Mon–Sat 10am–6pm; Sun noon–6pm.

Shop of the Two Sisters Upscale "girly" items: throw pillows, lamps, sconces, accessories, unique accent pieces (with an emphasis on florals and fruits), and upholstery. It's consumerism at its most beautiful, but be prepared to pay for it. 1800 Magazine St. ℂ **504/525-2747**. Mon–Sat 10am–6pm.

Thomas Mann Gallery This is a design store conceived by "techno-romantic" jewelry designer Thomas Mann. It aims at "redefining contemporary living" with its eclectic collection of jewelry, lighting, and home furnishings. There's another location at 829 Royal St. in the French Quarter. 1804 Magazine St. ℂ **504/581-2113**. Fax 504/568-1416. www.thomasmann.com. Mon–Sat 11am–6pm.

Three Dog Bakery Upon first glance, all the goodies here—cookies, petit fours, cakes—look incredibly yummy. Then you find out they are just for dogs. Which means they are made without ingredients that would appeal to human beings, like sugar or chocolate or fat or, really, anything with taste. These strictly canine delights are completely healthy for pooches. Cute names abound (Snicker Poodles, Ciao Wow Cheese Pizza), and dogs do love them. You might sneer at those who would splurge on such a gimmick. Dog owners, not to mention guilty ones away from home, go right ahead and drop lots of money. We recommend the Pawlines (the dog-friendly version of the local pralines), which went over big with some dogs we know. 827 Royal St. ℂ **504/525-2253**. Fax 504/525-2252. threedognola@yahoo.com. Daily 10am–6pm.

MUSIC

In addition to the giant **Tower Records** at 408 N. Peters St. (ℂ **504/529-4411**), there are a few other places you should check out for music, especially if you still have a turntable.

Beckham's Bookshop It's better known for its fine collection of used books (see earlier in this chapter), but Beckham's also has a large selection of secondhand classical LPs. 228 Decatur St. ℂ **504/522-9875**. Daily 10am–6pm.

Louisiana Music Factory This popular store carries a large selection of regional music—including Cajun, zydeco, R&B, jazz, blues, and gospel—plus books, posters, and T-shirts. It also has frequent live music and beer bashes—shop while you bop! 210 Decatur St. © 504/586-1094. Daily 10am–10pm.

Record Ron's   You'll find thousands of 45s, CDs, and cassettes plus a good selection of LPs covering classic rock, jazz, Cajun, zydeco, R&B, and blues. T-shirts, posters, sheet music, rubber stamps, music memorabilia, and jewelry are also available. 239 Chartres St. © 800/234-6889 or 504/522-2239. Daily 11am–7pm.

Rock & Roll Records & Collectibles   The name says it all—kind of. The owners say (and who are we to dispute?) that this is the largest and best collection of vinyl anywhere,—including 45s and 78s—which means hardly just rock 'n' roll. This is record nerd heaven. The walls are lined with classics, and floor space is at a minimum thanks to boxes and crates full of records. Prices are negotiable. 1214 Decatur St. © 504/561-5683. www.rockcollectibles.org. Daily 10am–8pm.

THE OCCULT

The Bottom of the Cup Tearoom   At the Bottom of the Cup Tearoom, psychics and clairvoyants specialize in palm reading, crystal gazing, tea-leaf reading, and tarot. You can also get your astrological chart done. It's been open since 1929 and bills itself as the "oldest tearoom in the United States." In addition to having a psychic consultation, you can also purchase books, jewelry, crystal balls, tarot cards, crystals, and healing wands. 732 Royal St. © 504/523-1204. Mon–Fri 10am–6pm; Sat–Sun 11am–7pm.

Marie Laveau's House of Voodoo   The place for voodoo dolls and gris-gris bags. It's tourist voodoo, to be sure, but such items make great souvenirs for the right friends, and it's a fun store to poke around in. 739 Bourbon St. © 504/581-3751. Daily 10am–midnight.

7

New Orleans After Dark

New Orleans is one of the most beautiful cities in the United States, possibly the world, but we won't mind if you never see a bit of it—provided, however, that the omission is because you are spending the daylight hours recovering from the equally extraordinary nightlife.

This is a city of music and rhythm. It is impossible to imagine New Orleans without a soundtrack of jazz, Cajun, and zydeco. Music streams from every doorway, and sometimes it seems people are dancing down the street. Sometimes they really are. (After all, this is the town that sends you to your grave with music and then dances back from the cemetery.) You walk down Bourbon, for example, and with every step you hear music of all varieties. Maybe none of it is world class, but that doesn't seem to matter. It's darn infectious.

This is also the city of decadence and good times rolling. Not to mention really loose liquor laws and drinks in "go" cups (plastic containers you can take with you; many bars and clubs even have walk-up windows for easy refills). And all this increases four-fold at night. We aren't just talking about the open-air frat party that is Bourbon Street some (okay, most) evenings. In fact, we prefer not to talk about that at all.

Most important is that, virtually every night, dozens of clubs all over town offer music that can range from average to extraordinary but is never less than danceable. Cover prices vary, of course, but rarely will you have to pay more than $10—and then only for more high-falutin' places like the House of Blues.

When the clubs get too full, no matter; the crowd spills into the street, talking, drinking, and still dancing right there on the sidewalk. Sometimes the action outside is even more fun than inside.

Club hopping is easy, and some of the better choices will require leaving the Quarter by cab or some other vehicle. Don't worry—most are a cheap cab ride away, if not walking distance of each other. And only steps away is the scene in the Faubourg Marigny, where at least five clubs are going at once within 3 blocks of each other.

For information on what's happening around town, look for current editions of *Gambit, Offbeat,* and *Where,* all distributed free in most hotels and all record stores. You can also check out *Offbeat* on the Internet (www.nola.com; once you get to the Nola home page, go to the music and entertainment section). Other sources include the *Times-Picayune*'s daily entertainment calendar and Friday's **"Lagniappe"** section of the newspaper. Additionally, **WWOZ** (90.7 FM) broadcasts the local music schedule several times throughout the day. If you miss the broadcasts, call ☎ **504/ 840-4040,** WWOZ's "Tower Records Second Line," for the same information.

1 Jazz & Blues Clubs

THE FRENCH QUARTER & THE FAUBOURG MARIGNY

Donna's A corner bar at the very northern edge of the Quarter, Donna's has become one of the top spots for the revival of the brass band experience and for jazz and blues traditions. The main asset may be Donna herself, monitoring the door to make sure you don't bring in drinks from outside and making sure you do order something inside. She's been a true booster of new generations of New Orleans music (she's managed both the hip-hop–edged brass band Soul Rebels and the new-funk ensemble Galactic) and has helped promote awareness of veteran brass bands like Treme and Olympia. As with most real New Orleans hangouts, atmosphere is minimal, but spirits (liquid and otherwise) are high. *Note:* Donna's is in a transitional neighborhood, so be careful entering and leaving. 800 N. Rampart St. ☎ 504/596-6914. Cover varies according to performer.

Dragon's Den Imagine a hippie hangout–cum–opium den turned performance space and you'll have an idea of the Dragon's Den. Before show time, it's a pillows-on-the-floor, nouvelle-Asian restaurant. After the lights go down, however, the place transforms into one of the funkiest jazz venues in the city. The standing-room bar and floor-bound seating area both look into the performance area, which is something short of a stage. Actually, it's the floor—be careful that the performers don't step on you. Tables are often taken by diners who don't leave, but there's room in some corner for everyone, even if it's on the balcony overlooking Esplanade. Now imagine the whole place bopping to the ReBirth Brass Band and you've got the idea. 435 Esplanade Ave. (above Siam Café). ☎ 504/949-1750. Cover $4–$10.

Fritzel's European Jazz Pub You might walk right past this small establishment, but that would be a big mistake because the 1831 building brings some of the city's best musicians to play on its tiny stage. In addition to the regular weekend program of late-night jazz (Fri and Sat from 10:30pm, Sun from 10pm), there are frequent jam sessions in the wee hours during the week when performers end their stints elsewhere and gather to play "Musicians' Music." The full bar also stocks a variety of schnapps (served ice-cold) and German beers on tap and in bottles. 733 Bourbon St. ℭ 504/561-0432. No cover; 1-drink minimum per set.

Funky Butt Fret not—this is not a strip bar. Jazz aficionados will connect the name with a tune associated with New Orleans's own Buddy Bolden. There was another Funky Butt club in the early days of jazz; this one is a more recent arrival, operated by the owner of the Magic Walking Tours. Downstairs is a typical funky bar; upstairs is a slightly more pleasing and mature performance space than that at other clubs in town. It's leaning toward, if not totally achieving, smoky jazz nightclub ambience. Bookings emphasize jazz but can also include anything from the Wild Magnolias (the most famous of the Mardi Gras Indians; it's something special to see them here) to an amazing Billie Holiday tribute band to the New Orleans Klezmer All-Stars. Creole and vegetarian food is available.

Note: Although the club itself is safe, the neighborhood around it isn't. Take a cab to and from this area unless you're in a large group or during a crowded time (Mardi Gras, Jazz Fest). Better yet, get a cop to escort you. 714 N. Rampart St. ℭ 504/558-0872. www.funkybutt.com. Cover varies.

Funky Pirate Decorated to resemble a pirates' lair, the Funky Pirate lives up to its name—especially the "funky" part. The Pirate is as far from urbane modern jazz as you can get, so there's no chance you'll confuse it with the Funky Butt (see above). The place seems to be perpetually full of loud beer drinkers, and at night it can get jam-packed. "Big" Al Carson and the Blues Masters hold court here playing live blues, and Big Al lives up to his name—especially the "big" part. 727 Bourbon St. ℭ 504/523-1960. 1-drink minimum.

John Wehner's Famous Door Open since 1934, the Famous Door is the oldest music club on Bourbon Street. Many local jazz, pop, and rock musicians have passed through the Famous Door. One of them, Harry Connick Jr., played his first gigs here at the age of 13. The owner is actually a young musician; his group (John Wehner's Dream Band) plays at night, offering a tourist

New Orleans Nightlife

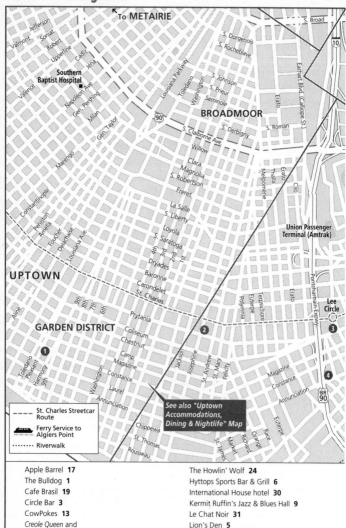

To METAIRIE

Southern Baptist Hospital

BROADMOOR

Union Passenger Terminal (Amtrak)

UPTOWN

GARDEN DISTRICT

Lee Circle

See also "Uptown Accommodations, Dining & Nightlife" Map

- - - St. Charles Streetcar Route
▬▬ Ferry Service to Algiers Point
····· Riverwalk

Apple Barrel **17**
The Bulldog **1**
Cafe Brasil **19**
Circle Bar **3**
CowPokes **13**
Creole Queen and
the *Cajun Queen* **20**
Dos Jefes Uptown Cigar Bar **8**
Feelings **15**

The Howlin' Wolf **24**
Hyttops Sports Bar & Grill **6**
International House hotel **30**
Kermit Ruffin's Jazz & Blues Hall **9**
Le Chat Noir **31**
Lion's Den **5**
Mermaid Lounge **4**
Michaul's on St. Charles **32**
Mother-in-Law Lounge **10**

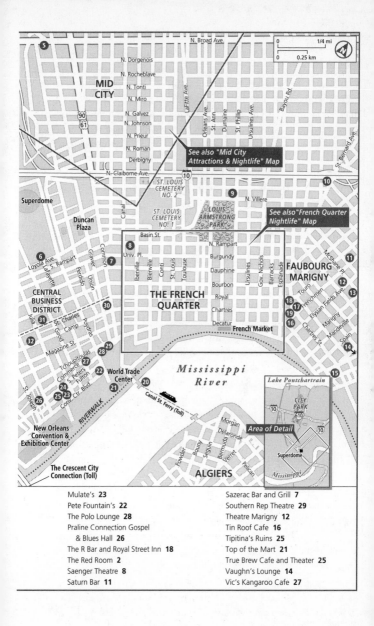

The following legend entries appear at the bottom of the map:

Mulate's **23**	Sazerac Bar and Grill **7**
Pete Fountain's **22**	Southern Rep Theatre **29**
The Polo Lounge **28**	Theatre Marigny **12**
Praline Connection Gospel & Blues Hall **26**	Tin Roof Cafe **16**
The R Bar and Royal Street Inn **18**	Tipitina's Ruins **25**
The Red Room **2**	Top of the Mart **21**
Saenger Theatre **8**	True Brew Cafe and Theater **25**
Saturn Bar **11**	Vaughn's Lounge **14**
	Vic's Kangaroo Cafe **27**

crowd–pleasing selection of Motown, funk, and swing. 339 Bourbon St. ℂ 504/522-7626. Occasional cover. 1-drink minimum per set.

Maison Bourbon Despite its location and the sign saying the building is "dedicated to the preservation of jazz" (which seems a clear attempt to confuse tourists into thinking this is the legendary Preservation Hall), Maison Bourbon is not a tourist trap. The music is very authentic, and often superb, jazz. Stepping into the brick-lined room, or even just peering in from the street, takes you away from the mayhem outside. From about midafternoon until the wee hours, Dixieland and traditional jazz hold forth, often at loud and lively volume. Patrons must be at least 21 years old. 641 Bourbon St. ℂ 504/522-8818. 1-drink minimum.

Mama's Blues A new addition to the continuing renaissance of Rampart, and thus very welcome indeed. A cousin to the Funky Butt, this lacks the FB's ambience (yes, it has quite a lot, actually, so stop it), largely due to the nearly complete absence of decor (just a bar—featuring some truly bad beer—and a stage at this writing), but then again, it has something the FB doesn't have nearly enough of—sightlines. You can actually see the performers and the stage! Anyway, figure on an emphasis on the blues (Marva Wright is a regular) and perhaps an evolution in terms of looks. 614 N. Rampart St. No phone at this writing. www.mamasblues.com.

Palm Court Jazz Café This is one of the most stylish jazz haunts in the Quarter. It's an elegant setting in which to catch top-notch jazz groups Wednesday through Sunday. If you have a collection of jazz records at home, peek at the records for sale in a back alcove. You might want to make reservations—it's that kind of place. 1204 Decatur St. ℂ 504/525-0200. Cover $5 per person at tables; no cover at bar.

Praline Connection Gospel & Blues Hall There are two Praline Connections in New Orleans, both operated by the same company. One is a restaurant (see chapter 4). The 9,000-square-foot Praline Connection Gospel & Blues Hall is a restaurant as well (with the same cuisine), but here you get live music with dinner on Thursday, Friday, and Saturday nights. Sunday brings a great gospel buffet brunch. Reservations are strongly recommended. 907 S. Peters St. ℂ 504/523-3973 for reservations and information.

Preservation Hall The gray, bombed-out building that looks as if it was erected just shortly after the dawn of time doesn't seem like much, but it's a mecca for traditional jazz fans and an essential spot for any visitor. It doesn't get any more authentic than this.

French Quarter Nightlife

With no seats and constant crowds, you won't be able to see much, but you won't care because you will be having too fun and cheerfully sweaty a time. Even if you don't consider yourself interested in jazz, there is a seriously good time to be had here, and you very probably will come away with a new appreciation for the music.

Patrons start lining up at 6:15pm—the doors open at 8pm, so the trick to avoid the line is to get there either just as the doors open or later in the evening. The band plays until midnight, and the first audience usually empties out around 10pm.

A 30-year-old sign on the wall gives prices for requests, but it's out-of-date. As the doorwoman said, "If we still took $5 for 'Saints Go Marchin' In,' they'd be playing it all night." (One night, some big spenders tossed seven $100 bills for seven rounds of "Saints.") Try about $10, and for other requests, "just offer something."

Thanks to the casual atmosphere, not to mention cheap cover, Preservation Hall is one of the few nightspots where it's appropriate to take kids. Early in the evening, you'll notice a number of local families doing just that. 726 St. Peter St. ℂ **504/522-2841**, or 504/523-8939 after 8pm. www.preservationhall.com. Cover $5.

Snug Harbor   If your idea of jazz extends beyond Dixieland and if you prefer a concert-type setting over a messy nightclub, get your hands on Snug Harbor's monthly schedule. On the fringes of the French Quarter, Snug Harbor is the city's premier showcase for contemporary jazz, with a few blues and R&B combos thrown in for good measure. Here, jazz is presented as it should be: part entertainment, part art, and often, part intellectual stimulation. This is the surest place to find Ellis Marsalis (patriarch of the Marsalis dynasty) and Charmaine Neville. Not only does Snug offer good music, but the two-level seating provides universally good viewing of the bandstand. Be warned: Waiting for a show usually means hanging in the crowded, low-ceilinged bar, where personal space is at a minimum. 626 Frenchmen St. ℂ **504/949-0696**. www.snugjazz.com. Cover $12–$20, depending on performer.

Storyville District   Nope, it's not in (or even all that near) the old Storyville District, nor does it have anything to do with bordellos. This is the brand-new brainchild of (in part) Quint Davis, the man who helps bring us Jazz Fest every year, and that alone inspires confidence. The idea is to bring high-quality jazz back to Bourbon Street in a non-frat party atmosphere, and we completely support it. Music plays much of the day, starting in the red-walled parlor room in the afternoon, with bigger bands playing in a larger, more club-like space at night. It's not stuffy or pretentious, though the clean, somewhat sophisticated atmosphere makes for an almost disconcerting contrast with the rest of Bourbon Street. The level of booking, thanks to the owner, is high, while New Orleans–style nibbles are available courtesy of Ralph Brennan. 125 Bourbon St. (C) 504/410-1000. Mon–Wed 2pm–12am; Thurs–Sat 2pm–1:30am; Sun (jazz brunch) 10am–2pm.

ELSEWHERE AROUND THE CITY

Kermit Ruffins' Jazz & Blues Hall   Once the teenaged front-man of the ReBirth Brass Band, trumpeter-vocalist Ruffins (with his own Barbecue Swingers group) has been one of the most popular fixtures in New Orleans jazz for a decade. He takes not only his accomplished and entertaining Louis Armstrong–inspired mix of styles to various local clubs, but also often his barbecue pit trailer. Now he has his own home, opened in spring 2001 in the cozy one-time location of the old Trombone Shorty's club in Ruffins' native Treme neighborhood. He went so far as to offer free horse-and-buggy rides to late-night patrons during the 2001 Jazz Fest—a gesture that made tourists more comfortable hanging out in a neighborhood that doesn't have the best reputation. A recent regular rotation at the club, open Fridays through Tuesdays, had the Treme Brass Band on Fridays, ReBirth on Mondays, and Kermit himself holding court on Saturdays and, starting at 4 p.m., Sundays. 1533 St. Philip St. (C) 504/299-0790. Cover varies.

The New Showcase Lounge   Even though it has the patina of an age-old joint, this is indeed a new showcase—the *new* means it's one of the newest clubs in town, and the music it showcases is modern jazz with an occasional blues singer. It's in the same family of clubs with Snug Harbor, and it is another place to look for members of the Marsalis clan. The bar is shaped like a piano, and the room is very comfortable—just small enough to ensure that everyone pays attention to the music. If you're lucky, there will be a buffet of soul food to go with your jazz. Tuesday night is "In a Mellow Mood" night. 1915 N. Broad Ave. (near St. Bernard, at Bruxeles, well northeast of the Quarter). (C) 504/945-5612. Cover varies.

Pete Fountain's   Pete Fountain has managed to make his name synonymous with New Orleans music. He grew up playing around town, moved to Chicago with the Dukes of Dixieland, joined Lawrence Welk's orchestra, and then, for more than 20 years, held forth in his own Bourbon Street club. These days, you'll find him here in a re-creation of his former Quarter premises, with seating for more than twice as many as the old club. The plush interior—gold chairs and banquettes, red velvet bar chairs, lacy white iron-railed gallery—sets the mood for the popular nightspot. Pete is featured in one show a night, Tuesday through Saturday at 10pm. You'll need reservations. In the New Orleans Hilton, 2 Poydras St. ℂ **504/523-4374** or 504/561-0500. Cover $19 (includes 1 drink).

The Red Room   Swing has finally caught on with a vengeance in New Orleans, helped no doubt in part by this hot, fairly new, 1940s-style jazz and supper club. Live music happens every night, with jazz and swing performed by both established names and talented up-and-comers. It's a lively place, perfect for dancing and romancing in the way your parents (or, depending on your age, you yourself) did. It's all housed in an odd-looking structure that puts you in mind of the Eiffel Tower. (That's because it once was the restaurant there; the disassembled pieces somehow got transported to New Orleans and then were abandoned for some years before the recent transformation.) Dress appropriately; the staff won't hesitate to send you on your way if you are wearing jeans. 2040 St. Charles Ave. ℂ **504/528-9759.** Jacket and tie recommended for men. No cover.

Vaughn's Lounge   Tucked deep in the Bywater section of New Orleans, Vaughn's Lounge is way down home. It's in a residential neighborhood and feels almost as though you're in someone's house. The long bar takes up so much room that people almost fall over the band at the end of the room. Thursday—Kermit Ruffin's night—is the night to go to Vaughn's. Go early and get some of the barbecue Kermit is usually cooking up before a show—he tends to bring his grill along with him wherever he is playing. Or you might catch a Mardi Gras Indian practice. Be sure to call ahead to see if there will be live music on a given night, and be sure to take a taxi. 800 Lesseps St. at Dauphine St. ℂ **504/947-5562.** Cover varies.

2 Cajun & Zydeco Joints

Michaul's on St. Charles   Michaul's attempts to re-create the Cajun dance hall experience, and for a prefab kind of place, it does it well enough. If you've experienced the real thing, you'll turn up your nose, but if you haven't, it'll do. Come for the free dance lessons. 840 St. Charles Ave. ℂ **504/522-5517.** No cover.

Mid City Lanes Rock 'n' Bowl   Anything we just said about tourist traps and inauthentic experiences does not apply here. It does not get any more authentic than a club set in the middle of a bowling alley, which is itself set in the middle of a strip mall. Actually, as a bowling alley, Mid City bowling is nothing to write home about unless you like lanes that slope. But as a club, it's one of the finest experiences in New Orleans. Certainly it's the best place for zydeco, particularly on the nights devoted to Zydeco Wars. It also features top New Orleans rock and R&B groups. On good nights (though we do wonder if Mid City has any that aren't), the dance floor is crowded beyond belief, the noise level is ridiculous, the humidity level is 300%, and you won't want to leave. You might even bowl a few frames. 4133 S. Carrollton Ave. ✆ 504/482-3133. www. rockandbowl.com. Bowling: daytime and Sun–Thurs evening $12 per hour; Fri–Sat evening $10 per hour. Show admission $5–$7.

Mulate's   A branch of the original (out in Cajun country) and a not-unlikely place to find authentic, and decent, Cajun bands. The stage and dance area are relatively spacious, and the food isn't bad. It's in the same neighborhood as Michaul's (see above), so if you get the Cajun bug, you can easily do both places in a night. 201 Julia St., at Convention Center Blvd. ✆ 504/522-1492. No cover.

3 Rhythm, Rock & the Rest of the Music Scene

Most clubs in New Orleans feature an eclectic lineup that reflects the town's music scene; the ReBirth Brass Band, for example, attracts as many rock fans as it does brass band fans. Consequently, the bulk of the club scene escapes categorization (and, of course, booking policies are often subject to change)—even the local papers refer to club lineups as "mixed bags." Check listings night by night. Some places are generally good fun on their own regardless of who is playing; any night at the **Maple Leaf** is going to be a good one, while wandering from spot to spot in the Frenchmen section is a well-spent evening. Really, in New Orleans, you can't go too wrong going just about anywhere simply to hang out. And in the process, you might be exposed to a new, wonderful genre of music or an incredible band.

THE FRENCH QUARTER & THE FAUBOURG MARIGNY

Cafe Brasil   Day (when it is a great place to get a cup of coffee) or night (when it delivers danceable music), Cafe Brasil is the center of the increasingly lively and popular Frenchmen section of the Faubourg Marigny. It features Latin or Caribbean music, R&B, or jazz almost every night, and chances are whatever is playing will be infectious. Anticipate a hip and trendy, though still casual, crowd and be prepared to act cool. The decent-size dance floor fills up quickly, and the crowd spills into the street to see and be seen. 2100 Chartres St. ✆ 504/949-0851. Cover varies according to performer.

Checkpoint Charlie's   Somewhere between a biker bar and a college hangout, the dark Checkpoint Charlie's only *seems* intimidating—an effect that's helped by the hard rock sounds usually blaring from the stage. It's easy to overlook straight rock with all the other New Orleans sounds around, but this would be the place to start trying to find it. R&B and blues sneak into the mix as well. A full bar, food, and pool tables help soften the ambience for the easily intimidated, and it's open 24 hours, making it a less touristy place for a quick drink during the day. Plus, there's a coin laundry, so a dusty traveler can clean up while enjoying the music. And right across the street is a fire station known for its hunky firemen, who on sultry nights sit outside and admire the views. Admire them right back. 501 Esplanade Ave. ✆ 504/949-7012. No cover.

House of Blues   New Orleans was a natural place for this franchise to set up shop, but its presence in the French Quarter seems rather unnatural. With all the great, funky music clubs in town, why build one with ersatz "authenticity" that wouldn't be out of place in Disneyland? And while it's noble that they've patronized many deserving Southern "primitive" artists, whose colorful works line the walls, there's a certain Hearst Castle grab-bag element to that, too, which diminishes the value and cultural context of the works.

That isn't to say the facility is without its qualities. The music room has adequate sightlines and good sound, and the chain's financial muscle assures first-rate bookings, from the Neville Brothers to Los Lobos. The nouvelle Orleans menu in the restaurant, too, is high quality, from a piquant jambalaya to fancy-schmancy pizzas. But patronizing this club rather than the real thing, like Tipitina's (which lost considerable business after the HoB opened), is akin to eating at McDonald's rather than Mother's. 225 Decatur St. ✆ 504/529-2583. www.hob.com. Cover $5–$25.

Shim-Sham Club   After taking over a longtime jazz club space, the Shim-Sham club has evolved into an interesting scene—"a little decadent, a little bohemian," says one local who frequents the place. The club books perhaps the most eclectic lineup in town. In one recent week, in addition to the regular '80s and S&M nights, were shows by Louis Prima protégé and torch-carrier Sam Butara, proto-grunge legends the Melvins, and a surprise late-night show by Counting Crows lead singer Adam Duritz and friends. Seating can be either cabaret style (tables and chairs) or standing room. There is also a secret scene that revolves around the upstairs bar, which you only get to enter by invitation. Act nice and look like fun and maybe you'll get lucky. 615 Toulouse St. ✆ 504/565-5400. www.shimshamclub.com. Cover varies.

ELSEWHERE AROUND THE CITY

Throughout this book, we keep nagging you to leave the Quarter, especially at night. It's not that there aren't worthwhile clubs in the Quarter or at the fringes. It's just that there are so many terrific (and, in some cases, outright better) ones elsewhere. And not only do they feature some of the best music in town, they aren't designed as tourist destinations, so your experience will be that much more legitimate.

Amberjack's   Amberjack's is one of a number of spots at Lake Pontchartrain where you can pass a festive evening. It's on the Lake Pontchartrain marina, and most nights it's crowded with local boaters. When the weekend rolls around, Amberjack's becomes a stomping ground for young revelers with a penchant for tropical drinks. Friday and Saturday nights bring live pop, rock, and R&B bands, while Sunday is New Orleans music night—Neville Brothers covers abound. Pizzas and sandwiches are available if you get the munchies. 7306 Lake Shore Dr. ✆ 504/282-6660. Cover on Fri–Sat only.

Carrollton Station   A long, narrow space means that folks at the back won't get to see much of what's up on stage, but hey, that puts them closer to the bar, so everyone wins. Way uptown in the Riverbend area, Carrollton Station is a gourmet beer house that schedules local and touring blues, classic New Orleans, and R&B musicians (plus some singer-songwriter types) Wednesday through Sunday, generally beginning at 10pm. (The bar opens at 3pm.) The crowd is a good mix of college students, music aficionados, and fans of whatever act is appearing on a given night. 8140 Willow St. ✆ 504/865-9190. Cover $3–$10.

The Howlin' Wolf   This is arguably the premier club in town in terms of the quality and fame of its bookings, especially since a remodeling job increased capacity nearly fourfold—and made it a competitor with the House of Blues. Good. Better a local non-chain gets the business. Howlin' Wolf draws some top touring rock acts, though it is not at all limited to rock—El Vez, the Mexican Elvis, is as likely to play as a country band or the latest in indie and alternative rock (recent performers included Frank Black, the Jon Spencer

Blues Explosion, and Iris DeMent). 828 S. Peters St., in the CBD. ℭ 504/ 522-WOLF. www.howlin-wolf.com. Cover none–$15.

Lion's Den   A true neighborhood dive, but it's well worth stopping by should Miss Irma Thomas be in residence. She usually is, and sometimes, if you're lucky, she's even cooking up some red beans and rice. Thomas has only one hit to her credit ("Wish Somebody Would Care"), but she's still a great, sassy live R&B and soul act with a devoted following, who can never get enough of "You Can Have My Husband, But Please Don't Mess with My Man" and other delights. She puts on one hell of a show, and it's well worth treading into this otherwise unsavory neighborhood to see it. *Note:* At press time, Ms. Thomas had taken up a regular residency at the new Levon Helm's Classic American Cafe. She was/is still performing regularly at the Lion's Den—and arguably, that is *the* place to see her—but the French Quarter location might be far more convenient and comfortable for the average tourist. 2655 Gravier St., at N. Broad Ave. in Mid City. ℭ 504/821-3745. Cover varies.

Maple Leaf Bar   This is what a New Orleans club is all about. It's medium-size but feels smaller when a crowd is packed in. And by 11pm on most nights, it is, with personal space at times becoming something you can only wistfully remember. But that's no problem. The stage is against the window facing the street, so more often than not, the crowd spills onto the sidewalk and into the street to dance and drink (and escape the heat and sweat, which are prodigious despite a high ceiling). You can hear the music just as well and then dance some more. With a party atmosphere like this, outside is almost more fun than in. A good bar and a rather pretty patio make the Maple Leaf worth hanging out at even if you don't care about the music on a particular night. But if Beausoleil or the ReBirth Brass Band is playing, do not miss it; go and dance till you drop. 8316 Oak St. ℭ 504/866-9359. Cover $3–$10, depending on day of week and performer.

Mermaid Lounge   Although it's very hard to find, thanks to a series of one-way streets (that all seem to lead away from the club) and its location in a cul-de-sac on the edge of the Warehouse District, the Mermaid Lounge is worth the effort. (You might call the club and ask plaintively how to get there. They might tell you.) An eclectic booking policy attracts everything from the Hackberry Ramblers (the Grammy-nominated Cajun band that has been playing together for nearly 70 years!) to hard-core grunge—and yet, the blue-haired pierced kids still come to dance to the Cajun bands in the tiny, cramped, dark space (yes, there is a mermaid motif throughout). It all adds up to one of the coolest vibes in town. 1102 Constance St. ℭ 504/524-4747. Cover none–$10.

Rock 'n' Bowl Cafe   Located right under Mid City Lanes (hence the name), this is a huge room (bowling-alley size) that helps take care of the constant overflow from upstairs. Dark and bleak, thanks to the black paint job and lack of windows, the Rock 'n Bowl Cafe offers essentially the same acts as Mid City, though perhaps not as much zydeco. 4133 S. Carrollton Ave. ℭ 504/482-3133. www.rockandbowl. com. Cover usually $5–$7.

Tipitina's   Dedicated to the late piano master Professor Longhair, Tip's was long *the* New Orleans club. But due to circumstances both external (increased competition from House of Blues and others as well as the club's capacity being cut in half by city authorities) and internal (locals say the bookings have not been up to snuff for some time), its star has faded considerably. It remains a reliable place for top local bands, though. The place is nothing fancy—just four walls, a wraparound balcony, and a stage. Oh, and a couple of bars, of course, including one that serves people milling outside the club, which is as much a part of the atmosphere as what's inside. They also have two other rooms; Tips French Quarter and the Ruins at this point are only being used for special events. 501 Napoleon Ave., Uptown. ℭ 504/895-8477, or 504/897-3943 for concert line. www.tipitinas.com. Cover $4–$15, depending on the performer.

4 The Bar Scene

You won't have any trouble finding a place to drink in New Orleans. Heck, thanks to "go" (or *"geaux"*) cups, you won't have to spend a minute without a drink in your hand. (It's legal to have liquor outside as long as it's in a plastic cup. Actually, given the number of people who take advantage of this law, it almost seems illegal *not* to have such a cup in your hand.) Note that many of the clubs listed above are terrific spots to hoist a few (or a dozen), while some of the bars below also provide music—but that is strictly background for their real design. Piano bars, in particular, have begun to pop up; they're everywhere; in addition to the ones listed below, you can find a piano bar in almost every large hotel.

THE FRENCH QUARTER & THE FAUBOURG MARIGNY

In addition to the places below, you might consider the clubby bar at **Dickie Brennan's Steakhouse,** 716 Iberville St. (ℭ 504/

522-2467), a place where manly men go to drink strong drinks, smoke smelly cigars (they have a vast selection for sale), and chat up girlie girls. Or you could enjoy the low-key sophistication found at **Beque's at the Royal Sonesta,** 300 Bourbon St. (✆ **504/586-0300**), where a jazz trio is usually playing. No cover unless noted.

The Abbey Despite the name, this place is more basement rumpus room (walls covered with stickers and old album covers) than Gothic church (well, there are some motley stained-glass windows). But the jukebox plays The Cramps and "I Wanna Be Your Dog," and the clientele is very David Lynchian (and maybe still left over from the place's heyday 15 years ago!), so it's OK by us. 1123 Decatur St. ✆ **504/523-7150.**

Apple Barrel A small, dusty, wooden-floored watering hole complete with jukebox and darts (of course). You can find refuge here from the hectic Frenchmen scene—or gear up to join in. 609 Frenchmen St. ✆ **504/949-9399.**

The Bombay Club This posh piano bar features jazz Wednesday through Saturday evenings. On Fridays and Saturdays, the music runs past 1am. Apart from the piano, the Bombay Club is a restaurant and a martini bar—the drink has been a specialty here for years, so don't accuse the club of trying to ride the current martini trend. In fact, the Bombay's martinis are hailed as the best in town. The bar bills itself as casually elegant—a polite way of saying don't wear jeans and shorts. 830 Conti St. ✆ **504/586-0972.**

Carousel Bar & Lounge There is piano music here Tuesdays through Saturdays, but the real attraction is the bar itself—it really is a carousel, and it really does revolve. The music goes on until 2am, and who knows if the carousel ever stops revolving. In the Monteleone Hotel, 214 Royal St. ✆ **504/523-3341.**

El Matador This place was once a bar called the Mint; there are no big aesthetic changes from its previous incarnation except that the vibe is more straight than gay now. This is not necessarily an improvement. Still, it's bigger than most local corner bars and enough steps above seedy that it is worth going to, regardless of whether or not the evening features local hard rock and punk bands. 504 Esplanade Ave., at Decatur St. ✆ **504/586-0790.**

Feelings Cafe Here's a funky, low-key neighborhood restaurant and hangout set around a classic New Orleans courtyard, which is where most folks drink—unless they are hanging out with the fabulous piano player, singing the night away. It's authentic in the

Pat O'Brien's & the Mighty Hurricane

Pat O'Brien's, 718 St. Peter St. (✆ **504/525-4823**), is world famous for the gigantic, rum-based drink with the big-wind name. The formula (according to legend) was stumbled upon by bar owners Charlie Cantrell and George Oechsner while they were experimenting with Caribbean rum during World War II. The drink is served in signature 29-ounce hurricane lamp-style glasses. The bar now offers a 3-gallon Magnum Hurricane that stands taller than many small children. It's served with a handful of straws and takes a group to finish (we profoundly hope)—all of whom must drink standing up. Naturally, the offerings and reputation attract the tourists and college yahoos in droves. Some nights, the line can stretch out the door and down the street, which seems quite silly given how many other drinking options there are mere feet away.

Which is not to say that Pat's isn't worth a stop—it's a reliable, rowdy, friendly introduction to New Orleans. Just don't expect to be the only person who thinks so. Fortunately, it's large enough to accommodate nearly everyone—in three different bars, including a large lounge that usually offers entertainment—with the highlight, on non-rainy days at least, being the attractive tropical patio.

Even if it is a gimmick, what trip to New Orleans is complete without sampling the famous Hurricane? There's no minimum and no cover, but if you buy a drink and it comes in a glass, you'll be paying for the glass until you turn it in at the register for a $2 refund.

right ways but is also more cheerful than some of the darker, hole-in-the-wall spots that deserve that adjective. A bit out of the way in the Faubourg Marigny, but everyone who goes there comes back raving about it. 2600 Chartres St. ✆ 504/945-2222. Cover varies.

Hard Rock Cafe Gag. When the Hard Rock Cafe was simply a place for homesick Americans in London who were longing for a real burger, it had some value. Now it's a chain—there must be one in Katmandu by this time—and it's particularly offensive here, where there is real music to be had at every turn. It bemuses us to

see tourists lined up outside this place when original experiences—
as opposed to prefab, assembly-line experiences—are just feet away.
Better burgers and better beer are to be found elsewhere. Go there
instead. 418 N. Peters St. ⓒ **504/529-5617.** www.hardrock.com.

Kerry Irish Pub   In a few short years, Kerry Irish Pub has established that the French Quarter can indeed handle a little bit of
the green. This traditional Irish pub has a variety of beers and other
spirits but is most proud of its properly poured pints of Guinness
and hard cider. The pub is a good bet for live Irish and "alternative"
folk music; it's also a place to throw darts and shoot pool. 331 Decatur
St. ⓒ **504/527-5954.** www.kerryirishpub.com.

Lafitte's Blacksmith Shop   It's some steps away from the main
action on Bourbon, but you'll know Lafitte's when you see it.
Dating from the 1770s, it's the oldest building in the Quarter—
possibly in the Mississippi Valley—and it looks it. In other towns,
this would be a tourist trap. Here, it feels authentic. Definitely
worth swinging by even if you don't drink. 941 Bourbon St. ⓒ **504/
523-0066.**

Napoleon House Bar & Cafe   Set in a landmark building, the
Napoleon House is just the place to go to have a quiet drink (as
opposed to the very loud drinks found elsewhere in the Quarter)
and maybe hatch some schemes. Like Lafitte's, it's dark, dark, dark,
with walls you really wish could talk. Also like Lafitte's, it seems too
perfect to be real—surely this must be constructed just for the
tourists. It's not. Even locals like it here. 500 Chartres St. ⓒ **504/524-
9752.** www.napoleonhouse.com.

O'Flaherty's Irish Channel Pub   Over the years, the city's Irish
Channel (uptown along Magazine Street) has become visibly less
Irish in character. O'Flaherty's is taking up some of the slack. This
is the place to go hear the best in local Celtic music, and on
Saturdays, there's also Irish dancing. The supposedly haunted courtyard in the 18th-century building is almost as big a draw as the Irish
atmosphere. 514 Toulouse St. ⓒ **504/529-1317.** www.celticnationsworld.com/
oflahertys.htm.

The R Bar and Royal Street Inn   The R (short for Royal Street)
Bar is a little taste of New York's East Village in the Faubourg
Marigny. It is a quintessential neighborhood bar in a neighborhood full of artists, wannabe artists, punk rock intellectuals, urban
gentrifiers, and well-rounded hipsters. It's a talkers' bar (crowds
tend to gather in layers along the bar) and a haven for strutting,

overconfident pool players. On certain nights, you can get a haircut and a drink for $10. Sometimes the cuts aren't bad, depending on how much the gal wielding the scissors has had to drink. 1431 Royal St. ℭ 504/948-7499. www.royalstreetinn.com.

Saturn Bar   Genuine barflies or just slumming celebs? It's so hard to tell when they are passed out in the crumbling (and we mean it) booths or blending in with the pack-rat collection that passes as decor. The Saturn Bar is among the hipster set's most beloved dives, but it's hard to decide if the love is genuine or comes from a postmodern, ironic appreciation of the grubby, art-project (we can only hope) interior. Must be seen to be believed. 3067 St. Claude Ave., in the Faubourg Marigny. ℭ 504/949-7532.

ELSEWHERE AROUND THE CITY

In addition to those listed below, check out the bar at the **International House hotel,** 221 Camp St., in the CBD; it's a hip and happening hangout. There is no cover unless noted.

Acadian Brewing Company and Beer Garden   If you want to sample beers from a variety of regional brewing companies, head here. Acadian brews two brands, Acadian Pilsener and Acadian Vienna Amber, which are sold across Louisiana. In its first few years, Acadian has won a lot of loyal beer drinkers, and the beer garden has become a favorite Mid City hangout; it serves Acadian draught beers, those from local brewers, and imported beers. 201 N. Carrollton Ave., Mid City. ℭ 504/483-3038. www.acadian-beer.com.

The Bulldog   The Bulldog has become a favored hangout for uptown's young post-college and young professional crowd (though some frat-party types can still sneak in). In the early evening as work lets out for the day, you can see people filing in and filling up the benches out front on Magazine Street. At night, the Bulldog draws a larger, more lively group. It is likely drawn by the bar's beer selection—at more than 50 brews, probably the best in town. 3236 Magazine St., Uptown/Garden District. ℭ 504/891-1516.

Circle Bar   This is the new happening bar, courtesy of the slightly twisted folks behind Snake & Jake's. Ambience is the key; they've chosen the ever-popular "elegant decay" look, from peeling wallpaper to a neon glow from an old K&B drugstore sign on the ceiling. The jukebox keeps the quirky romantic mood going, thanks to bewitching, mood-enhancing selections from the Velvet Underground, Dusty Springfield, and Curtis Mayfield. The clientele is real and real laid-back. Live music includes local acts such as the sarcastically depressed Glyn Styler. Bet you'll see us there. 1032 St. Charles Ave., in the CBD at Lee Circle. ✆ **504/588-2616.**

Dos Jefes Uptown Cigar Bar   Dos Jefes has a post-college, young, yuppie-ish clientele (mostly men, it seems). The patio outside has banana trees and iron chairs, and it's nicer than inside—carpet and cigars are a bad combination. The bar has a good selection of beer on tap and piano music until midnight Tuesdays through Saturdays. 5535 Tchoupitoulas St., Uptown. ✆ **504/891-8500.**

Madigan's   Madigan's is a casual watering hole that has been home to blues musician John Mooney on Sundays. You might want to call and see if his residency is still ongoing. 800 S. Carrollton Ave., Uptown. ✆ **504/866-9455.** No cover most nights.

Mother-in-Law Lounge   Ernie K-Doe may be gone, but this shrine to his glorious self and funky lounges everywhere lives on, thanks to wife Antoinette, the keeper of the K-Doe legend and the bar's owner. Named after his biggest hit, a rousing 1961 number-one pop/R&B novelty, this is a true neighborhood dive bar, distinguished by the K-Doe memorabilia that lines the walls. You may want to be careful in the neighborhood, but once you're there, be sure to play one of K-Doe's songs on the jukebox and drink a toast to the man who billed himself as "Emperor the Universe." 1500 N. Claiborne Ave., northeast of the Quarter. ✆ **504/947-1078.** Call for hours.

Nick's   The slogan here is "Looks like the oldest bar in town!"—and it does. Behind the barroom, you'll find billiards and occasional performances by live musicians. Special drink prices are offered on weekdays—Nick's is famous for shots of drinks with vulgar names. 2400 Tulane Ave., Mid City. ✆ **504/821-9128.**

The Polo Lounge   The Windsor Court is, without a doubt, the city's finest hotel, and the Polo Lounge is the place to go if you're feeling particularly stylish. Sazeracs and cigars are popular here. Don't expect to find any kids; if you like to seal your deals with a drink, this is likely to be your first choice. In the Windsor Court hotel, 300 Gravier St., in the CBD. ✆ **504/523-6000.**

Sazerac Bar and Grill   In the posh Fairmont Hotel, the newly renovated Sazerac Bar is frequented by the city's young professionals and was featured in the movie *The Pelican Brief.* The African walnut bar and murals by Paul Ninas complete the upscale atmosphere. In the Fairmont Hotel, University Place, in the CBD. ✆ **504/529-4733.** www.fairmont.com.

Snake & Jake's Xmas Club Lounge   Though admittedly off the beaten path, this tiny, friendly dive is the perfect place for those looking for an authentic neighborhood bar. Co-owned by local musician Dave Clements, decorated (sort of) with Christmas lights, and featuring a great jukebox heavy on soul and R&B, this is the kind of place where everybody not only knows your name, they know your dog's name 'cause you bring the dog, too. There is almost no light at all, so make friends and prepare to be surprised. Naturally, Snake & Jake's can get really hot, crowded, and sweaty— if you are lucky. *Gambit* readers voted Jose the bartender the best in the city. 7612 Oak St., Uptown. © 504/861-2802.

St. Joe's Bar   An agreeably dark (but not pretentious), non-seedy corner bar, this is a very typical New Orleans friendly-but-not-overbearing place. Its Upper Magazine location means it's more neighborhood- than business-oriented. The place is often seasonally decorated: At Halloween, the cobwebs look as if they should be permanent. There is a pleasant patio and a well-stocked jukebox with the likes of Ray Charles and the Grateful Dead. 5535 Magazine St., Uptown. © 504/899-3744.

5 Gay Nightlife

For more information, check **Ambush,** 828-A Bourbon St. ((© 504/ 522-8049; www.ambushmag.com), a great source for the gay community in New Orleans and for visitors. The magazine's website has a lot of handy-dandy links to other sites of gay interest, including info on local gay bars (www.gaybars.com/states/louisian.htm). Once you're in New Orleans, you can call the office or pick up a copy at Tower Records, 408 N. Peters St., in the French Quarter, or at Lenny's News, 5420 Magazine St., uptown.

BARS

In addition to those listed below, you might try the **Golden Lantern,** 1239 Royal St. (© 504/529-2860), a nice neighborhood spot where the bartender knows the patrons by name. It's the second-oldest gay bar in town, and one longtime patron said that "it used to look like one half of Noah's Ark—with one of everything, one drag queen, one leather boy, one guy in a suit." If Levi's and leather is your scene, the **Rawhide,** 740 Burgundy St. (© 504/525-8106), is your best bet; during Mardi Gras, it hosts a great gay costume contest that's not to be missed. The rest of the year, it's a hustler bar. Both of these places are in the French Quarter, as are the establishments listed below.

The Bourbon Pub-Parade Disco   This is more or less the most centrally located of the gay bars—it's right at ground zero, and many of the other popular gay bars are nearby. The downstairs pub is the calmer of the two; it's open 24 hours daily and gets most crowded in the hour just before the Parade Disco opens. (*Tip:* From 5 to 9pm, a $5 cover charge gets you all the draft beer you can drink.) Upstairs, the Parade features a high-tech dance floor complete with lasers and smoke. Consistently voted as a top dance club (in all of America), it usually opens around 9pm except on Sunday, when it gets going in the afternoon. 801 Bourbon St. ✆ **504/529-2107.**

Café Lafitte in Exile   This is one of the oldest gay bars in the country, having been around since 1953. There's a bar downstairs, and upstairs you'll find a pool table and a balcony that overlooks Bourbon Street. The whole shebang is open 24 hours daily. This is a cruise bar, but it doesn't attract a teenybopper or twinkie crowd. One of the most popular weekly events is the Sunday evening "Trash Disco." 901 Bourbon St. ✆ **504/522-8397.** www.lafittes.com.

The Corner Pocket   While the boast that they have the hottest male strippers in town may be perhaps too generous, you can decide for yourself by checking out this bar Thursday through Sunday nights after 10pm. Locals who aren't a bit ashamed of themselves claim the cutest boys can be found on Friday nights, and sigh that the management has the strippers wear the sort of garments that prevent peeking. The bar itself is none too special, with the average age of the clientele around 70. 940 St. Louis St. ✆ **504/568-9829.** www.cornerpocket.net.

CowPokes   Looking for a gay country bar? Never let it be said that Frommer's lets you down. This is a particularly nice gay country bar, though it resides in a transitional neighborhood, so take a cab out for some of the weekly activities, including free line-dance lessons on Tuesdays and Thursdays and karaoke on Wednesdays. 2240 St. Claude. ✆ **504/947-0505.** www.cowpokesno.com.

Good Friends Bar & Queens Head Pub   This bar and pub is very friendly to visitors and often wins the Gay Achievement Award for Best Neighborhood Gay Bar. They describe themselves as "always snappy casual!" The local clientele is happy to offer suggestions about where you might find the type of entertainment you're looking for. Upstairs is the quiet Queens Head Pub, decorated in the style of a Victorian English pub. The bar is open 24 hours. 740 Dauphine St. ✆ **504/566-7191.** www.goodfriendsbar.com.

LeRoundup   LeRoundup attracts the most diverse crowd around. You'll find transsexuals lining up at the bar with drag queens and well-groomed men in khakis. Expect encounters with working boys. It's open 24 hours. 819 St. Louis St. © **504/561-8340.**

T.T's Lounge   We have locals who tip us off to things, and though it's perhaps too much for our delicate selves, we can report that this great little bar turns into something else all together around 5pm on Fridays and 8pm on Saturdays. In other words, come see local "entertainers" shake their moneymakers as they strut on the bar, and fortify yourself as you do so with a stiff cocktail from bartender Charles. 818 N. Rampart St.

DANCE CLUBS

In addition to those listed below, you might also try the **Red Room** (see "Jazz & Blues Clubs" earlier in this chapter) for some 1940s jazz swing dancing.

Oz   Oz is the place to see and be seen, with a primarily young crowd (like its across-the-street neighbor, the Bourbon Pub-Parade Disco). It was ranked the city's best dance club by *Gambit* magazine, and *Details* magazine named it one of the top 50 clubs in the country. The music is great, there's an incredible laser light show, and from time to time there are go-go boys atop the bar. There are frequent theme nights here, so call ahead if you're going and want to dress accordingly. 800 Bourbon St. © **504/593-9491.** www.ozneworleans. com. Cover varies.

735 Night Club & Bar   Oz continues, for the moment, to rule as top NOLA dance club, but this new-ish venue might be making them work harder. For one thing, 18-year-olds can join in the fun, and for now at least, straight guests don't have to pay extra. (Yes, we all wonder how anyone can tell.) The result is a mixed crowd that works a good-size dance floor and is happy to catch their collective breath admiring a decor of velvet and animal prints (timeless, both of them). 735 Bourbon St. © **504/581-6740.**

Index

See also Accommodations and Restaurant indexes below.

RESTAURANTS